More Praise for

THE BIG FIX

"If you want to know how the biggest scandal in U.S. congressional history really took place, and why it is likely to happen again, Jim Adams's book vividly illuminates in readable narrative who did what for whom with our money—hundreds of billions of dollars worth."
—Warren T. Brooks, Syndicated Columnist
The Detroit *News*

"James Ring Adams has the eye of a novelist and the pen of a journalist. He is honest and fair. He tells a story of the savings and loan crisis that every citizen should know."
—Lewis Lehrman, Managing Director
Morgan Stanley Asset Management

"There are two things to know about James Ring Adams: number one, he's an ace reporter; and number two, he really knows how to tell a good yarn. If anybody can get to the bottom of one of the worst scandals of the twentieth century, Jim Adams can. I'm very pleased he's written this book."
—Thomas J. Bray, Editorial Page Editor
The Detroit *News*

THE BIG FIX

Inside the S&L Scandal

□ □ □

*How an Unholy Alliance of Politics and Money
Destroyed America's Banking System*

JAMES RING ADAMS

John Wiley & Sons, Inc.

New York   Chichester   Brisbane   Toronto   Singapore

To Jared, Jonathan and Abigail,

who gave up so much,

and to Miss Jane Marple—

and to Laurel, too.

Publisher: Stephen Kippur
Editor: Karl Weber
Managing Editor: Ruth Greif
Editing, Design, and Production: Impressions Publishing Services, Inc.

LIBRARY OF CONGRESS CATALOGING-IN-PUBLICATION DATA

Adams, James Ring
The big fix/James Ring Adams
p. cm.
ISBN 0-471-51535-3
ISBN 0-471-53844-2 (Paper)

Printed in the United States of America
91 92 10 9 8 7 6 5 4 3 2 1

Contents

Preface

EVERY DAY, thousands of drivers must cross the 14th Street Bridge in Washington, D.C. Few, I'm sure, pause to notice the small plaque that marks the structure as the Arland Williams Bridge. Yet Williams is a genuine American hero. He was a passenger on the Air Florida jetliner that lost altitude while leaving National Airport in January 1982 and crashed into the bridge. As the survivors struggled in the icy Potomac, a rescue helicopter lowered a lifeline. Williams repeatedly passed the buoy to other passengers, assisting their rescue, until he lost his grip and disappeared into the dark river.

Williams's heroism almost remained anonymous forever; it was months before the rescuers could confirm his identity. But his conduct was, in a way, typical of his profession. Williams was a bank examiner for the Federal Reserve Board. At the time of the crash, he was engaged in a sensitive examination of the Metropolitan Bank and Trust of Tampa, Florida, where he had displayed another form of quiet heroism. Like most of the banks and thrifts whose stories are told in this book, the Metropolitan Bank had been infiltrated by crooks and con artists who appeared to enjoy a measure of political protection. It was Williams's job to shut them down. Those examiners who worked with him admired his skill and perseverance in unraveling the bank's tangled criminal affairs. The work of men and women like Williams goes on continually, in total secrecy. It often requires great courage.

In recent years, the bank examiners have been a front line of sorts, striving to protect the depositors, the financial institutions, and ultimately the taxpayers against an epidemic of fraud, a coordinated wave of white-collar crime unlike anything in history. Too often, the examiners have been our only defense. They have been outnumbered, outmaneuvered, and overwhelmed. And they have often been made into scapegoats for losing a fight in which they had been given few weapons, few reserves, and scant support of any kind. In many battles, they have been betrayed by their leaders.

This book will show what the examiners have been up against. Even more, it will show why their defeat has been such a costly disaster for the American taxpayer. By current calculations, every person in this country—man, woman, and child—will be at least $6,000 poorer because of the $1.5 trillion savings and loan calamity. The damage inflicted on our political morality is incalculable. The defeats at the front have been caused by a political betrayal of the public as heinous in its way as the crimes of Laval and Quisling. The criminals who plundered the country's banks and thrifts succeeded in draining off their billions and tens of billions because they could buy political protection. United States senators and representatives pressured the bank regulators on behalf of large contributors. They often made no discernible effort to understand the concerns of the regulators and even less effort to judge the moral character of the people giving them the money.

The result has been serious, endemic corruption, in the precise meaning of that word. Although publicity so far has focused on such figures as former House Speaker Jim Wright, former House Majority Whip Tony Coelho, and former House Banking Committee Chairman Fernand St Germain, the corruption has spread far and wide. Former luminaries such as Senators Alan Cranston and John Glenn have been tainted. Several statehouses have been implicated. And the political milieu in Washington has become so degenerate that many of its elected officials don't even realize that they are corrupt.

The standard that has been abandoned was well defined by the late United States Senator Paul Douglas, a model of integrity in public service. In his manual *Ethics in Government*, Douglas wrote, "A legislator should not immediately conclude that the constituent is always right and the administrator is always wrong. but as far as possible should try to find out the merits of each case and only make such representations as the situation permits." By contrast, the House Committee on Standards of Official Conduct, the so-called Ethics Committee, now says, in effect, that members of Congress are free to do whatever big campaign donors ask, with no obligation to determine whether it is right or wrong, good policy or bad, beneficial or injurious to the public interest.

This book shows the temptations that helped produce this corruption. The accidents of history and a series of understandable but ill-conceived policies helped turn federal deposit insurance for the savings and loan industry into a virtually unlimited government subsidy for fraud. A network of experienced swindlers stood ready to exploit the opening. These figures, whom we will meet in the coming pages, often in surprising contexts, found it easy to cultivate the political friendships that helped them close the loop. Their system of bank fraud protected by political fund-raising connections was as elegantly simple as it was disastrous for the nation.

The cases we will examine show a progression amid the luxuriant growth of scandal. Each incident is bolder and more expensive than the previous one. From the exotica of drug-infested South Florida banking, through the down-home thievery of the Butcher brothers in Tennessee, to Ohio's corruption of its state insurance system, to the monumental expropriation of the nation's entire savings and loan industry, each coup has brought more open involvement by the politicians. Subtlety has dropped away, until members of Congress applied crude extortion on behalf of their pet swindlers.

We will look at the impact of this politicization on the tortured careers of two chief regulators: William Isaac, former chairman of the Federal Deposit Insurance Corporation, and Edwin Gray, former chairman of the Federal Home Loan Bank Board. Their stories illuminate the burgeoning scandal and financial crisis our country is only now beginning to face.

If the atmosphere of this book is sometimes oppressive, I apologize. There is little relief from the corruption, and the frustration suffered by the decent and the honest appears overwhelming. Perhaps the only consolation—a considerable one—is the repeated discovery that there were and are a few good men and women, anonymous heroes like Arland Williams, who fought the corruption every step of the way. This book is written in their honor.

JAMES RING ADAMS

Weston, Connecticut
September 1989

Acknowledgments

So MANY PEOPLE have helped in so many ways to bring this project to completion that I don't know how to thank them properly. I'm afraid of not naming people who would appreciate it, and of naming some who might be inconvenienced by the mention. Let me state my gratitude to you all, and especially to those who took some risk in cooperating.

Several belong at the top of the list. My special thanks to the Lynde and Harry Bradley Foundation, whose foresight made this book possible, and Karl Weber and Ruth Greif of John Wiley and Sons, whose hard work helped bring it to fruition. Ruth broke all speed records for production and yet turned out a very handsome volume. Lewis Lehrman and Nick Rizzopoulos provided the logistics for my research. I should also thank Robert Bartley of the *Wall Street Journal* editorial page, who put me on the trail in the first place and Brooke Manville of McKinsey & Co., who introduced me to Karl Weber.

My thanks to the American Spectator, Barron's and H. C. Wainwright Economics, for allowing me to use material I originally wrote for them. I would also thank Vince Tirola and Alan Neigher, Alan for his help in negotiations and both for their patience.

Many "well informed sources" have pointed me in the right direction, patiently explaining things and putting up with my endless opportuning. Let me thank a few, Raymond B. Vickers, Craig Kiser and the irrepressible Ken Muszynski. And William G. Batchelder, George Freibert and R. Jerome Sanford. Also Tom Tew and Marc

THE BIG FIX

Raymond of Miami. Also Lawrence Kane of Cincinnati and Edward
Kane of Columbus (who aren't related). Diana Fong, my researcher
during one tumultuous period, did such outstanding work that I have
been drawing on it ever since. I've relied on the excellent work of
many in the press, both for printed sources and personal advice.
Notable among them are Allen Pusey, Byron Harris, David McNeely,
Adrienne Bosworth, Georgiana Vines, Sandra Duerr, Andy Hall, John
Dougherty and Terrence Jeffrey.

The regulators themselves have given their time generously to
help set the record straight, but no one has been as generous as
Edwin Gray. This book takes his side on many points, not because
I have found him so thoroughly likable and helpful, which I have,
but because I think he is right. I also thank Irvine Sprague, William
Isaac, John Heimann, H. Joe Selby, all of whom helped beyond the
call of duty. People on the other side have also been generous. I
thank especially Jesse Barr and Jake Butcher for their good humor.

Others have played essential roles that are hard to categorize.
Special thanks to Ron and Jenni for the use of the water bed. Regards
to my valued friends Bob Asahina, David Asman, Virginia Armat,
Elinor Bachrach, Warren Brookes, Hillel Fradkin, Allan Dodds
Frank, John Fund, Michael Joyce, Alan Keyes, Bill Kristol, Art Laf-
fer, Susan Lee, Jose Luis Llovio-Menendez, Ed McDowell, Reba
McEntire, Gigi Mahon-Theobold, Huber Matos, Jr., Marc Miles,
Wladi Pleszczynski, David Ranson, Diane Rennell, Jon Rothchild,
Abe Shulsky, and many, many more, who encouraged me through
this ordeal.

The ordeal has been hardest, not on me, but on my family. They
suffered very real hardship during the four years this work has been
under way, and they deserve the glory. Thank you, Laurel, Jared,
Jonathan, Abigail and the ever faithful Miss Marple.

PROLOGUE

How to Start a Depression

□ 1 □

BANK RUNS ARE THE BOGEYMEN of American bank regulators. Their ultimate nightmare is a line of angry depositors clamoring for their money at the doors of a closed savings institution. Often it seems that all other concerns, including preventing and punishing bank fraud, take second place behind shoring up confidence in the savings system.

History would make one fear a bank panic. In the past 150 years, the mobs at the closed brass doors of a bank have been more directly tied to the onset of depression than have the most violent of stock market crashes. The run itself though isn't the problem. It's what government does afterward that causes the damage.

Runs, however, do tend to catch peoples' attention. Even more than a stock market crash, they are the most extreme example of market forces in action. A simple run may be thoroughly "rational." Depositors may suddenly have received new information and question the safety of their bank. Knowing the bank can't pay everyone, they rush to get there while it still has money. It's rational, but turbulent.

"The crowd immediately entered the Bank *vi et armis*, and commenced the demolition of every thing they could lay their hands on," begins a contemporary description of the Cincinnati Bank Riot of 1842. "Books, papers, desks and counters were thrown into the street, together with reams of unsigned sheets of bank notes. The mob then attacked with crowbars, sledge hammers, etc."

The mob was reacting to a court decision outlawing bank notes issued by certain banks. The good workers of Cincinnati also dispensed some summary justice to suspected swindlers:

> An attack was now made on Lougee & Co.'s broker's office. This Lougee had put into circulation a large amount of irresponsible paper which came under the decision of the Court in Bank alluded to above. This building was also destroyed, and the safe opened by violence, but everything valuable had been removed hours before, as the attack had been anticipated. During these proceedings, Charles Fox, Esq., a lawyer of this city, attempted to read the riot act, when the mob dismounted him from his hobby, and made him take to his heels; he was chased by about three hundred men to the Pearl Street House, where he obtained shelter.

"Irrational" runs are even more dangerous. The Cincinnati workmen trashed only the banks that they felt had cheated them with worthless currency. What regulators truly fear is that a "rational" run, if not quickly contained, will spread to healthy banks. If a solvent bank has trouble paying its depositors, the crisis of confidence could shake the entire financial system. The outstanding example is the onset of the Great Depression, which was marked by not one but three waves of bank panics before President Roosevelt declared the Bank Holiday of March 1933.

Bank failures by themselves do not trigger a panic. The trauma of the Great Depression has obscured the memory of a wave of bank closings during the 1920s. From a high point of 29,211 in 1921, the total number of state, national, and private banks and "loan and trust companies" in the United States had shrunk to 24,806 in 1928, before the Crash. Some 4,400 savings institutions closed during the 'Roaring Twenties,' and few were mergers. In the 1920s, general prosperity masked a surge of bank failures.

A high proportion of the failures could be blamed on fraud. That is the conclusion of Raymond B. Vickers, a lawyer and graduate student who has examined this period from an unusual perspective. Early in his career, in the late 1970s, Vickers was the chief appointed bank regulator of the state of Florida, where he saw financial and political corruption at close hand. As a student, he pored over the examiners' reports on the banks that failed after the Florida land boom collapsed in 1926. He was amazed to discover the same patterns he had seen in his days as Florida's chief deputy comptroller. He found insider abuse and over-concentration of loans, as developers bought banks and turned them into piggy banks for their own pet projects. He uncovered political protection and high-level interference with the regulators. Perhaps to a greater degree than today, he was able to trace financial interests to major national officials, including then Vice President Charles Dawes, a former Comptroller of the Currency. Says Vickers about both his research and his work experience, "I haven't found a single bank failure that didn't involve a conscious conspiracy to defraud."

The pattern of the 1920s—a prosperous economy obscuring the significance of a wave of bank failures and an epidemic of fraud and corruption in the banking system—has been ominously repeated in the late 1980s.

As an example of the role of fraud in the 1920s bank failures, Vickers cites the Palm Beach National Bank, controlled by the architect Addison Mizner. Called "one of the great charlatan-geniuses of the Twenties" by the Southern historian George Tindall, Mizner dreamed of making Boca Raton the world's leading resort, complete with medieval castle. The Palm Beach Bank lent most of its capital to the Mizner Development Corporation, which featured a prominent United States senator and the chairman of the House Judiciary Committee as board members. (The congressman used his influence to get a regulatory approval from the office of the United States Comptroller of the Currency three weeks before the bank filed the application.) The Palm Beach Bank also made loans to Florida State Comptroller Ernest Amos and his chief bank examiner, who regulated the closely related state-chartered Palm Beach Bank and Trust

Company. After both banks collapsed in June 1926, a Palm Beach grand jury indicted the Florida comptroller for "wholly and shamefully" failing in his duty to safeguard depositors. (Amos was arrested two more times on similar charges, but never convicted. The Florida Supreme Court dismissed the charges each time.)

The Florida land bust of 1926 devastated the state's shadier banks, just as the downturn in Texas laid low the high-flying savings and loans six decades later. In both cases, wild and fraudulent lending helped substantially to cause the economic collapse. But neither led, not immediately at least, to a national panic.

The first of the depression-era banking crises began in October 1930 and reached its peak in the failure of the Bank of United States in New York City on December 11. More than 440,000 New Yorkers, many of them hard-pressed Jewish immigrants, had placed their earnings in the bank's 57 branches. Some thought from its name that it was government-owned. Although that wasn't true, never had a commercial bank of its size, with $220 million in deposits, been forced to close its doors. The day before the failure, "terrific runs" hit branches throughout the city. At the Southern Boulevard branch, the line turned into a near riot. As depositors pushed and clamored in a cold afternoon drizzle, two emergency squads rushed to the scene, and mounted police charged the crowd. The shock went deep, and memories last to this day. In 1988, when a call-in show on a Miami radio station turned to the current S&L crisis, one of the listeners phoned in to invoke the Bank of United States. "I was 13 when it failed," he said. "We all thought it was as solid as the government."

The controversy over the closing also persists. No less an authority than Milton Friedman maintains that the bank could have been saved. For two months before the run, New York State Bank Superintendent Joseph A. Broderick had been negotiating a merger. Two days before the Bank of United States closed, says Friedman, all Broderick lacked was an agreement from the New York Clearing House, the association of the city's largest commercial banks, to contribute $30 million to the proposed new bank. The Clearing

House refused, amid charges that the Wall Streeters disliked the brash Jewish owners of the "pantspressers" bank.

The Clearing House committee met until 3:00 A.M. the morning of the bank's demise. After cooling his heels for hours, Superintendent Broderick was allowed into the board room at 1:00 A.M. for a last-minute plea. Failing to budge the committee members, Broderick told them that, they were "making the most colossal mistake in the banking history of New York."

There is another version. The Clearing House, say other historians, harbored a strong and justified suspicion that the Bank of United States owed its spectacular growth to fraud. The bank's owners had been funneling its cash into dummy subsidiaries, using the money to manipulate the price of its stock. The merger plans were provoked by a much delayed state examination, which stated in "severe and drastic" terms that the bank was busted. Its two principal owners received three-year terms in Sing Sing for their manipulations. Superintendent Broderick himself was indicted by a New York County grand jury for neglect of duty; in an all too familiar pattern, he was accused of ignoring his examiners' urgent warnings. (Broderick's first trial ended in a mistrial, and he was acquitted at the second.)

The Bank of United States crisis climaxed a spate of failures that claimed more than 600 banks in November and December of 1930. Confidence stabilized with the new year, and according to Milton Friedman, the indicators at that time showed what should have been the bottom of a traditional recession and the beginning of recovery. Instead the nation endured two more waves of bank panic, each worse than the one before. Starting in March 1931, a European bank crisis fanned another spate of runs and failures in the United States. Groping for a solution, President Hoover proposed establishing the Reconstruction Finance Corporation to give last-resort loans to businesses such as banks.

The second respite ended as the 1932 election repudiated the Republican era. President-elect Franklin Delano Roosevelt didn't take office until March, and the lack of leadership in the interregnum fostered the greatest bank panic of all. Nevada declared a statewide bank holiday in November, and the practice spread across the country as local crises erupted from Louisiana to Michigan.

On the eve of February 4, 1933, Louisiana Governor Huey Long needed a day to save a New Orleans bank in which he had a personal investment. He woke the city librarian and ordered him to find an excuse for declaring a state holiday. The librarian reported that nothing at all of interest had happened on that date. On February 3 1917, however, the United States had broken diplomatic relations with Germany. The Kingfish declared that such an important event must have taken two days to put in effect, and he proclaimed his holiday.

Although Huey Long's ruse apparently worked in New Orleans, which welcomed any excuse to party, the public couldn't ignore Michigan's decision ten days later to close all of its banks. Congress delivered an even heavier blow to confidence through a standard case of scandal making. The Democratic House was still enraged by an incident from the 1932 panic involving Charles Dawes, who had moved on from Vice President of the United States to head of the Reconstruction Finance Corporation. Shortly after leaving the RFC in June 1932, Dawes was in Chicago trying to save his family-owned bank from a run sweeping the city. Dawes threatened to close his bank, the last major institution in the city to stay open, unless he received a $90 million loan from the RFC. The Democratic national convention happened to be meeting in Chicago at the time and immediately seized on the issue. Emotions ran higher when Dawes's bank failed anyway. At the beginning of the next session of Congress, the House ordered the disclosure of RFC loans. When the names of rescued banks became public, their depositors immediately began pulling out money, even though some of the banks had regained relative health. This incident has been burned into the brains of generations of regulators; it is the main excuse for their extreme concern for secrecy.

As panic spread across the country, and the lame duck Hoover did nothing except antagonize Roosevelt, state after state declared its own bank holiday. Maryland and Ohio were among the first. By the time Roosevelt boarded the Baltimore and Ohio railroad in Jersey

City to head for his inauguration, all 48 states had either limited withdrawals or closed their banks.

"It's incredible," complained one of Roosevelt's cabinet appointees as the festive train rolled south to Washington. "The country is in ruins, and we seem to be on a kind of Sunday picnic." But there were plenty of reminders, passing the smokeless smokestacks of the industrial belt, that the depression had reached its deepest trough. Unemployment reached 25 percent, national income was 50 percent below that of 1929, and the stock market had fallen to one-fourth of its 1929 high. With the suspension of banking, parts of the country no longer had the use of money and had to make do with scrip and barter. Capitalism had collapsed.

The merriment on Roosevelt's inauguration train was somewhat excusable, however, because he already had a clear plan of action. Using groundwork laid by Hoover's Treasury Department and retaining some of its senior professionals, he would invoke the Trading with the Enemy Act of 1917 to proclaim a national Bank Holiday. Its legality may have been as dubious as Huey Long's history, but it showed decision and leadership. The enemy in the banking crisis, Roosevelt told the nation in his March 4 inaugural, was "fear itself—nameless, unreasoning, unjustified terror." His Bank Holiday and its administrative aftermath ended bank panics for the next 50 years.

□ 2 □

WHAT WAS THE DIFFERENCE between the routine bank failures of the 1920s and the waves of bank closings in the early depression? Why did "rational" runs on tottering banks turn into "unreasoning, unjustified terror" that engulfed the good along with the bad? And perhaps the most important question, could it happen again? Could the United States suffer a general bank crisis on the order of 1930 to 1933?

The most persuasive answer is that the depression bank panics were part and parcel of the mechanism that created the Great Depression in the first place. As explained by Milton Friedman and

Anna Schwartz in their classic *Monetary History of the United States*, the downturn of 1929 would have ended in 1930 as a severe but standard recession if it had not been for disastrous bungling by the men in charge of the nation's money supply. Friedman is a modern reviver of the economic doctrine called monetarism; he maintains that the economy waxes and wanes in direct response to expansion and contraction in the money supply. To state his technical analysis more simply, the bank runs caused the money supply to contract by taking deposits out of circulation. The Federal Reserve System, then just two decades old, should have compensated by pumping more money into the system. Instead it did just the opposite. The money stock fell at an annual rate of 10 percent from 1929 to 1933. By taking ultra-conservative measures to contract the available money, the Fed strangled the economy. Bank runs became more intense, removing even more deposits from the financial system, and diminishing the money stock even further.

In this light, perhaps the bank panics of 1932 and 1933 were not so unreasonable and unjustified, after all. If the banking system as a whole is riding a downward spiral, it makes sense to try to step off. Blaming the runs on the depositors becomes a backward logic (even though Friedman himself seems to indulge in it). Sound banks become swept up in a panic along with the bad because a disastrous economic policy was victimizing both.

Could it happen again? Probably not in the same way. Friedman's work, once dismissed as right wing crankery, now has a following at all levels. The Fed has already announced plans to counter S&L runs by making funds available. The danger may lie in another quarter. What if the rescue plan, costly as it is, still fails to cover the problem? Any number of bad breaks—rising interest rates, the long-awaited recession, a collapse of the junk bond market—could create new thrift failures. FSLIC's troubles could spread to the FDIC and the commercial banks. When the FDIC moved into thrift supervision, it seriously diluted its attention to bank problems, which are substantial. According to one private analyst, 10 percent of the 13,000 commercial banks are troubled. The FDIC itself has suffered the first major loss in its history, $4.2 billion in 1988. A stiff recession could leave its funds seriously depleted.

Much is unpredictable, but the Great Depression offers little comfort. Eerie similarities are accumulating, from the surge in fraud-related bank and thrift insolvencies, to the stock market crash, to the possibility of major runs. The S&L debacle isn't over.

□ 3 □

ROOSEVELT KNEW, and others were to learn much later, that it's easier to close banks than to reopen them. On Monday, March 6, using a proclamation originally drafted for Hoover, Roosevelt suspended "all banking transactions" for four days. The country took it with relief and good humor. A patron of an Oklahoma City hotel paid his bill with a pig. The governor of California suspended executions, declaring "a bank holiday was no time to hang a man." In the meantime, the Treasury had to work out what to do next.

Treasury decided to divide the banks in three classes, following the plan of Ogden Mills, Hoover's Treasury Secretary and now an adviser to Roosevelt's appointees. Solvent banks would reopen as soon as possible. Banks which were insolvent but still savable, the second class, would reopen gradually, with government help. The third class, the hopelessly busted, would stay closed. When Roosevelt proposed his Emergency Banking Act to legalize and extend the Bank Holiday, Mills's plan was Title II. Congress received the bill on March 9, its first day in session, and passed it in less than six hours.

This bill, harrumphed one of Roosevelt's advisers, allowed "the present system to be regenerated." The Treasury secretary had the job of licensing national banks for reopening after reassurance from federal regulators that they were reasonably sound. The acting Comptroller of the Currency, one of Hoover's men, argued for liberal standards. Politicians and lobbyists flocked to the Treasury to plead on behalf of their clients, sometimes successfully. By the end of the month, nearly 13,000 banks, both state- and federally chartered, had reopened.

The Treasury applied much stricter standards to the rest, merging and selling them when possible and closing the remainder. In one year, 1,005 state and national banks were liquidated. The banking system had not only been regenerated, it had been purged of its weakest members. Failures among the reopened banks were low. Other bank reforms had the advantage of starting with a system as pristine as it was ever going to be.

These hectic rescues went on without the benefit of federal deposit insurance. That idea was so controversial that Treasury simply set it aside during the emergency. The initiative came from Congress. In the hindsight of 55 years later, deposit insurance was a deeply flawed notion, a federal subsidy destined eventually to run haywire, threatening to devastate a financial system it purported to save. Those were the arguments of the time as well.

Populist congressmen had pushed the idea of deposit insurance since the beginning of the depression. All banks would be required to contribute a premium equal to a small portion of their deposits to an insurance fund. Whenever a bank failed, the fund would pay off depositors. All depositors would get back their money, and there would be no need for runs. The fund would bolster confidence in the system. Sound banks would no longer have to worry about irrational panics. New York State had tried the idea as far back as 1819. After the panic of 1907, eight states, mainly in the Midwest and Southwest, had guaranteed deposits in state-chartered banks.

After the shock of the Bank Holiday wore off in 1933, the push for bank reform in Congress took the shape of the Glass-Steagall bill. Repeal of Glass-Steagall has been a watchword in recent years as large banks fought furiously with stockbrokers over its provisions forbidding commercial banks from peddling stocks and bonds. This rule was the Glass half of the bill, pushed by Senator Carter Glass, a veteran financial reformer who had helped draft the Federal Reserve legislation under Woodrow Wilson. In 1933, surprisingly, separation of banking and underwriting had become almost a non-controversial issue as New York banks realized that by endorsing it they could improve their PR and hobble J. P. Morgan. The furious fight swirled around Representative Henry Steagall's half of Glass-Steagall, a House bill to give all deposits a full federal guarantee.

All the previous guarantee funds had failed, argued Steagall's opponents, and they failed for the same reason. If only a few banks collapsed in a crisis, their losses would be more than enough to wipe out the fund, and the other members would be worse off than before. A federal fund was unnecessary, moreover, because the Bank Holiday had cleaned up the banking system, and new safeguards would keep it clean.

But the strongest argument came from the most self-interested parties, the financially strong northeastern banks. As the banks with the largest deposits, they would pay the highest premium for insurance they didn't need, thus subsidizing a fund for small and poorly run banks in the rest of the country. Their stake in the outcome was evident, but the large banks still made a cogent case. Deposit insurance removed market restraints on incompetent banking. The depositor would no longer shop for the bank with the best reputation. With the federal guarantee, all banks were the same. According to a National City Bank bulletin of July 1933:

> The element of character in the choice of a bank is eliminated, and the competitive appeal is shifted to other and lower standards, such as liberality in making loans. The natural result is that the standards of management are lowered, bankers may take greater risks for the sake of larger profits, and the economic loss which accompanies bad bank management increases.

The bank concluded that the bill "puts the burden of maintaining sound banking upon regulation by the Government, and takes it off the public."

These points impressed one important person, President Franklin Delano Roosevelt. "As to guaranteeing bank deposits," he said in his first press conference in office, "the minute the government starts to do that, . . . the government runs into a probable loss." He added prophetically, "We do not wish to make the United States government liable for the mistakes and errors of individual banks, and put a premium on unsound banking in the future." As Senator Glass and his committee worked on the bill, Roosevelt met with them personally to oppose deposit insurance. Word leaked out that if the provision stayed in the bill, Roosevelt would veto it.

Roosevelt's mind began to change when Republican Senator Arthur Vandenberg attached the program to Glass's bill in a floor amendment. (Vandenberg later claimed the insurance idea as his own, to Steagall's great annoyance.) A flood of letters from victimized depositors pleaded for guarantees. Roosevelt's own vice president, John Nance Garner, told him, "You'll have to have it, Cap'n." In mid-June, Roosevelt negotiated a compromise that provided insurance on a sliding scale. After a one-year interim, the bill would establish the Federal Deposit Insurance Corporation, which would fully insure deposits up to $10,000. Larger amounts would receive partial coverage. Roosevelt signed the Glass-Steagall Act on June 16. Later, to the amusement of spectators like Vice President Garner, he claimed credit for the bill.

Once the banks were given deposit insurance, it wasn't long before the savings and loan associations asked for it. The S&Ls (then called building and loan associations) were in desperate shape, along with homeowners in general. By 1932, nearly one-quarter of the country's home mortgages were delinquent. Foreclosures clogged banks and thrifts with unwanted and unsellable real estate. Some 1700 S&Ls had closed. The industry, largely organized as mutual societies in which depositors became shareholders, had lost nearly 20 percent of its clientele. Washington urgently wanted to rescue the S&L. The pleas of desperate homeowners rubbed a raw nerve in Congress. The government also reasoned that if home mortgage lending could be revived, millions of masons, carpenters, handymen, loggers, sawmillers and brickmakers could go back to work, enlivening the economy.

Hoover inaugurated the rescue by setting up the system of Federal Home Loan Banks. Modelled on the Federal Reserve, they were supposed to pump loans to troubled thrifts and, at first, even to homeowners. But like many of Hoover's efforts, this system ran into a frustrating Catch-22. If you were desperate enough to need their loans, you were probably too bad a risk to get one. Roosevelt broke the stalemate with two housing acts. The first, passed in tandem with Glass-Steagall, put the Home Loan Bank Board in the business of chartering federal savings and loans. Federal thrifts were needed, said New Dealers, because the state-chartered system was so inadequate. The state S&Ls, went a familiar refrain, had run into trouble because of lax supervision, and they were using their Home Loan Bank advances to pay off shareholders instead of to make fresh loans. The National Housing Act of 1934 topped off this structure.Along the lines of the bank deposit guaranty, the act set up the Federal Savings and Loan Insurance Corporation to insure accounts to $5,000.

From the beginning, federal deposit insurance rode under false colors. It was really a form of government subsidy, not an insurance policy. Legislation for the S&Ls made it explicit. The Bank Board, the federal chartering of institutions and FSLIC were means "to build up home ownership." The FDIC served a political as well as an economic function; it helped restore depositors' confidence in the regenerated banking system. Neither fund seriously tried to match premiums to risk. (As anyone who has had a minor auto accident can testify, a private insurance company will eagerly jack up the premium on an "unsafe" driver. That is how they stay in business.) Loss projections and reserves, so vital to managing a real insurance company, were completely arbitrary. When premiums did increase, they did so across the board, so that, as Roosevelt warned, the healthy institutions wound up pulling the weight of the sick ones.

But it took decades for these problems to emerge, partly because of Roosevelt's scruples. His initial opposition kept Congress from passing a total guarantee. The small depositor could sit back and rely on federal insurance, but those with more than $10,000 to bank still had to worry about their uninsured balance. These depositors, who were more financially sophisticated anyway, maintained market discipline on the banks and thrifts. Deposit insurance started out with another advantage. Thanks to the Bank Holiday and the massive S&L failures of the 1930s, it began with a relatively clean slate. The victims of the economy or of their own bad management had largely been removed from the field.

So for the first five decades, deposit insurance seemed to be a good idea. The funds grew steadily, untested by any major waves of failures. Economists of all stripes praised the guarantees as the most important structural change to come from the 1933 bank panic. Wrote John Kenneth Galbraith,

> With this one piece of legislation the fear which operated so efficiently to transmit weakness was dissolved. As a result one grievous defect of the old system, by which failure begot failure, was cured. Rarely has so much been accomplished by a single law.

Not until the 1980s did the bad effects become apparent. All of a sudden, the forebodings of Roosevelt and the New York bankers have come true with a vengeance. Any praise for deposit insurance these days must be dampened by its role in generating the $300 billion savings and loan debacle.

PART ONE

The Fix Is In

CHAPTER ONE

The Biggest Scam in History

□ 1 □

THE DOWNHILL SLIDE to the $300 billion savings and loan disaster began one night in mid-1980 in a high-ceilinged conference room in the United States Capitol. The push came from one man, the slick and not overly scrupulous chairman of the House Banking Committee, Fernand St Germain. A congressman from Woonsocket, Rhode Island, since 1960, St Germain vigorously enjoyed the perquisites of office, including frequent nights on the town with the lobbyists of the United States League of Savings Institutions. Once handsome, his features now drooped in jowly dissipation, and his evening meetings sometimes ended with the arrival of hard and beautiful young women whose expertise lay elsewhere than banking.

St Germain had other business in hand at this conference committee. In time-honored congressional routine, members of the House and Senate had come together to produce a bill that compromised between versions passed by each chamber. On this night, they were thrashing out the first major attempt to revise the New Deal banking regulations. Over the years, deposit insurance had inched up to cover accounts of $40,000. The Senate bill had raised the limit to $50,000. The House hadn't voted on the issue. In the conference, St Germain pulled off a fateful coup. He proposed a "compromise" limit of $100,000. "It was a United States League [of Savings Institutions] special," says one thrift regulator. "But they were surprised they got it." Adds Tim McNamar, then a Deputy Secretary of the Treasury, "We were lucky they didn't get a million."

What was so bad about raising the deposit guarantee? For starters, it changed the nature of the program. Roosevelt's compromise in 1933 had focused deposit insurance on the small saver. It seemed reasonable to protect a middle-class nest egg, to cover the necessaries of life, but why guarantee the affluence of the rich? Besides, the depositor with an uninsured balance would be forced to take a keen interest in the soundness of his bank. Money would drain from the poorly run banks and wind up in safe ones. This market discipline would help limit the losses that might be charged to the insurance funds.

St Germain's coup more than doubled the guarantee, changed the incentives to banks and thrifts, and created a new subsidy for the rich. Bankers quickly figured out how to market the subsidy. Even in the midst of the S&L debacle, when the perversion of deposit insurance was widely discussed, Citibank mailed a brochure to its customers showing how to stretch FDIC coverage to $1.4 million. (Both FDIC and FSLIC offered separate guarantees not only for individual accounts but for trust accounts, joint accounts and the like. So the trick was to split deposits into individual accounts for each family member and use all the available permutations to set up joint and trust accounts. By creating joint accounts for husband and wife, husband and child, wife and child, child and child, each could be insured to $100,000.)

An even greater perversion of deposit insurance was underway in the sales rooms of the big brokerage houses. National firms such as Merrill Lynch and Drexel Burnham were turning the populist program of Steagall and Vandenberg into a new fixed-income investment vehicle. They were pioneering the national market in "jumbo CDs." The brokers packaged funds to buy certificates of deposit in amounts just under the federal guarantee; they shopped thrifts across the country for the highest interest rates, then sold their clients shares in the CD as an absolutely safe, high return, federally guaranteed investment. Some experts trace the origin of this market to St Germain's coup. The increase to $100,000, they say, made the jumbo CD feasible. Others think the scheme would have developed anyway. In either case, St Germain helped turn deposit insurance on its head.

It took one more element to convert this program from just another haywire government subsidy into the most costly scam in history. With the increased guarantee, thrift owners soon realized that no matter what they did, they had access to almost unlimited deposits. Buyers of jumbo CDs cared only about the interest rate, which was almost always highest at the weakest thrifts. "Hot money" flowed into the hands of the worst managers at a phenomenal rate. Their thrifts grew a thousandfold and more in just four years and kept growing as their losses mounted.

By mid-1983, the regulators were finding brokered deposits in their problem cases. An excited Edwin Gray, chairman of the Home Loan Bank Board, later complained to the Senate Banking Committee, "It was the easy, instantaneous access to very willing money brokers, willing to provide high-priced federally insured money to any institutions which sought it—in virtually unlimited amounts— which fueled the rapidly made investments and loans that have become very bad assets in some of the most significant thrift failures we have seen." William Isaac, Gray's counterpart at the FDIC, added that more than a third of the brokered funds in his system had gone to troubled banks. In some of his basket cases, "hot money" made up almost half of their deposits. Many depositors taking advantage of these jumbo CDs were themselves federally insured banks, thrifts and credit unions.

The broker business was a ready-made scam, and some took full advantage. As regulators pored over the books of failed banks, one name kept popping up. The FDIC surveyed all 80 of the banks that closed from 1982 to 1985 and found that 25 of them had drawn funds from the First United Fund, Ltd. of Garden City, Long Island. This outfit was the brainchild of Mario Renda, a New Yorker who pioneered the technique of linking his deposits to a reciprocal favor. In Kansas, according to the indictment in a later case, he pumped deposits into a failing bank on the condition that it funnel loans to the people he named. Renda pleaded guilty in that case, as well as in a separate case in the Federal District Court in Brooklyn, where he was charged with receiving kickbacks for providing deposits from two union welfare funds.

Monies provided by people like Renda were the elixir of life for insolvent thrifts which miraculously stayed open, institutions regulators were beginning to call the "living dead" or the "zombies." By the mid-1980s, the S&L industry had begun to defy the elemental laws of business. Any other business that lost more than it made would quickly fold. But a thrift in the hole not only stayed open, it thrived. Even stranger, its deposits grew faster than in the rest of the industry. According to one study, sick thrifts in 1986 held $315 billion in liabilities (deposits and borrowings), about 40 percent of the amount held in the well thrifts; by the second quarter of 1988, holdings of the sick thrifts had grown to 50 percent of their healthy competitors' total. How to explain this phenomenon, where the bankrupt not only survived but outcompeted the solvent? Answered one critic, "a zombie has transcended its natural death from accumulated losses by the black magic of federal guarantees."

The deposit brokers had become agents of a Ponzi scheme. This device, named after a Boston businessman of the 1920s, paid off early investors with the funds from later investors, creating the illusion of high profits. Of course, nothing was left for the last people enticed into the scheme. The brokers provided the new money that covered the zombies' operating losses and paid off their old depositors. But when the scam collapsed, the new depositors weren't penniless; they merely collected their money from FSLIC and ultimately from the taxpayer. The zombies had to pay high interest to stay alive; federal insurance took care of all the risk; so for the brokers, jumbo CDs were a legitimate business. And in fact the largest broker of all was Merrill Lynch, whose former chairman Donald Regan became Chief of Staff in the White House.

Renda was an extreme case, but he merely drove the logic of deposit insurance to its extreme conclusion. As FDR had warned, the program became a subsidy for bank fraud. Why did this happen when it did? The answer is that the early 1980s produced the worst possible combination of pressures. The increase in deposit insurance coincided with the first major effort to revise the depression era structure of bank law. Some circles try to blame the thrift crisis on this movement or, more polemically, on Reagan deregulation. This scapegoating misses the point. Market pressures dating from the Carter administration and earlier had forced some damaging changes, but the problem lay in the failure to deregulate enough. Congress reacted to a series of crises by enacting piecemeal reforms that created even more severe crises. Each change left the industry ever more exposed to the baleful effects of deposit insurance.

For example, consider the fate of the federal ceiling on bankbook rates, Regulation Q. Since the depression, banks and thrifts had been permitted to offer only a fixed interest rate. The rule was ultimately untenable, but it did prevent depositors from shopping around for the highest rate. In principle, competition was based on reputations for safety and sound management. The depositor could not get maximum return on his dollar, but there was no national hot money market.

By 1980, pressure had been building for years to eliminate Regulation Q. Depositors could not shop among the thrifts for higher interest rates, but as soon as the choice of uncontrolled (and uninsured) money market funds became available, money flowed away from the traditional savings institutions. This money flight was called "disintermediation," which became one of the buzz words of the 1970s. Regulation Q, like all price controls, produced a shortage of the controlled product, namely deposits. Reacting to pleas from the thrifts and banks, Congress in 1980 created a commission to phase it out. (This bill was also the vehicle for St Germain's coup on deposit insurance.)

This reform put the thrifts in another bind. They could now hold on to their depositors by offering higher interest rates, but they couldn't change the return they were earning on most of their mortgages. The combination of high cost of money and low earnings put a deadly squeeze on their profitability. As profits vanished, thrifts began dipping into their capital, the money originally put up by investors and owners when the thrift was formed. This nest egg provided the first line of defense against losses. By 1982, on an industrywide average, capital was nearly exhausted. Some 50 S&Ls had failed, a shocking number for the time. The crisis produced another deregulation bill, the Garn-St Germain Act of 1982.

Garn-St Germain shifted the focus to rebuilding capital. Reasoning that thrifts couldn't profit on their traditional mortgages, the bill greatly expanded the types of investments they could make. A new breed of owner was invited in, aggressive risk-takers who presumably would help the thrifts earn their way out of their hole. States such as Texas, California, and Florida went even further in broadening investment powers for state-chartered thrifts. California led the way with the 1983 Nolan Act, which has been called the "most liberal banking law ever passed anywhere." As a means of rebuilding capital, these acts resembled calling in a fox to repopulate a chicken coop.

Garn-St Germain unleashed a horde of habitual risk-takers without subjecting them to any risk. The Bank Board compounded the problem by relaxing capital requirements almost to nonexistence. With expanded deposit insurance and reductions in the amount of capital thrifts were required to keep on hand, the new owners had every incentive to be as reckless as possible. They would reap the benefits of a long-shot business deal but bear none of the cost. In the words of one regulator, "Heads, they win. Tails, FSLIC loses." Insurance professionals have a term for it, "moral hazard." The policy offers too much temptation to cheat.

As fraud ran rampant in the system, some argued that officers at failing thrifts had been corrupted by the perverse incentives, that they had taken one desperate gamble too many in the attempt to recoup their fortunes. In Brooklyn Federal Court, Judge Jack Weinstein dismissed a criminal case against a thrift president on the grounds that the government had encouraged his high-risk lending. Yet it's more likely that thrifts in 1982 had become a juicy target for those who knew a scam when they saw one and wanted to get in on it.

Consider the unhappy careers of two men we'll name Jack Tieg and Wilmer Strait. This is the only fiction in the book. Tieg and

Strait are composites; we'll see enough of their real-life equivalents later on.

□ 2 □

JACK TIEG, graying and a bit heavy around the middle, was still proud of his condition for a 55-year-old. His great passion was golf, although he hadn't had much chance to play recently. Jack was president and majority stockholder of a small thrift in the small city of Westward, commercial center for the dairy farms in the valley and the vacation towns in the hills. His father had started the Westward Savings and Loan Association with friends from his country club, a doctor, several lawyers, the head of the local sprocket factory. When Jack took it over in 1976, it gave him an easy life. He made mortgage loans to local farmers and the town shopkeepers, many of whom he'd grown up with. He took in deposits at 5.5 percent, the limit set by the Federal Reserve under Regulation Q. He could count on a spread of two percentage points between his fixed rate mortgages and the interest he paid to depositors. It gave him a steady profit but not a spectacular rate of return on his stock. On Wednesday afternoons, he headed to the club in the foothills for a brisk 18 holes. He participated in his trade association, the United States League of Savings Institutions, calling his congressman when the League put out the word. The representative always answered the call, since Jack's father had helped arrange his nomination.

Jack took pride in his position. Every December, he invited friends over to watch Jimmy Stewart in "It's a Wonderful Life." He always choked up when the guardian angel showed the suicidal thrift executive the tract houses that had been built because he had made the loans. But around 1978, life stopped being so wonderful. Interest rates on government securities surged as they had before, but this time small investors tapped into the market. The druggist, the lawyer, and several of the larger dairy farmers had withdrawn several thousand to put into the new money market accounts advertised by the broker in the big city across the river. For the first time he could remember, deposits in Westward S&L declined.

Jack went to Washington with the state trade group to complain about disintermediation, a fancy word their congressman always mangled. Jack preferred to say that the thrifts just couldn't compete for depositors with Regulation Q tying their hands behind their backs. The Home Loan Bank Board gave them some relief, allowing the S&Ls to offer an experimental Small Savers Certificate at money market rates. Jack called it the "Super-Thrift," and it attracted funds at an alarming rate. By the end of the year, these accounts amounted to one-third of his deposits. Congress promised help too. By mid-1980, Jack was hearing about the Diddymac, a jabberwockian acronym for the Depository Institutions Deregulation and Monetary Control Act.

The Diddymac was definitely going to change the business. It signalled the beginning of the end for Reg Q, although a federal commission was supposed to supervise a gradual phase-out. The act gave Jack another lure for customers, interest-bearing checking accounts. (Actually, the state regulator had let him try that a year before, but now the rest of the country could follow suit.) Jack could now make consumer loans and even offer credit cards if he wanted to. And he had to change all his stationary to reflect the increase in the FSLIC deposit guarantee. Jack's life was becoming more interesting, and he wasn't sure he liked it.

He soon realized what was bothering him. He began paying more to his depositors, a lot more as the national prime interest rates hit 20 percent. But his income still came from the fixed-rate mortgages he had been making since he started out as his father's loan officer 20 years ago. His "spread" narrowed to the vanishing point. One day as he sat in his wood-panelled office lined with sporting trophies, his chief financial officer came in with a worried expression. Westward S&L was now running a loss and starting to dip into its capital for operating expenses. Westward S&L wasn't alone. Jack had been reading that the negative interest rate spread, or as he put it, paying out more than you take in, was sinking thrifts around the country. Washington had solved his old problem, declining deposits, but it left him with a bigger and potentially fatal crisis. It was time to lobby Congress again.

The legislators that Jack and his colleagues talked to weren't just politely concerned; they were frightened. The thrifts faced a widespread collapse. Who knew what could happen to the entire financial system? Just two years after the Diddymac, the House and Senate Banking Committee chairmen put their names on a bill designed mainly to rescue the savings and loan industry. The Garn-St Germain Act of 1982 expanded on the Diddymac. Jack could offer a true money market account, indistinguishable from the product of the mutual fund broker. He could expand his NOW accounts, the interest-bearing checking. He no longer had to worry about Regulation Q. These measures didn't lower his cost of doing business, however, so Garn and St Germain gave him the means of increasing his earnings—or so they thought—as they greatly expanded the kinds of investments Jack could make. Jack found that he was no longer simply in the mortgage business. He could invest up to 55 percent of his assets in commercial real estate and other loans. He could make consumer loans of up to 30 percent of assets. (His counterparts in Texas and California were thoroughly liberated. State-chartered thrifts there could plunge 100 percent of their assets into practically anything.) A lawyer at the Bank Board told Jack that its legal staff had drafted Garn-St Germain to make a federal thrift charter "the best charter in the world." But Jack didn't feel comfortable. He understood home mortgages, but commercial real estate was a new and tricky field. Besides, he had some problems with the regulators.

The cash position at Westward S&L had declined sharply during the interest rate squeeze. On top of that, a drought hit the dairy farmers and some were behind on their mortgage payments. Jack was willing to carry them, but his balance sheet suffered. His regulatory capital, his treasurer reminded him, had fallen from 5 percent to 2 percent of assets. Jack understood that the first buffer against bad loans was his tangible capital (the money put up by investors plus the part of the thrift's earnings that it kept for itself rather than paying to stockholders). When that buffer was exhausted, FSLIC would have to step in. As part of its response to the interest rate squeeze, the Bank Board lowered the minimum capital requirement from 5 percent to 3 percent, but that still didn't help Westward. Jack had an unpleasant choice. He could try to raise fresh capital in a new stock issue or he could sell the thrift.

Jack wanted to get out of this business, and his decision was sealed when he found a buyer. Actually, the buyer found him. "The name is Wilmer Strait," said the hearty voice on the telephone. "I hear you have a thrift for sale." Strait made a generous offer, a good price for Jack's stock and recapitalization of Westward. Jack would stay on the board for the transition. The regulators said Strait was okay, and the directors voted for the sale with relief. Only Jack's wife, Sally, had reservations.

"Something about him isn't right," she said to Jack one afternoon as she dressed for dinner at the club. Sally had been a reporter when she married Jack ten years earlier. Jack respected her judgment, but she was touching a sore spot. "Don't worry about it," he snapped. "He'll do fine."

□ 3 □

WILMER STRAIT was born 40 years ago in one of the hardscrabble hill towns, to a poor Yankee family that had settled there 200 years ago and had not done much since. The valley establishment—Jack Tieg's world—was an alien place. His main contact with it had been to work in the kitchen of Jack's country club as a teenager; he had not been left with endearing memories. He went to business school in the Southwest and stayed there to make his fortune. Folks in Westward hadn't heard much from him until he returned, dressed in cowboy boots and a guayabera shirt and apparently flush with success.

Jack might have shared Sally's concern if he had known more about Strait's career. Wilmer achieved moderate success in real estate in Texas until he met a gentleman from Louisiana. This benefactor owned a pyramid of banks and insurance companies and always seemed willing to back Wilmer's riskiest ventures. One day he took Wilmer aside and explained that he was taking control of a new bank. "I have a happy family of borrowers," he said, "And I expect they'll show their gratitude by purchasing some of this stock."

"How much?" Wilmer replied.

The Louisiana backer had strange friends from New Orleans. One of Wilmer's partners, a transplanted New Yorker, called them the "bent noses." Wilmer noticed that the banks his benefactor bought made loans in Arizona, Nevada, and California, and they invariably wound up in trouble. One chain of Texas banks collapsed in the mid-1970s, inspiring a congressional investigation, but the Louisianan emerged unscathed. The Louisianan passed on ideas about exploiting thrifts to Wilmer and suggested that he might want to try the business. The regulators for Westward would have shuddered if they knew the source of Strait's financing.

Strait promised to recapitalize Westward, and he did inject about $5 million. But he did better with intangibles. As the buyer of a troubled thrift, he had permission from the Bank Board to book "goodwill" as capital. He announced that he planned to get the thrift out of its hole by "growing" it out. Once he was in control, he began breakneck lending in the areas Jack had avoided. He liked real estate loans in Florida and Texas. Even though they were well out of the Westward market area, they seemed highly profitable. Wilmer used his own appraiser for the Sunbelt shopping malls and condos. The appraised value would be the starting point for the loan. Wilmer then added enough to cover interest payments for two years. The loan also included a reserve for fees, which were substantial. So the loans looked highly profitable. Westward controlled the interest reserve and booked the payments when they were due. As long as the reserve lasted, the loans would be current, no matter what happened.

The treasurer came in Wilmer's office to complain about these loans. As a veteran of 35 years with Westward, and a good friend of Jack's father, he usually carried weight in setting policy. "We're not really earning money from these interest reserves," he said. "We're just paying ourselves back our own money and calling it profit. The loan could go bad, and we wouldn't know it for two years."

"The fees are good money," chuckled Wilmer from behind his huge desk. "Some of these developers pay us 4 percent each time we renew the loan, and they have six-month renewals." He toyed with a brass model of a condominium that a friend of the Louisianan had sent up from Dallas. "Who says the loans will go bad, anyway? We have good appraisals."

"That's another thing," the treasurer plunged on. "We don't really know these appraisers. The loans are way out of our area. What if the land is only worth $4 million instead of $10 million?"

"Let me worry about that," said Wilmer. "I'll be going down there myself." At the next board meeting, Wilmer suggested that the treasurer was out of touch with the rapid changes in the industry. He announced the treasurer's resignation with great appreciation for his long service. Jack was away with Sally on a cruise.

True to his word, Wilmer starting touring his far-flung investments. To save time, he told the board, he ordered a Lear jet for the company. Soon Westward had its own hangar at the municipal airport. Wilmer incorporated Westward Aviation to hold the jet and the hangar, and using the broad new investment powers of the Garn-St Germain Act, bought the company with Westward S&L money.

Wilmer started setting up other corporations as well, making them subsidiaries, or subsidiaries of subsidiaries of Westward. The thrift, now Westward Service Corporation, found itself the owner of entities such as ArgEquine, a stud farm for Argentine racehorses; Westward Cycles and Ascensions, Ltd., devoted to Strait's passions of motorcycling and ballooning; and WestInvest, S.A., a money-management office in Geneva, Switzerland, that no one at the thrift seemed to know much about. The thrift made frequent loans for deals handled by these subsidiaries, although it soon became hard to keep track of the money. Some of the old directors quietly left the board. Others took generous loans and bought into Wilmer's multitude of deals. Strait recruited new directors from among his friends. One, a carpenter, became a major builder, filling the river basin with his Westward-financed condos. Driving by one day, Jack Tieg remembered how four feet of water had covered that plain in the hurricane of 1955.

Strait was going far afield for his other banking business. Every once in a while, a loan participation from Florida, Texas or Louisiana would show up on his books. "It's a way of sharing the risk," he explained to his junior officers. "They make a loan for $30 million and sell parts of it to five other thrifts, so we all have a $5 million asset in a region with a different economic cycle." He began to shuffle his own loans through this network, although he didn't have an economic theory to explain why he and several trusted officers would work late to send them out in batches just days before the FSLIC examiners were due.

Westward grew by leaps and bounds. From a modest $25 million in assets under Jack Teig, it swelled to $300 million in Strait's first year. In his second, it broke $500 million, and by the end of his third it passed $1 billion. The community didn't have the economy to provide these deposits. They came from all across the country, attracted by the high interest on the jumbo CDs. Strait spent much of his time on the phone with deposit brokers in New York, Miami and Beverly Hills. Instead of adding tellers, he hired a fax and telex operator and installed a state-of-the art wire room. By the end of his fourth year, more than half of his deposits came from just four brokers. At the same time, local mortgages had fallen to less than one-third of his portfolio. One week, while Wilmer frenetically closed deals in Florida and Texas, a local dairy farmer came in for a loan to rebuild his herd. Wilmer turned him down.

As Westward grew, so did Wilmer's influence. He devoted a lot of energy to cultivating the district congressman, who had enough seniority to be in line for a committee chair. The two flew to Texas to shoot deer with Wilmer's business buddies or to Florida to fish. Strait started raising money for campaigns and helped the congressman set up his own PAC to channel funds to his House allies. The representative began to think about a leadership position. Strait gave him free use of the company jet for speaking engagements in his House colleagues' districts. Strait even began to handle his finances, cutting him in on some of the sounder condo projects.

A national horizon was opening before Wilmer Strait, and he decided to cut back his daily involvement in Westward. He resigned as chairman and brought in a well-known former thrift president from the large city to the east. The new chairman, whom we'll call Parker Ritwire, had just completed a term as president of the state savings and loan trade group. With Wilmer's backing, he had been elected to the board of the regional Federal Home Loan Bank. But Ritwire wasn't the buttoned-down stuffed shirt that Westward employees expected. Recently divorced, he drove a fancy Porsche, dated elegant women and did whatever Strait told him to. Ritwire was a handy acquisition, because Westward was heading towards a major crisis.

FSLIC had started its annual examination of Westward. The man in charge was one of the agency's few veterans; in fact, he was the regulator who had pushed Jack Tieg to recapitalize five years ago. He ran into Jack at the dingy café on Main Street and over coffee started to ask him just what was going on. "We're seeing loan participations from some of our real problem cases in the Southwest," he said. "How did they get up here? You know, a lot of the condos down there don't have anyone living in them. There's no rental money, no cash stream, nothing. And whatever happened to your old treasurer?" These were questions Jack had tried not to ask over the years. Although he'd stayed on as director, he hadn't had the heart to pay close attention. It was time, as he had known it eventually would be, to have a searching talk with Wilmer Strait.

After a walk around the block, he entered the marbled lobby of Westward's new building and stood outside Strait's southwestern style office. In the anteroom, several examiners were pulling loan files. When Strait ushered him in, Jack had the feeling he had been expected. "Hell, yes, I took risks," Strait said, interrupting Jack's questions. "Some paid off; some didn't. That's what happens when you throw the long bomb. But this examination won't stop us. I want you to stay on, Jack, to reassure the locals. Tell them their money's safe. It's all insured."

Jack left the building, expecting to see it padlocked the next day. But the morning came with no news. When he checked in later, the examiners had left the anteroom and Ritwire was sitting in Strait's office. Ritwire handed Jack a paper, his gold chains jingling as he reached across the desk. It was a Memorandum of Understanding with the Bank Board in Washington. The agreement said that Westward would slow down its growth and improve its lending procedures, and Ritwire would replace Strait as the chief executive.

"This is a wrist-slap," said Tieg. Ritwire smiled seraphically. Jack called the chief examiner to compare notes.

"I can't talk about it," his friend replied. "Washington took the case away from us and closed it. I'm being transferred."

□ 4 □

So THE STORY ENDS with the good guys frustrated, the bad guys unpunished, and the system in the throes of corruption. Eventually Westward will collapse, and the FSLIC will take responsibility for nearly $1 billion in deposits, most of them from money brokers. Most of the loans will be found worthless. The Justice Department will charge Wilmer Strait and his associates with nearly $200 million in bank fraud and embezzlement. FSLIC will sue Jack Tieg and the other directors for failing to perform their fiduciary duty, but the suit will be quietly settled when Jack's lawyers subpoena the Bank Board's records on the decision to transfer the examination to Washington.

The elements of this case show up in nearly every major thrift disaster and in many of the bank failures. A strong personality with strange national connections comes into control of a sleepy institution and makes it grow geometrically. He twists the thrift's investment policy away from traditional family homes into a bizarre array of corporate gambles and real estate schemes. The perverse incentives of deposit insurance make this growth possible. They encourage the reckless plunge for the big payoff. The Westward S&Ls of the industry attract jumbo CDs but not searching scrutiny because the federal insurance funds bear the risk. But the saga of Wilmer Strait raises the ultimate question: What happened to the federal scrutiny? Why weren't the insurance funds able to protect themselves?

All the history, all the economic theory and all the criminal investigations ultimately bring us to this question: What went wrong with the regulators? The framers of deposit insurance showed some awareness of its temptations and tried to build restraints into the system. Chief of these restraints were the bank and thrift examiners and their powers to discipline. It may be a second-best solution to have the defects of one government program ameliorated by another, but the checks and balances can make a difference. The failure of supervision was the fatal blow to the system.

To see its importance, compare the performance of the thrifts and of the commercial banks. Both presumably fell under the same perverse influence of deposit insurance. But the clients of FSLIC ran wild while those of the FDIC remained under some restraint. The difference is that in the thrift industry, the check of federal supervision almost totally collapsed. Also, as Treasury officials argue, capital standards were much stricter in banking. Many factors contributed to this breakdown, including confusion in the early Reagan administration about the meaning of deregulation. But FSLIC's problems aren't unique either.

Five years ago, the FDIC suffered its own disasters. The failures of the FDIC are less well known and their cost dwindles to insignificance next to a debacle measured in terms of the gross national product. But at the time, $1 billion seemed a lot of money to lose to fraud. Even worse, one saw the shadow over the FDIC that later took shape and substance as the nemesis of FSLIC. The suspicion of political interference emerged well before the crude extortions of Speaker of the House Jim Wright.

Wilmer Strait and dozens of real-life counterparts had discovered a simple secret. The best way to steal is to share a portion of the proceeds with those in a position to provide protection. The protectors may be in Congress or the White House or a governor's mansion. They may not understand just what they are doing, and their cut can be incredibly small. But they have stripped the defenses from the financial system, weakened banking and allowed the destruction of the savings and loan industry. The cost is $1200 and rising for every man, woman, and child in the United States.

The following chapters trace the rise of this system of political intervention. The many names and the intricate relations constitute a seamless web that has compromised some of our most important financial agencies. In the process there have been many victims: examiners, law enforcement agents, stockholders, depositors, and ultimately every taxpayer in the country.

CHAPTER TWO

□□□

"Proper and Consistent Conduct"

□ 1 □

JIM WRIGHT WAS SWEATING. As Speaker, he was the most powerful man in the United States House of Representatives, the second in succession to the presidency, the leader of the Democratic opposition. Yet the whispers in the marble lobbies and panelled cloakrooms of Congress had taken an ominous tone. It was the week of April 1, 1989, the cherry blossoms ringed the Tidal Basin with pink, and the House Ethics Committee was springing a series of damaging leaks about its forthcoming report on the Speaker's misconduct. The independent counsel had done an exhaustive job, in spite of acerbic exchanges with Ethics Committee members. He was dumping a 1,000-page report (including appendix) on the committee table and it listed 137 charges. The *Wall Street Journal* had run the story about the free Cadillac Wright had forgotten to report, and the Ethics Committee was going back into session to hear testimony about a Florida land deal that had just been uncovered.

No Speaker of the House had been in such trouble since the Progressive revolt against Uncle Joe Cannon in 1912. Even though Wright was staying very visible, flexing his bushy white eyebrows behind his wire rim glasses virtually every night on C-Span, the strain was beginning to tell. The Capitol buzzed over the tale that he had cancelled a press conference, then encountered a group of reporters in a hall and on the spot invited them to lunch. Over sandwiches, he had begun to muse about the possibility of stepping down from his post. It took his staff most of the next week to reassure nervous House Democrats.

With the help of his staff, Wright pulled himself together for a counterattack. One of the charges concerned a book deal that looked like a conduit for channeling campaign funds to Wright's own pocket. So House Democrats lodged their own ethics complaint about the promotion of a book by Newt Gingrich, the gadfly republican congressman from Georgia who had become Wright's main tormenter. Wright leaked his own preemptive confession to some of the more technical charges and offered to accept a wrist-slapping letter of reprimand. But as his aides tantalized leak-thirsty reporters with intimate chats in hideaway offices, Wright divulged his greatest triumph: the news that the Ethics Committee had voted to dismiss charges about his interference with federal savings and loan regulators.

As *Washington Post* reporter Tom Kenworthy wrote, on being favored with this break:

> In the absence of any financial interest by Wright in the thrifts, committee members argued that the speaker's conduct was proper and consistent with his role as a member of Congress, sources said.

So, without another word, the *Washington Post*, home of Woodward and Bernstein, heroes of the Watergate scandal, passed over the attempted cover-up of the greatest scandal of our generation. The House Ethics Committee would not only *not* condemn Wright's substantial role in destroying the American savings and loan industry, it would condone what he had done as "proper and consistent conduct" for Congress.

□ 2 □

THE ETHICS COMMITTEE VOTE tried to distance Wright and Congress from the costliest debacle of modern times. Estimates of losses in the savings and loan industry had reach $165 billion by early February, when President Bush offered a rescue plan that put the disaster squarely on the national agenda. The cost overwhelmed even the $1.2 trillion federal budget. So Bush proposed borrowing through an elaborate shell corporation to keep the cost off the budget. Interest payments on these 30-year bonds nearly doubled the cost of the rescue, to around $300 billion—more than $1200 for each man, woman, and child in the United States.

The financial holocaust had engulfed one-third of the savings and loan industry, which over the past five decades had lent millions of Americans the mortgages to buy their own homes. Nearly 1,000 of the nation's 3,100 thrifts were dead or dying. By the end of 1987, 435 thrifts had less cash on hand than the regulators considered the absolute minimum for safety, and just over 500 thrifts were insolvent by any standard. These last 500 were gone beyond hope, the "living dead," the regulators called them, but they stayed open. Even worse, they grew like cancers, at a faster rate than the rest of the industry. Desperate for cash, they offered the highest passbook rates in the country, pushing up costs for healthier thrifts. And every day they stayed in business, they lost up to $30 million.

More damaging even than the cost was the reason for the disaster. It wasn't the fall in oil prices, although many in the S&L industry were glad to say so. Nor was it drought, farm belt foreclosures or the southwestern regional recession. The most common elements in thrift failures, as the regulators began saying openly and even vehemently by mid-1987, were management misconduct, insider abuses, and outright fraud.

William K. Black, an intense red-haired, red-bearded lawyer who at the time served as deputy director of the Federal Savings and Loan Insurance Corporation, took the lead in trying to alert Congress. In testimony given in mid-June 1987, he warned that insider abuse and fraud, along with a pattern of quick growth and risky investments "are overwhelmingly responsible for virtually all recent failures, FSLIC's growing insolvency, and the huge coming losses that we have already identified." The biggest failures on FSLIC's books, he said, "have borne an uncanny resemblance to each other," a pattern of takeover, rapid growth, and "insane" loans designed to create the illusion that the thrift was running a huge profit. This pattern distinguished a group of interconnected thrifts that Black called the "Texas 40." On average, he said, institutions in this group were insolvent "by the end of 1984—well before the steep 1986 drop in oil prices."

Black described a problem that was becoming worse and spreading far beyond the thrift industry. Just three years earlier, a congressional survey blamed "criminal misconduct" for one-fourth of the savings and loan failures between 1980 and 1983. In early 1989, when the General Accounting Office reviewed the worst thrift failures from 1985 through 1987, it found fraud in all of them.

The same virus was infecting banking, legally a separate industry with its own layers of regulation. Several of the competing federal bank regulating bureaucracies have tried to downplay the problem, but the Office of the Comptroller of the Currency, the most venerable of the lot, faced it head on. It went back over nine years of the bank failures in its jurisdiction and found that no more than 7 percent could be blamed solely on the economy. Greed and bad management had caused the rest. Said Comptroller of the Currency Robert L. Clarke, "banks continue to fail the old-fashioned way."

These old-fashioned failures had become a ten-year obsession for a small group of professional staff hidden away on the Commerce, Consumer, and Monetary Affairs Subcommittee of the House Committee on Government Operations. Similar to Ralph Nader in outlook, they sometimes found that their investigations exceeded the curiosity of the congressmen they worked for. From 1982 on, this subcommittee, led by the precise and graying Staff Director Peter S. Barash, had tormented the federal regulators with hearings and reports on their inexplicable failures. (The staff also worked on at least one report that Subcommittee Chairman Doug Barnard Jr., Democrat of Georgia, saw fit not to publish.) In October 1988, Staff Director Barash produced a grand summation of his work under the misleadingly mild title, "Combating Fraud, Abuse and Misconduct in the Nation's Financial Institutions: Current Federal Efforts are Inadequate." Barash blasted the regulators for minimizing the problem, law enforcement for incompetence in fighting it, and even judges for their lenience in sentencing the perpetrators.

Barash pointed to the apparent coordination of players in whole series of bank and thrift failures, a network with more than a hint of Mafia involvement. "Many of these outsiders, primarily borrowers, loan brokers, money brokers and appraisers, know each other and identify institutions which are easy targets," he wrote. Even before the full onset of the savings and loan disaster, federal lawmen were swamped by bank fraud. As of June 30, 1988, there were 7,350 open FBI and federal grand jury investigations, one-third of them concentrated in Texas, California, and Florida. Oliver Revell, executive assistant director of the FBI, told Barash, "We have a serious endemic problem out there and it is getting worse and we have probably only seen the tip of the iceberg." Concluded Barash, "The United States Government is now confronting a growing and long-term epidemic of insider and outsider abuse, misconduct, and criminality in financial institutions."

Even Barash, however, declined to look too deeply into the cause of this epidemic of fraud. The stock answer was to blame the poorly trained, underpaid bank and thrift examiners for not catching the theft and book-cooking. With a starting salary of $14,000, the FSLIC examiners were easy prey for this scapegoating. But these examiners, although vastly outgunned, often performed well and even heroically. "The grunts are doing some good work," said one FDIC veteran, "but they're not getting support from higher up."

In case after case, when it was time for the supervisors to act on the recommendations from the field, a strange paralysis would set in. Bankers whom the examiners thought should be removed would stay on the job. Strictly enforceable penalties such as a cease and desist order would be replaced by less binding Memoranda of Understanding, which the bank or thrift would then ignore. Urgently needed follow-up examinations would be postponed, sometimes for years, or would produce equally toothless warnings.

Major scandals lurked in the files of nearly every bureaucracy in the country's patchwork, overlapping system of financial regulation. One hundred and fifty years of states' rights and Jacksonian resistance to central banking had created a dual banking system, in which both state and federal governments would charter and supervise their own banks and thrifts. It was understood that some state regulators would be incompetent or corrupt. But for the past decade, demoralization had spread through the supposedly superior federal ranks, even affecting the august Federal Reserve Board.

The extent of the paralysis depends on the history and structure of the regulatory agency. The Board of Governors of the Fed may be the most insulated, self-consciously defending itself from politics as it manipulates interest rates and money supply in its marble fortress on the fringe of the four blocks of offices that make up Washington's financial policy ghetto. But the twelve regional Federal Reserve Banks, which supervise the system's members and all bank holding companies, are open to local pressures.

The Office of the Comptroller of the Currency (OCC) has supervised all national banks since 1863, when the pressure of financing the Civil War brought the federal government back into the business of granting bank charters. As the oldest supervisor, the OCC jealously guards its independence, but its failures—Penn Square, Continental Illinois—have been among the biggest.

The deposit insurance agencies are the most far-reaching and the most vulnerable of the federal regulators. Because the FDIC and FSLIC provide deposit insurance to nearly the whole of their industries, their bureaucracies must face all the lobbying pressure a bank or thrift can buy. The FDIC insures and examines 13,000 commercial banks, whether chartered by the states or by the federal Comptroller of the Currency. It exerts discipline in its role as protector of the insurance fund. Its main lever is the threat to withdraw insurance coverage, since only states can close the banks they have chartered. This apparently technical point becomes important in some of the FDIC's most lurid cases.

The FDIC is so widely exposed to the rough and tumble of the industry that it is bound to take heavy bruising, but in some of its cases, according to critics from the Fed and the OCC, it has also taken unexpected dives. Some failures have been so egregious that it is ironic that the FDIC emerged as the white knight of President

Bush's thrift rescue. "The FDIC looks good mainly because it has FSLIC to be compared with," says one former state regulator.

For years, FSLIC and its parent, the Federal Home Loan Bank Board, were the doormats of financial regulation. Pay was lower, staffs were smaller, legal weapons were punier than in the agencies for bank regulation. The Bank Board structure put examiners in a perpetual hobble. Although it was modelled after the Federal Reserve Board, with 12 regional Home Loan Banks, it lacked the Fed's independence and prestige. The original role of the Bank Board, as outlined in the National Housing Act of 1934, had been to promote the founding of federally chartered savings and loan associations. The 12 Home Loan Banks were literally owned by the industry, which held part of their outstanding stock. Until late in the game, FSLIC examiners, directed from Washington, depended on the supervisory staff of the regional banks to enforce their findings. We will see how this system collapsed, fomenting low morale and scandals ranging from rings for expense account cheating to outright collusion with some of the industry's worst elements.

But the problems grew worse when, starting in late 1983, the Bank Board tried to clean house. The senior regulators ran squarely into the thrift industry's legendary political influence. Thrifts, the friendly neighborhood mortgage lender, had that down-home Norman Rockwell appeal. Banks were impersonal and plutocratic, but the savings and loans made you think of Jimmy Stewart in "It's a Wonderful Life." (Appropriately enough, however, Frank Capra's sentimental movie plot revolved around a case of embezzlement.) The thrift lobby and its largest group, the United States League of Savings Institutions, worked the grass roots image hard, mustering local executives in nearly every congressional district to lobby for its interests. Edwin Gray, the FHLBB's former director, complained that ever since the founding of the Bank Board, the industry's wishes had prevailed.

Until the early 1980s, the industry was so tightly hedged by the 1930s legislation that its power over the Bank Board did little harm. But with the wave of deregulation under President Carter and Reagan, something went wrong. A new breed of owners took over, hyperaggressive developers and dealmakers who saw the thrifts as giant cash cows ready to be milked. More than a few of these high-flyers ran into indictments when their thrifts later failed, but at the time they seemed to speak for the industry. The United States League threw its weight behind their interests, not those of the older, traditionally managed thrifts, or of the depositors. Congressional leaders around Fort Worth Democrat Jim Wright, soon to be Speaker, eagerly embraced the new men, who had become a major source of campaign funds. Ultimately, Jim Wright's circle turned a $20 or $30 billion savings and loan debacle into a $300 billion disaster by taking actions that the House Ethics Committee later concluded were "proper and consistent" with the conduct of a congressman.

□ 3 □

BY 1985, WHEN THE BANK BOARD IN WASHINGTON began to realize just how serious a fraud problem it had on its hands, FSLIC was in desperate shape. The fund, which backed the federal guarantee of thrift deposits, had come close to doubling its payouts in each of the past three years. At the 1985 loss rate of $3.5 billion, it was close to running out of money. FSLIC started 1986 with $3.8 billion in its main reserve and knew it would be gone in a year.

Edwin J. Gray, the square-jawed affable Bank Board chairman, began to plead with Congress for more money. In October 1985, he told the House Banking Committee, "The fund must be recapitalized. The alternative—that of deferring action on cases now before us and projected to come before us in the future—can only result in greater costs to the FSLIC down the road." Gray, a former public relations executive and press secretary for Ronald Reagan's 1980 campaign, sounded shriller and shriller warnings over the coming months. While Gray rang the public alarm, the Bank Board learned that FSLIC's problems exceeded its worst nightmares. Failures soared, and the FSLIC no longer had the cash on hand to pay off depositors. The best it could do in most cases was to replace the incompetent or crooked thrift managers with its own teams of care-takers. Yet even under FSLIC control, these thrifts kept losing money at a rate of $1 billion a month. Through 1986, FSLIC paid out more than $13 billion, wiping out all of its reserves and current income. It ended the year more than $6 billion in the hole.

At first, Congress seemed willing to help. In May 1986, the Bank Board and the Treasury Department sent a $15 billion recapitalization bill to the Hill, where Fernand J. St Germain and Chalmers Wylie, the chairman and the ranking minority member of the House Banking Committee respectively, put their names on it. In mid-September, Gray warned Chairman St Germain that FSLIC reserves were dropping rapidly. Within a week, the Banking Committee cleared the bill by a vote of 47 to 1. St Germain asked House leaders to vote on it under the "suspension calendar." This standard procedure suspends House rules and speeds up bills considered non-controversial.

If this bill had passed in 1986, it might not have solved the full problem, but it would certainly have kept the cost well below $60 or $150 or $300 billion. At this point, however, reports Richard Phelan, the House Ethics Committee's Special Outside Counsel, Jim Wright began to hear from Dallas businessmen. On September 15, Wright summoned Gray and several Bank Board staff to his office to pass on complaints that the regulators were using "heavy-handed" or "Gestapo-like" tactics. Wright and several Texas congressmen* did most of the talking, hammering at Gray for nearly two hours. Gray left the meeting in a somber mood. "Why wouldn't a good standard Democrat understand the need for regulation?" he asked an aide.

Within a few days, Gray had an answer. Wright followed up the meeting with a phone call about a Dallas real estate syndicator named Craig Hall. With a pencil-thin moustache and a salesman's oily smile, Hall had emerged as one of the town's busiest wheeler-dealers, packaging around 325 real estate partnerships, backed by a billion dollars of mortgages held by dozens of savings and loans.

*Republican Steve Bartlett and Democrats John Bryant and Martin Frost.

Many of Hall's partnerships were close to defaulting on their payments, and he was trying to arrange a global restructuring of his debt. His main obstacle was a stubborn FSLIC receiver at a California thrift.

Hall had gone to Wright for help in early September 1986 and found immediate sympathy. As Hall sat in Wright's Fort Worth district office, the majority leader (soon to be Speaker) made phone calls to Banking Committee Chairman St Germain and Congressman Tony Coelho, then head of the Democratic Congressional Campaign Committee. By the third week in September, Wright had asked Gray to review the FSLIC receiver's intransigence. To make his point, Wright pulled the recapitalization bill from the suspension calendar.

Gray and his staff got the message that the only way to get FSLIC more money was to satisfy Craig Hall. Over the last weekend in September, Gray replaced the recalcitrant conservator, and Hall managed to reshuffle his loans. Mollified, Wright returned the recapitalization bill to the calendar, and it passed the House by a voice vote.

But FSLIC's troubles were just beginning. In the Senate, the recapitalization bill bogged down in a separate controversy, and Congress adjourned for elections before the two Houses could agree. The 100th Congress convened in January 1987 with recapitalization high on the agenda. But Wright was now Speaker, and the thrift industry smelled blood. The United States League of Savings Institutions concluded that if FSLIC had too much money, it would close too many of the League's members. Some of the Texas "high-flyers," perhaps emboldened by Hall's success, may have thought Wright offered them a last chance to roll the Bank Board. It helped that two of these figures, Thomas Gaubert and Don Ray Dixon, had become important fund raisers for congressional Democrats. Gaubert, in fact, was finance chairman for Tony Coelho's Democratic Congressional Campaign Committee.

The full story of these two characters and their roles in the "Texas 40," the network of corrupt and failing thrifts, will come later. Suffice it to say that both of their thrifts, Gaubert's Independent

American and Dixon's Vernon Savings and Loan, were well past the point of collapse, and when they were finally closed, they cost FSLIC around $2 billion. Gaubert, the bluff, hearty entrepreneur, and Dixon, the high-living hometown boy, were sued for bank fraud in civil actions. (Gaubert was indicted but acquitted in a criminal case. Dixon, as of this writing, has not faced criminal charges.) But for a short time, their influence helped induce Congress to abandon the rescue of FSLIC, with disastrous consequences.

In early November 1986, after the 99th Congress had adjourned without providing for FSLIC, Wright called Gray about Thomas Gaubert. Bank Board supervisors had already removed Gaubert from his Independent American Savings Association two years earlier and, in January 1986, signed an agreement barring him from all FSLIC-insured thrifts. Gaubert complained to Wright that he had been unfairly pressured. In Wright's own words:

> I called Ed Gray. I said, "Ed Gray, Tom Gaubert." He said, "Yes, I know of him." I said, "Do you know the circumstances surrounding his situation?" He said, "No."

Wright summarized Gaubert's claims and then asked Gray, " 'Would you hear him? Would you let him come talk to you?' He said, 'Yes.' "

Gray's "Yes," raised administrative embarrassments because the informal contacts with Gaubert barred Gray, under Bank Board rules, from sitting in judgment on the Independent American case. But Gray felt himself in a bind. "Speaker Wright had the power to stop and kill our FSLIC recap legislation," he explained to Special Counsel Phelan. Gray's solution was to have the Bank Board lawyers appoint an outside investigator to review FSLIC's treatment of Gaubert, a step apparently without precedent. More than three years later, Gray was astonished to read in the Phelan report that the investigator had been chosen from a list supplied by Gaubert.*

Wright made his call for Don Dixon shortly after Christmas. Dixon's Vernon Savings and Loan, based in North Dallas, had al-

---

*The investigator, a distinguished Nashville defense attorney named Aubrey Harwell, concluded that, aside from some minor arbitrary behavior, the Bank Board had treated Gaubert appropriately.

ready become notorious; the former president of the Dallas Home Loan Bank told Phelan that the thrift was "the worst-run, worst-managed debacle that he knew of in the savings and loan industry." But Dixon was close to Wright's number three man, California Congressman Tony Coelho. Among other favors, Dixon had placed Vernon's 112-foot yacht "High Spirits" at the disposal of the Democratic Congressional Campaign Committee and neglected to bill for the charter fee. Wright's staff heard from Coelho that FSLIC was going to shut down Vernon that day, and Wright agreed to ask Gray for more time.

Wright called Gray from Fort Worth, just before catching a plane back to Washington, and perhaps it was the haste that created a disastrous misunderstanding. When Wright asked about plans to "shut down" Vernon, Gray thought he meant to put the institution in receivership, and he answered that the Bank Board hadn't voted to do that. In fact, the supervisors had taken a lesser step, putting Vernon up for a merger if a taker could be found. When, after Wright's call, Gray learned about the lower level action, he spent two hours trying to locate Wright's chief of staff to explain the difference. The explanation didn't work. As the Phelan report concluded, "Wright thereafter became wed to a mistaken version of the facts. He believed that Gray had promised that the Bank Board was not going to 'close down' Vernon, but that it did so anyway."

(Vernon ultimately stayed out of receivership for another three months, even though it was losing $10 million a month. In a still-pending civil suit, the receivers charged Dixon with siphoning off millions for his personal use.)

Wright now had a real grudge against the Bank Board, based on the Dixon and Gaubert cases. As he complained later, he got involved with the regulators on three issues. The first, involving Craig Hall, "was handled very satisfactorily and worked out very well." The other two, he said, "had been extremely unsatisfactory." His dissatisfaction had an easy target, the FSLIC recapitalization bill.

St Germain and Wylie had reintroduced the bill in the first week of January 1987 and, as promised, planned to speed it to the House floor in March. But on January 22, Wright sent up a flare. Gray was

testifying for the bill before Banking Subcommittee Chairman Doug
Barnard, sponsor of so many hearings on bank fraud, when to general astonishment, Barnard asked about "overly rigorous and arbitrary" supervisory actions. "For example," said Barnard, "in Texas
people are especially concerned over situations like Vernon Savings
and Loan and Independent American Savings and Loan." Gray soon
learned that the question had come down directly from the Speaker.
"Before the hearing was even over, Congressman Barnard or one
of his immediate assistants had talked to my assistant," Gray told
Phelan, "and said to her very apologetically that he was really sorry
he had to ask those questions, but he had to do it because the Speaker
had told him he had to do it."

On January 29, Wright went to lunch with St Germain and several other congressmen to talk about the Bank Board. The men from
Texas complained about FSLIC's "high-handedness," and St Germain agreed to investigate. The lunch also sparked a congressional
movement for "forbearance" provisions, riders in the recapitalization bill that would tie FSLIC's hands in dealing with troubled
thrifts. By March 1987 St Germain had junked his original bill and
offered FSLIC a much smaller $5 billion bailout over two years. His
new bill contained restrictions on Bank Board examiners unheard
of for other federal regulators.

The minimal recapitalization, one-third the size of the original,
had one widely understood effect. It would prevent FSLIC from closing all but a handful of thrifts, because the fund simply would not
have the money to pay off depositors. The United States League of
Savings Institutions said explicitly in a letter introduced in floor
debate, "We are seriously troubled about the FSLIC's ability to use
wisely monies provided to it. Thus, we have structured a proposal
for funding the FSLIC that has strong and effective congressional
oversight built into it."

At this point, however, FSLIC had no monies at all to use, wisely
or not. The General Accounting Office, in conducting its annual
audit, had concluded that the fund was insolvent by at least $6 billion.
On March 2, Chairman Gray wrote Senator William Proxmire,
chairman of the Senate Banking Committee, that public disclosure

of the GAO's finding could have "wide-ranging" impact, including a series of bank runs that FSLIC might not be able to handle. Copies of the letter went to House Banking Chairman St Germain and Speaker Wright.

This letter had less impact on Wright, it appears, than another impending embarrassment. On March 20 1987, Vernon went into receivership. On April 27, FSLIC sued Dixon and former officers and directors of Vernon, in a civil action, charging fraud, self-dealing, and breach of fiduciary duty. Files in the Federal Courthouse in Dallas bulged with Don Dixon's dirty linen. On April 28, Wright and St Germain issued a joint press release dropping their opposition to a $15 billion recapitalization. Wright may have taken himself out of the front line, but Tony Coelho, now the House Majority Whip, and a friend of Dixon, kept up the fight. When the House took up recap in early May, Wright and St Germain spoke in favor of $15 billion. Coelho insisted on $5 billion. The House sided with Coelho, by a vote of 258 to 153.

The conference with the Senate somewhat modified the damage. Under threat of a presidential veto, the conferees approved a $10.8 billion bailout, more than either chamber had voted. The bill, absurdly named the Competitive Equality Banking Act of 1987 (CEBA), was signed into law on August 10. Even on its own merits, CEBA was a national scandal. In the face of overwhelming evidence to the contrary, it presumed that Bank Board examiners were too effective and legislated a range of detailed interferences with their work. It expressly rescinded some of the measures the Bank Board had adopted to cope with rampant fraud. Above all, it deliberately starved FSLIC, not even providing the means to restore the fund to solvency. Both the United States League and the House leaders wanted to keep FSLIC from closing insolvent thrifts, but every day the "living dead" opened their doors for business, they lost another $30 million, and the cost of rescuing the thrift industry grew geometrically.

But the story goes well beyond the details of the FSLIC recapitalization bill. It involves a Congress willing to sacrifice the public good to the narrow interests of cronies and big contributors, and congressmen who react to opposition with a mixture of arrogance and petty spite. For another look at the spirit behind the FSLIC disaster, consider the conduct of Speaker Wright toward its Deputy Director William K. Black.

Black, a young and slightly built redhead who was considered one of the Bank Board's brightest men, acted as its "point man" on recapitalization. But he was also cursed with an abundance of moral courage. "He doesn't like perversion of the process," said former Bank Board Chairman Edwin Gray, who made Black his right-hand man. "He doesn't like corruption."

Black ran into trouble with Wright in early February 1987 when a group of Bank Board and Dallas Home Loan Bank officers met with the Speaker in his offices. The regulators asked for the meeting, using Dallas and Washington power-broker Robert Strauss as go-between, to try to allay Wright's problem with recapitalization. The talk seemed to go smoothly until Wright brought up his phone call with Gray about "shutting down" Vernon Savings. Wright grew vexed about Gray's "misrepresentation" and Black tried to correct him. Black remembers that Wright accused him of "prevaricating."

"I'm a midwesterner," Black replied, he thought humorously, "and midwesterners don't prevaricate."

Instead of laughing, recounts the Phelan report, "Wright began shouting. He went on for a while and then stopped. No one spoke for about 20 seconds." The meeting was over.

Neither Black nor Gray met with Wright again. Yet they still had a public forum in congressional testimony, or so they thought. In the last days of the recapitalization fight, Black trudged up Capitol Hill for a hearing at the House Banking Committee. Chairman St Germain's letter of invitation had asked, in part, for the Bank Board's thoughts on "the possible causal relationship between bank fraud or insider dealings and bank failures." Black delivered the answer, quoted earlier, that bank fraud was "overwhelmingly responsible for virtually all recent failures." He described in excruciating detail the way that Texas high-flyers such as Don Dixon had structured their loans like a Ponzi scheme, to create high profits out of bookkeeping fictions. "Congress can help," he said, "by deleting the so-called forbearance language in the House recapitalization bill—which would be used by those engaged in fraud and insider abuse to delay the Bank Board from ending their misconduct." He added a barb about the cost of delay. "Over $2.5 billion in net operating losses have occurred," he said, "since the FSLIC recapitalization bill was first put on hold in October 1986."

St Germain had an advance text, and the message was more than he could bear. As Black waited in the hearing room, St Germain sent a letter to the Bank Board cancelling the hearing. "You have obviously misinterpreted our letter in terms of the primary purpose of the hearings," St Germain wrote. "I'm convinced he acted at the behest of the Speaker," says Gray.

Gray's term as Bank Board Chairman was almost up, and Black's days in Washington were numbered. On July 1, 1987, Gray turned his job over to M. Danny Wall, former Republican staff director of the Senate Banking Committee. Black left for the the Federal Home Loan Bank of San Francisco. As the largest of the Home Loan Banks, it was legally and temperamentally an independent entity. But Wright hadn't forgotten him.

Shortly after taking office, Danny Wall paid a courtesy visit to Speaker Wright. As he waited in the Speaker's anteroom, some of Wright's staff asked if Black still worked for the Bank Board. When Wall walked into Wright's office, the Speaker asked him the same. Wall answered that Black was out of his jurisdiction, and the matter dropped for a time. By the end of 1987, however, Wright went after Black again. An aide to the Speaker named Phil Duncan called the Bank Board's director of congressional affairs and said they couldn't accept the argument that the San Francisco Bank was independent. Said the Phelan report, "He wanted Black fired."

Special Counsel Phelan seemed baffled by this episode. "William Black, in our opinion," he wrote, "was one of the most impressive witnesses to appear before the Committee." It was Wright himself who wanted Black fired, concluded Phelan, yet "the grievance seems completely personal." Phelan called it a clear violation of House ethics.

Although Special Counsel Phelan devoted one-third of his final 1989 report to Wright's pressures on the Bank Board, the House Ethics Committee didn't share his outrage. Neither the order to fire Black, the tirades on behalf of Dixon and Gaubert, the extortion to bail out Craig Hall, or the attempt to hold the financial integrity of FSLIC and the safety of the banking system hostage to the needs of some shady constituents, none of this behavior struck the Committee as beyond the bounds for a member of Congress. On a series of bipartisan votes, in which up to four Republicans sided with all six Democrats, the Ethics Committee voted to dismiss all charges that Wright "exercised undue influence" in dealing with the Bank Board. Explained the Committee's report:

> The assertion that the exercise of undue influence can arise based upon a legislator's expressions of interest jeopardizes the ability of Members effectively to represent persons and organizations having concern with the activities of executive agencies.

The Committee was somewhat less forgiving than the *Washington Post* reporter who passed on the phrase "proper and consistent" conduct. It did admit that Wright may have been "intemperate." But the damage was done. Jim Wright's personal drama had ratified a new brand of institutional corruption. The focus of the inquiry shifted away from the $300 billion savings and loan disaster, which Wright and his congressional coterie had certainly helped foster. The spotlight of the press fell instead on personal business deals involving perhaps $200,000. Badly tarnished as Wright may have been, the inquiry had become a prime example of Washington's rush to trivialize its scandals.

□ 4 □

AS THE ETHICS COMMITTEE BLUNTLY ACKNOWLEDGED, Congress had an interest of its own to protect. Its members wanted to preserve all the tools they could muster "to represent persons and organi-

zations having concern with the activities of executive agencies."
Who were these "persons and organizations"? In the case of the
thrifts, they were certainly not the public, the depositor, or even
the honest businessman. They were the large contributors who had
a very practical reason for giving money to politicians. They were
people who were worried about the regulators and wanted to buy all
the protection Congress could offer.

The S&Ls, and banking in general, fell prey to a pattern of
institutionalized bribery, or "honest graft," as *Wall Street Journal*
reporter Brooks Jackson described it in a valuable book of that name.
"High-flyers" bent on plundering a thrift or bank had discovered
that if they invested a small portion of their take in campaign contributions they could buy enough political clout to keep the examiners off their backs for a year or two or five, long enough anyway
to develop a $20 to $50 to $100 million scam. And, since to pocket
one dollar they had to lend $20, the loss at a single corrupt thrift
could easily exceed a billion.

Congress was an easy mark. After a decade of campaign finance
hypocrisy, its members needed the money more than ever. The
growth of television advertising had made the multi-million dollar
campaign a common event. With the right technology, an incumbent
could virtually guarantee his seat; the rate of re-election in the 1988
House campaign exceeded 98 percent.

Campaign finance laws, designed to reduce the power of political
"fat cats," had increased the leverage of bankers and their go-be-
tweens. The reforms shifted power to people who could easily raise
a large number of maximum donations. Lawyers with a wide range
of clients fit the category (especially if their practice dealt with
government). Bankers, with their many economic dependents, also
fit. This power shift accompanied a more sinister development, the
spread of the notion that with the right political pressures, the bank
and thrift regulators could be swayed.

This pattern had received official sanction from the House Ethics
Committee and even worse, from the keepers of Washington's pub-
lic opinion. A spate of newspaper columns and editorials treated
Wright's troubles as the product of a shift in ethical standards, a

"new Victorianism" that was exposing Congress to much higher levels of personal scrutiny. The pendulum was swinging indeed, but in a much different direction. Without arousing much protest, one branch of government had declared that it was all right to politicize the regulators, on behalf of the high-flyers who most needed to be controlled.

Just on the face of it—the thrift industry ruined at a public cost of $300 billion—the result was an incredible scandal. Congress had been willfully irresponsible; in the face of urgent warnings, it had delayed the rescue of FSLIC and then had saddled it with the harmful CEBA, and all to protect the worst elements of the industry. It is hard to think of a grosser betrayal of the public interest. The one-hundredth Congress may well be remembered as the most corrupt since the days of the Credit Mobilier scandal in the late nineteenth century. And the 101st Congress is an accomplice after the fact.

□□□

CHAPTER THREE

The Edge of the Meltdown

□ 1 □

"THEY GAVE US A BAND-AID AND SAID, 'Take care of it until 1989,' " said M. Danny Wall at a poignant and bitter occasion. He was speaking in Dallas at the 1989 annual meeting of its Federal Home Loan Bank. It was the last public gathering of the three members of the Home Loan Bank Board before they were disbanded by President Bush's S&L "rescue" plan. Wall was looking back over two years of makeshift temporizing, of desperate shuffling with grossly inadequate resources. He had been given a very small Band-Aid indeed and was told to avert the financial equivalent of a nuclear meltdown. Wall had scrambled under a threat not known since the depression, the possibility of widespread bank runs and a general panic. In attempting to protect a small group of corrupt thrifts, Speaker Wright and his cronies had jeopardized the stability of the country's savings institutions.

Danny Wall had replaced Edwin Gray as Bank Board chairman in mid-1987, at the tail end of the congressional mugging of FSLIC. Wall, with his trim, pointed beard and piercing gaze, was a product of Capitol Hill. He had worked as staff director of the Senate Banking Committee in the two years in which Republicans held the majority, and he had been tight with Republican Banking Committee Chair-

man Jake Garn since their days together in the municipal government of Salt Lake City, Utah. Wall seemed the man to mollify Congress after Ed Gray's open war with Jim Wright. Wall understood
that he somehow had to keep the lid on the savings and loan disaster
until after the 1988 elections.

Wall's first problem was Texas. More specifically, it was the
governor of Texas, the crotchety, blunt Republican William Clements, back for a second term after losing to the good ol' boy Democratic establishment and not really caring whose toes he trampled.
On August 10, 1987, the day President Reagan signed CEBA, the
FSLIC recapitalization bill, Governor Clements harrumphed to reporters from the *Amarillo Daily News* that the crisis was just beginning. The Bank Board was "defrauding the public," he said, by
keeping insolvent thrifts open.

"I'll predict what is going to happen," he told the reporters from
the Panhandle. "The federal government is finally going to belly up
to this problem, and when they do, they're going to pay off those
depositors like 30 cents on the dollar, and give them a piece of
paper, like a bond . . . like an IOU."

Some depositors in Amarillo were listening. Roy G. Cartwright,
president of the First Federal Savings & Loan, told the banking trade
journal *American Banker,* "I had one longtime customer who withdrew his $16,000, and told me, 'Roy, thanks, but I just can't take a
chance. The governor caused me to withdraw the funds.' " Other
thrifts in town reported that some customers were taking out their
life savings. The industry mustered its forces to denounce Governor
Clements and braced for a full-scale run.

The Texas Savings and Loan League sent out letters to its members telling them how to respond to their customers. The League's
somewhat inaccurate line was that the CEBA bill placed the "full
faith and credit of the government" behind FSLIC. Thrift presidents
around the state called Clements irresponsible. Said one, "I hope
people in Texas realize that the governor has a tendency to shoot
from the hip and retract things later." In Washington, Danny Wall
himself called a press conference to squelch the panic. "Wholesale
closings of thrifts is no answer," he said. "The governor is wrong."

Remarkably, the barrage against Clements worked, perhaps because the governor did have a reputation for shooting from the hip. None of the Amarillo thrifts were seriously threatened, and withdrawals elsewhere seemed normal. The Texas flap subsided quickly, and Danny Wall just as quickly took credit. "The preventative action worked," he said.

Yet the very ferocity of the attacks on Clements gave the tipoff that in many ways the governor was right. Clements stubbornly refused to retract his blast at FSLIC. Instead, he decided to appoint a task force to study the savings and loan industry. His task force ultimately produced one of the first detailed public warnings about the extent of the disaster.

In the meantime, Danny Wall had a stroke of good luck, the Black Monday stock market crash of October 19, 1987. The country watched in horror as the crumbling bull market in securities turned into a rout. By the lunch hour, the Dow Jones average had dropped a sickening 200 points. While the Wall Street brokers fell apart and stopped answering their telephones, shopkeepers and professionals stopped each other on Main Streets around the country, shaking their heads helplessly over the plunge. By the closing bell, the market had fallen 508 points, losing nearly a quarter of its value, a bigger fall than Black Friday, 1929. Thoughts of the Great Depression were everywhere. Federal Reserve Chairman Alan Greenspan announced that the Fed stood ready to avert any bank runs.

But the economy held firm, and the savings and loans, ironically, were the first to benefit. Investors who pulled their money from the stock market were putting it in certificates of deposit. The thrifts received $6.1 billion in fresh deposits that October, a new record for the month and the biggest monthly increase since 1984. The turnaround was dramatic. Deposits had been falling through most of the preceding year, and even with the October surge, net new deposits for the first ten months of 1987 dropped by $7.7 billion below 1986. Some analysts grumped that the inflow masked a "silent run" on the S&Ls. But most of those new CDs wouldn't be cashed until maturity. The stock market crash gave the thrifts about a year's reprieve.

Some thrift industry apologists even used the post-Crash deposits to argue that confidence in S&Ls was high. The United States League of Savings Institutions insisted, as always, that if the regulators just gave the thrifts more leeway to work out their problem loans, the crisis would diminish. But a game of doomsday leapfrog was starting to unroll over the size of the thrifts' losses. The Bank Board would offer an official, very conservative estimate. The General Accounting Office or a rival regulator would top it, and a private analyst would hit the newspapers with a number twice as large as either. Within three months, the Bank Board would accept the high estimate, and the GAO and the consultants would leapfrog it once more. The predicted cost of cleaning up the existing, identified problem grew in near geometrical progression, from $17.8 billion to $30 billion to $50 billion to $80 billion to $156 billion. By the end of 1990, the low official estimate was $325 billion, and the high private estimate (my own) was $1.5 trillion.

After several delays, Governor Clements released his report in January, 1988, at the start of this leapfrog, and its understated numbers showed just how desperate the situation had become. Of the 213 Texas state-chartered S&Ls, 66 percent had less than the already lax regulatory requirement of 3 percent capital (in principle, the cash available to absorb losses but in practice a bookkeeping fiction much diluted by intangibles such as "goodwill"). A full 40 percent of the state S&LS, a total of 85, were already insolvent. The bankrupt thrifts were still open because of "regulatory forbearance," a euphemism for the FSLIC's lack of cash to pay off the depositors. The State Commissioner of Savings and Loans had taken 69, most but not all, of the bankrupt state thrifts under his spotty supervision. The Bank Board had taken over 11 more.

Just these 80 cases, said Clements's Texas Task Force, were losing about $4.5 billion a year. It takes a while for this number to sink in, and the report spells out its meaning. Consider that CEBA, the bill that Congress had grudgingly passed in 1987 to rescue FSLIC, allowed the national fund to raise $10.8 billion over three years but not more than $3.75 billion a year. All of this money would be swallowed up by just 80 thrifts in Texas. And they would still be $750 million in the red each year. These were the S&Ls, moreover, that supposedly had been taken away from the crooks and incompetents and were being run safely by the regulators. What about all the undetected losses in the other Texas thrifts, not to mention the equally large disasters waiting to be uncovered in the rest of the country? The task force concluded, "The ultimate cost will be borne by the United States taxpayer." Governor Clements may have shot from the hip in his Amarillo interview, but he hit the target.

These numbers weren't lost on the Bank Board. One reason for Governor Clements's postponement of the report, it turned out, was his desire to cooperate with the Reagan administration, his ideological ally, and for several months his task force had worked closely with the federal regulators. Danny Wall wanted to produce at least the appearance of a solution. A week after the release of the Texas report, Wall held a press conference to announce his Southwest Plan.

□ 2 □

ARMED WITH CHARTS AND A POINTER, Wall laid out a strategy of "consolidation and new capital." He wanted to merge the sick thrifts with the healthy, reducing the total in Texas to around 160. With a number of sweeteners, some of them later very controversial, he hoped to attract investors with fresh money. The Bank Board would put up some of the new cash raised to revive FSLIC, but Wall wanted to stretch out his resources by writing blank checks and IOUs. He emphasized that his plan had the blessing of Governor Clements's Task Force.

As an attempt to deploy the Band-Aid Wall had been given, this plan showed remarkable ingenuity. As a real solution, it was far less. Three months passed before the first consolidation of four smaller thrifts took place under the auspices of the Southwest Plan. Several big deals came together during the summer, but they basically created one big FSLIC-controlled problem thrift out of clusters of slightly smaller problems. Said Texas Congresman Henry Gonzales, St Germain's successor as banking committee chairman, "they've taken a lot of dead horses and stitched them into one big horse that's just as dead and stinks even more." The outside money didn't come pouring in until almost the last minute, the last weeks of December, just before an important tax benefit was about to expire. In those hectic weeks, Danny Wall's lawyers found themselves facing some of the sharpest dealmakers in the country, such as the billionaire Bass brothers of Fort Worth and the corporate raider Ronald Perelman, famous for his conquest of Avon Cosmetics. Very few thought the Bank Board would come out ahead in the negotiations.

Chief among the skeptics were the auditors at the General Accounting Office, the respected independent watchdogs reporting to Congress. The GAO kept close watch over the Southwest Plan mergers, 15 in all, involving 87 insolvent thrifts, and it found plenty to worry about. The deals, it said, were creating thinly capitalized, FSLIC-subsidized super-thrifts that had strong potential for remaining super-problems. To make up for its lack of cash, FSLIC had provided notes, its IOU, and guarantees of profits on the most risky assets, essentially a blank check. No one really knew what numbers would eventually be written on the blank check, but it was a good bet they would be much larger than expected. When Danny Wall had first announced his plan, he had said that FSLIC could cover the cost out of its own resources, including the recap, industry insurance premiums and other income, which he estimated at $20 billion over the next three years. The subsidies and inducements had succeeded in attracting only a bit over $1 billion from outside investors. Now GAO concluded that the total cost of the Southwest deals would be $44 billion.

Coming from the impartial GAO, this criticism was fair comment. The more galling attacks came from congressmen who hammered on the Southwest deals as taxpayer-financed giveaways to the corporate sharks. Maybe they were, but Wall relied so much on notes, subsidies and tax breaks because he had no cash. And he had no cash because Congress had deliberately put a stranglehold on FSLIC.

By business standards, the Southwest Plan was a failure. Complaints and forebodings dominated that 1989 annual meeting of the Dallas Home Loan Bank, the last reunion of the three-man Bank

Board. One reporter described the atmosphere as a "dark and some-times bitter gripe session." One of the main gripes concerned the failure to break the "Texas premium," the extra interest that Texas thrifts (and banks) had to pay to attract funds, thanks to the bidding competition from the corrupt and insolvent thrifts. The premium did come down for a while, as FSLIC tried to drive out the "hot money." But by May 1989, the rates had edged up again. One speaker at Dallas blamed the rise squarely on government inter-vention. Insolvent thrifts that had been freshly seized by regulators were jacking up their CD rates on the principle that they had nothing to lose. They could gamble the deposits on high-risk investments and let their new owners, the deposit insurance funds, bail them out if they lost.

The new thrifts were still a long way from inspiring confidence. Even able managers were plagued by continuing losses and the pain of dealing with government bureaucracy. (FSLIC kept part owner-ship and insisted on approving large deals.) Standard and Poor's, the credit raters, hinted cryptically that the thrifts were dragged down by doubts about FSLIC's own solvency.

But these complaints missed the point. Wall's achievement wasn't economic, it was political. By creating the illusion of activity, he had kept the thrift scandal out of the 1988 election.

Not that anyone in Congress wanted to talk about it. By late 1988, it was apparent that CEBA was easily one of the most irre-sponsible acts ever produced by that institution. Remarkably, very few of the candidates had the wit to raise the issue. The Democratic presidential challenger Michael Dukakis, in one of his more naive moments, made a speech blaming the debacle on the Reagan ad-ministration's deregulation, presided over by Vice President Bush. Bush retorted that the Democratic Congress had some role in the problem, and the issue faded from the presidential debate. Only one race may have been decided by the thrift debacle, but that one was important. House Banking Committee Chairman Fernand St Ger-main had been weakened by House Ethics Committee and Justice Department probes of the lavish favors he had received from S&L lobbyists, and he lost by a narrow margin.

Although most politicians avoided the problem, it wasn't going away. With the election wrapped up, serious voices began to warn that the numbers were worse than ever. Lowell Bryan of the consulting firm McKinsey & Company reported in mid-November not only that it was a $100 billion crisis, but that in the last two years the unhealthy thrifts had become a much larger part of the industry, taking up one-third of its deposits. George Bush's transition team knew that it had to face the S&Ls immediately or jeopardize his presidency. "This isn't just a huge problem," one of his planners told the *Wall Street Journal*. "We've got huge problems all around. This one is the problem."

□ 3 □

THE PROBLEM, NOW, was far more serious than ever before. The specter of a bank panic, looming in the background ever since Governor Clements shot off his mouth in Amarillo, was on the verge of realization. A year had passed since Wall Street's Black Monday, and all those CDs purchased in the flight from the stock market crash were coming to maturity. Money was leaving the thrift industry as rapidly as it had come in. Withdrawals reached records of $7 billion in November 1988 and $8 billion in December. The "silent run" had returned as a thundering roar.

After the false solutions of CEBA and the Southwest Plan, the industry was in worse shape than ever. Losses in the fourth quarter of 1988 surged to $2.3 billion. More than half of the loss came from 77 insolvent thrifts in Texas. The red ink for the year reached a record $12.1 billion, a figure swollen by booking the cost of closing or merging 223 thrifts during the year. Danny Wall had stretched his Band-Aid through the election, but now it was shot.

A new approach was necessary, and it was brewing at the Treasury Department, which had kept suspiciously quiet during most of the year. A report in the fall gave the first sign that something was stirring. Nicholas F. Brady, the newly appointed Treasury Secretary, was puzzled by the leapfrogging figures on the size of the thrift crisis, and he set out to get his own numbers.

Brady had headed a commission to review Black Monday, and for his new assignment he turned to two professors from the Harvard Business School who had directed that study: Robert R. Glauber, who combined the stuffiness of a professor and an investment banker, and David W. Mullins, Jr., a wiry, sandy-haired idea man, who spilled out eager, nonstop policy analysis. They also had a talent for clandestine operations. Brady brought them into the Treasury in October 1988 and hid them in the office of a recently retired undersecretary. The ornate gold leaf title over the transom was whitewashed, and the office was identified only by Glauber's name. They were told to "compartmentalize," keeping their inquiries so limited that neither Treasury regulars nor the regulators could figure out what they were doing. They didn't even use the Treasury's computers. Says Mullins, "My first official action was to put in a requisition for personal computers for the staff." Personal computers were standard equipment at Harvard but an innovation at Treasury, and they helped maintain security.

Through November, their team turned the new, top-of-the line Compaqs to the task of assimilating data. They say that, using the procedure of the earlier stock market task force, they wanted to let their policy emerge from the facts. The crucial finding, to their mind, was the importance of adequate capital. The thrifts that were well capitalized, that had a substantial amount of the owner's money at risk, were less likely to take chances and get in trouble. This point, they said, may also explain why banks, which had to put up at least twice as much capital as thrifts, were less troubled.

After the election in November, it was time to grapple with policy. Among the wide range of issues, the one Glauber and Mullins insisted on most strongly was to increase capital requirements. In the congressional struggles, this issue would be one of the most contentious. In focusing on capital, however, they slighted the more basic structural problems of deposit insurance. The S&L rescue did almost nothing to deal with those perverse incentives, except to place some direct regulation on brokered deposits. Glauber and Mullins also took a complacent view of the broadened investment powers granted by Garn-St Germain. For the past decade, Treasury had consistently argued against regulation of investment decisions. Glauber even advanced the idea that the flexible thrift charter, coupled with the strength of the recapitalized insurance fund, to be renamed the SAIF, would attract smaller banks to change charters. He envisioned a rationalization of federal regulation in which the SAIF and the Treasury's Office of Thrift Supervision would become the haven for small neighborhood institutions, and larger commercial banks would stay with the FDIC.

But the immediate concern was to bring the thrift crisis under control quickly, even before their bill took its stormy way through Congress. Glauber and Mullins put a great deal of planning into an administrative coup, to take effect as soon as President Bush announced his plan. They would place the troubled thrifts under the jurisdiction of the FDIC immediately, thus sealing the doom of the Bank Board and permanently weakening the thrift lobby. Until Congress passed the bill and allowed funding, this stroke dealt more in form than substance. Its immediate practical effect was to stretch thin the manpower of the FDIC. And all the time Glauber and Mullins kept an anxious eye on the market reaction. The threat of a panic was never too far from their minds.

The secrecy was intended to decrease bureaucratic in-fighting and to avoid leaks that might spread public alarm. Brady's bunch soon had a chance to see how damaging a leak could be. Within a week of the Bush inauguration, word got out that the administration might try to replenish FSLIC by charging thrift depositors a 25 cent premium on each $100 in their account. The proposal was politically impossible, but it served one public benefit. It brought the thrift crisis home to average citizens. They could ignore the argument over incomprehensibly large numbers, but they would react vehemently to an attempt to extract a quarter from their pockets. The furor killed the idea on the spot. It also brought the nightmare of a run closer than ever.

Depositors reacted to the two-bits leak the way anyone would to news of a possible price rise; they looked for a cheaper place to put their money. Reports of heavy withdrawals from S&Ls began to flood the news. "There is no stampede," said Barney Beeksma, the new chairman of the United States League, "but the system is very fragile." Thrift chairmen were receiving anxious calls from their own parents. Treasury officials complained that their idea was misunderstood. The premium would tax commercial banks as well, so there would be no place to run to. Danny Wall passed on a public reassurance from the heads of his regional offices. "In the overall sense at the district bank level, they don't see anything of any significance," he said. But something of significance caught the attention of President Bush. On the Friday of his first full week in office, his aides told reporters to be sure to attend the daily session in the White House briefing room. On this short notice, President Bush called his first full-scale press conference. He quickly volunteered that S&L deposits "are sound, they are good, dollar-good. I just want to assure the American people of that." His aides passed the word that the two-bits fee idea had been dropped. Danny Wall went on television to say, "I think it's clear from the response that it's dead on arrival."

Wall didn't talk about it, but the response that made the most dramatic impression came from Jackson, Mississippi. The state capitol had just been shocked by a short but sharp run on one of its prominent thrifts. In a scene like something from the depression, depositors had lined up to withdraw millions of dollars in a few hours.

During the second week of January 1989, rumors had been flying about the imminent demise of Unifirst Savings Bank, ironically one of the stronger thrifts under the Home Loan of Dallas. On the morning of Friday the thirteenth, the lobby of the main branch seemed normal, to the surprise of television crews that had come to cover the run. Then shortly after 2:00 P.M., a panic struck. The lobby of the main branch filled with a cross-section of customers—elderly white-haired matrons, burly workers in red hunting caps—taking out savings accounts, cashing in CDs, even closing out their IRAs. Between 3:00 and 6:00 P.M., the thrift lost $20 million in deposits. The only spark that bank officials could detect came from several unscreened calls on the local radio talk show, repeating the rumors that the thrift was failing.

The thrift managed to beat the run by energetic public relations and by the traditional tactic of paying out as much cash as anyone wanted. TV cameras showed employees bringing the money into the lobby in large paper bags. Over the weekend, Unifirst held a press conference in its lobby with the governor, lieutanant governor and treasurer of Mississippi and the president of the Home Loan Bank of Dallas. It set up special monitors in the lobby on Monday to replay the broadcast, and the panic subsided.

Although the Unifirst run was an isolated incident, repeated in only a few other localities, it was sobering. Bush decided to speed up his rescue plan. On the night of Sunday, February 5, the eve of the plan's unveiling, senior officials met with Federal Reserve Chairman Greenspan in the Roosevelt Room of the White House. It may have been the first time since Roosevelt's first term that a White House meeting was held to develop a strategy for dealing with bank runs. Not everyone agreed that a major run was probable, but they all knew they had to be prepared. "Why take any risk?" one official said.

Greenspan, a repressed economist newly turned media star, came with a plan. The Fed would act as lender of last resort, the role it traditionally played for the banking system. If S&L depositors were clamoring for their money, and FSLIC or Home Loan Banks didn't have the cash on hand, the Fed would step in, making loans through its discount window. The "discount window" was jargon for the Fed's procedure of lending to its members and other banks to make sure money was in their vaults when they needed it. Banks used this service infrequently, and when they used it a lot, they usually were in serious trouble. Because the thrifts legally belonged to a separate system, the Fed would work with and through the Home Loan Banks and the Bank Board.

That left one serious hitch, what to do for collateral? When a bank came to the discount window, the Fed demanded that it put up its best assets before it walked away with a loan. But the thrifts that were most likely to need this service didn't have high-quality assets.

So Greenspan agreed to accept a note from a borrowing thrift, "secured with available collateral" and guaranteed by FSLIC. To Greenspan's many critics, this concession incredibly weakened the Fed's standards. It meant that the Fed was willing to take an IOU from an insolvent thrift backed by a guarantee from an insolvent FSLIC. Complained Congressman John LaFalce, "I fear that the Fed may be left holding poor collateral and the taxpayer left holding the bag." That the Fed would take this unprecedented step, however, shows how gravely worried it was about the S&L system. The worry was justified. Within two months the Fed would find itself lending, and lending heavily, to a troubled thrift in the throes of a run. (See Chapter Thirteen.)

With the very real fear of meltdown in the background, Bush announced his rescue plan three days early. It replaced Danny Wall's bandage with a comprehensive strategy, but it also gave a much higher price tag than any official had dared mention previously. The cost, said Bush, would be $156 billion over 10 years. The Treasury would try to raise $50 billion immediately to close down FSLIC's zombie institutions. Another $40 billion would cover the commitments FSLIC had already made during the year. The rest would go for interest, future losses, and a painful rebuilding of the insurance fund. At least $40 billion of the total would come from "Treasury funds," a euphemism for the taxpayer.

The rescue also virtually dismantled the agency it came to help. The bankrupt FSLIC would be replaced by a new fund with the acronym SAIF, a misspelled form of subliminal reassurance. FSLIC's case resolution duties, its administrative powers over the zombies, would be handed over to the better staffed FDIC, which was to embark on a campaign to seize thrifts, unequalled since FDR's 1933 Bank Holiday. The Bank Board itself was disbanded, to be replaced by a single chairman under the oversight of the Secretary of the Treasury. It was all an immense blow to the political power of the S&Ls, and some of Bush's advisers said openly that thrifts had outlived their social use. The outcome resembled a Greek tragedy, in which the hero brought on his own downfall by arrogance and over-reaching.

At first, the plan was hailed by many observers, if only because at last someone in Washington was facing the magnitude of the debacle. But within weeks the optimistic assumptions underlying the plan began to crumble. The Fed feared inflation as much as bank runs, and it pushed interest rates to a mid-February peak that threatened to sink up to 100 barely solvent thrifts. Deposits, furthermore, were not stabilizing. The silent run already evident in December now swelled beyond all fears. Net withdrawals in January 1989 reached a record $10.8 billion, perhaps showing the impact of asking the public to spare two bits. By the time the pace began to slow in March, the outflow for the first quarter had reached $28.5 billion. Some predicted that thrift deposits would shrink permanently from $1 trillion to $750 billion, completely destroying the Treasury's hopes of extracting more funding from deposit premiums.

Worst of all, the runs were no longer silent. Depositors had begun to target the potential problem thrifts, turning them into immediate crises. The FSLIC and the FDIC were now closing multibillion dollar thrifts in reaction to these sudden attacks on their liquidity. In explaining away the March 1989 withdrawals, the Bank Board released the hardly encouraging news that 20 thrifts in the West and the South had lost $5 billion in deposits. Only three of these 20 were insolvent at the time, meaning that 17 brand new problems had suddenly appeared.

The FDIC began to realize that its power grab had left it with more than it could handle. Supervision of its own banks began to deteriorate, raising the thought that the thrifts' troubles could spread to all savings institutions. The specter of a financial meltdown, present ever since the congressional bullying over CEBA, was more real than ever. By deferring the problem to 1989, the politicians had allowed it to grow to proportions that now threatened the general economy.

□ □ □

EVEN MORE OMINOUSLY, the problem extended beyond the thrift industry. The FDIC, now the most powerful of the bank regulators, had itself been compromised in an early set of scandals. Intimations of political interference predated the work of Speaker Wright.

PART TWO

The Strange Career of William Isaac

CHAPTER FOUR

□□□

The Road to Washington

□ 1 □

WILLIAM MICHAEL ISAAC—bright, deeply tanned, opinionated—could have been the perfect Reagan administration yuppie. As chairman of the Federal Deposit Insurance Corporation, he made a strong but nuanced case for deregulation. He wanted to make poorly managed banks pay higher premiums for deposit insurance, so the cost would reflect the risk. He proposed to inform the public when the FDIC disciplined rule-breaking bank officers, a radical idea that horrified the industry. He cultivated the press, especially the bright young financial writers who pushed the newly popular ideas of freer markets and smaller government. He fit so well into the atmosphere of the Reagan Revolution that many assumed he was one of Ronald Reagan's appointees.

Like other impressions about William Isaac, this assumption was false, even though some Democratic congressmen clung to it with strange stubbornness. It was President Jimmy Carter who named Isaac to the FDIC. Rumors of the nomination first circulated in mid-August of 1977. The formal nomination came on November 7. Because the Senate failed to act, the nomination was resubmitted the next year, and Isaac finally joined the board in March 1978. The confusion about this appointment matches the ambiguity of Isaac's career. From one perspective, he seems simply a distinguished, able public servant. From another, he is the victim of a bold attempt to corrupt federal bank supervision.

There is an underside to Isaac's career that he is loath to acknowledge. He can't be directly accused of wrong-doing, any more than any lawyer can be held accountable for the misdeeds of his client, but as a lawyer, Isaac was thrust into the biggest Miami scandal of the mid-1970s, a tangle of drug dealing, international embezzlement and suspected espionage. He deftly managed to extricate the powerful regional bank that employed him. Circumstances suggest that his reward was appointment to the FDIC.

No one disputes that Isaac was qualified for the job. Yet the intermediaries who claim to have brought his name to the White House, the Butcher brothers of Tennessee, were themselves later involved in another, separate scandal that directly impugned the integrity of the FDIC. As their chain of banks collapsed in 1983, some of the most corrupt figures in the banking industry felt they had a claim on Isaac, by now chairman of the nation's largest bank regulator, charged with the safety of 13,000 institutions. At the end of this saga an accused (and later convicted) member of a drug trafficking conspiracy subjected Isaac to something akin to blackmail. Ultimately, Isaac faced him down and emerged as something of a hero. As in the later career of FSLIC Chairman Edwin Gray, the regulator is constantly under pressure to compromise, but he can be destroyed if he yields.

□ 2 □

WILLIAM ISAAC WAS BORN IN BRYAN, OHIO, a small town in the far northwestern corner of the state, on December 21, 1943. His father's father had immigrated from Syria, his mother's, from Sweden. The family prospered, but, says a former colleague at the FDIC, Isaac experienced discrimination in his youth and still resents it. When it came time for college, he headed due south on Route 127 to Miami University in Oxford, Ohio, just north of Cincinnati. An outstanding student, he moved up to the Ohio State University College of Law in Columbus and received his Juris Doctor, summa cum laude, in 1969. After graduation, he took a job with Foley & Lardner, the largest law firm in Milwaukee, Wisconsin, and stayed there for five years.

So far, Isaac looked like any normal bright lawyer on the big-firm fast track. But in the summer of 1974, while only 30, he made a fateful move. He accepted an offer to head the legal department of the First National Bank of Louisville, Kentucky. The Louisville bank at the time was a highly regarded regional bank with around $2 billion in assets. Isaac had made a specialty of the law allowing one-bank holding companies, and he applied his expertise to the Louisville bank's parent company, the First Kentucky National Corporation. He soon held the titles of vice president, secretary and general counsel of First Kentucky.

These duties soon plunged Isaac into a world far removed from stolid midwestern banking. About five years earlier, the Louisville bank had tried to cash in on the fad for Third World lending. Another midwestern regional, the Mercantile Trust Co. of St. Louis, was getting into the business by buying into a ready-made outfit. A St. Louis Merc officer persuaded a friend at First Kentucky that it seemed like a good way to save the trouble of setting up an international department from scratch. So First Kentucky and the St. Louis Merc jointly invested in the WFC Corporation of Coral Gables, Florida.

First Kentucky thus put itself in the hands of a slick, cynical Cuban refugee named Guillermo Hernandez-Cartaya. Bill Hernandez, as his American banker friends called him, had been born in 1932 in a prosperous Havana banking family, a member of the privileged set that gathered at the Vedado Tennis Club in the days before Castro. His family held on for the first year of the Revolution, but as Castro purged opponents, Hernandez fled to the United States. He joined the CIA-sponsored invasion in 1961 and was a prisoner in Cuba until late 1962, earning entry into what may be the most important social network in Miami's Little Havana, veterans of the Bay of Pigs. A family friend recalls meeting him in Philadelphia early in his exile. Hernandez-Cartaya declared, "I am going to be very rich."

Hernandez-Cartaya pursued his dream in New York and Atlanta before coming to Miami, working in Chase Manhattan and the Citizens and Southern Bank. He launched WFC Corporation in 1971 with friends and contacts collected in his decade of banking. He dispatched them to offices in Panama, Colombia, Venezuela, Brazil and the tiny sheikhdom of Ajman on the Persian Gulf. Still marvelling at Guillermo's skilled use of his men and their networks, a former officer exclaimed, "He could play his staff like an organ." In Ajman, he set up a bank that became financial adviser to the Sheikh. His bank in Panama, co-owned with First Kentucky and the St. Louis Merc, received a full license rarely granted to foreigners. In 1975, he pulled off his biggest triumph, negotiating a $100 million loan to the Republic of Colombia. This was the kind of outfit First Kentucky had hoped for.

But Guillermo's dream had a dark side. WFC Corporation began to attract rumors about drug smuggling, money laundering, double agents and fraud. The troubles started on December 13, 1976, when Metro-Dade patrolmen answered a call from the Blue Ridge Farms Dairy in southwest Miami. Someone had been filling the store's dumpster with plastic trash bags. The police looked in the bags and found wads of marijuana leaves, stems and seeds. They also found a stack of parking tickets, bank receipts, electric bills, and, according to the official report, "records indicating $1,440,000 paid out for drugs."

Detectives traced their ample leads to a former state senator and two Cuban half-brothers, Alberto and Enrique (Kaki) Argomaniz. Kaki, they heard, was working at the National Bank of South Florida in Hialeah. When they called him there, the woman who answered said, "Try the WFC Corporation." At WFC, the police found a gathering of Miami's shadiest characters. One employee was a suspected agent provocateur for Castro. He had supplied explosives to several anti-Castro activists, blowing up one in the process. Hernandez-Cartaya's personal chauffeur was a heavy-set, buffoonish ex-veterinarian unabashed by his contacts with Cuban intelligence. A steady stream of informants filled the Metro-Dade files with news that Hernandez-Cartaya himself worked with an intermediary for Castro and the drug trade, an obscure head of Panama's military intelligence named Manuel Noriega. These developments were a bit much for the local police, and they asked for federal help.

On April 7, 1977, the United States Attorney in Miami, Robert W. Rust, called a seven-agency meeting to launch the strike force on WFC. He assembled 50 agents from the FBI, the DEA, the IRS, Customs, Treasury and the Office of the Comptroller of the Currency, not to mention the Metro-Dade detective bureau. But by this time, Hernandez-Cartaya was set to self-destruct. In May, a bank panic hit the Persian Gulf. Cartaya's Ajman-Arab Bank closed its doors, and the furious Sheikh discovered that $37 million was missing. Millions had been sent to Brownsville, Texas, home of Guillermo's father to build a country club. Hernandez-Cartaya flew out to mollify the sheikh, who clapped him into house arrest and threatened to ampute his hand.

Ajman, it turned out, was the main source of cash flowing through all of the WFC's branches. Without the liquidity, its other offices began to wither. First Kentucky discovered that its thriving partner was actually a giant check kite and that the bank stood to lose $2.5 million. William Isaac, First Kentucky's bright young vice president and general counsel, was charged with the task of sorting out the legal and financial mess. He began six months of shuttling to Miami. Isaac recalls trying to recover his bank's money from hard cases who were not glad to see him. The FBI tagged along behind him to one dinner meeting, just to make sure he survived. Says Isaac, "I was scared shitless the whole time."

Isaac's primary problem was to track his bank's money. First Kentucky had helped Hernandez-Cartaya set up his bank in Panama, the Union de Bancos, or Unibank, and was using it to make loans to Colombian businesses. Its largest borrower was a fertilizer factory called Monomeros Colombia-Venezolanos, S.A. Monomeros was paying back the loan, but the money never made it to Louisville. WFC would divert the payments to its Coral Gables expenses, and send the banks a duplicate promissory note from Monomeros. The staff called these fraudulent notes the "volidares," the "flying things." Around the end of July 1977, Isaac and his aides went to Coral Gables to collect on the Monomeros notes. A competent banker named Fernando Capablanca had come in as acting president and told them that the money from Panama was in the mail. Isaac retorted that they were beginning to think the notes were frauds. Capablanca says that when he heard that, he walked out of the meeting, cleaned out his desk, and left WFC.

Just days before this meeting, Hernandez-Cartaya had escaped from Ajman. A WFC employee had flown out to bring him a forged passport. (This employee was a good choice for clandestine work, since he reputedly had been a gunman for Raul Castro, Fidel's brother, in the Sierra Maestre.) The two walked nervously through the international airport at Dubai and boarded the first plane to London, sweating out another stop on Arab territory. When Guillermo came home, all his limbs intact, he took over the negotiations with Louisville. He wanted desperately to get Isaac off his back, but the best he could offer was a small bank he owned in Hialeah, the National Bank of South Florida. Louisville took a second lien on the bank, glad to come out with something tangible. But to recover Louisville's money, Isaac first had to dispose of the NBSF.

If WFC had been an embarrassment, the Hialeah bank was ten times worse. Isaac found himself on a bumpy tour of South Florida's drug and sleaze economy. Hialeah, an 80 percent Hispanic enclave in north-central Dade County, is the place Miami points to when it wants to look good in comparison. The town parades its racetrack and flamingoes, but it nestles jai alai and topless bars in a corner under the airport highway. Thousands of hard-working Cuban immigrants call it home, and so do drug dealers so tough that they have run the Italian Mafia out of town. Catholic churches coexist with Santeria shrines were mounds of chickens and small mammals die in sacrifice to deities of the Afro-Cuban folk religion. It's a place, in short, where a midwestern boy like Bill Isaac might have trouble feeling his way.

The National Bank of South Florida, moreover, had been in trouble with its regulator, the federal Office of the Comptroller of the Currency (OCC), since that February. Hernandez-Cartaya had bought the bank in July of 1976, paying more than $3 million in cash. About six months later, the regulators discovered that, contrary to statements at the time, much of the money was not Guillermo's own. The regional administrator mentioned this discovery at a weekly staff meeting, and his chief deputy exclaimed that he had been hearing about WFC from the Justice Department in Miami. The deputy, Lou Frank, pulled out the bank's quarterly reports and found an alarming pattern. In one quarter, the bank had nearly doubled its assets and deposits and had increased loans fourfold. On the face of it, something strange was going on. Frank went personally to take a closer look. Within hours of his arrival, he found "massive self-dealing, numerous violations of banking laws as well as possible criminal violations" and an apparent threat to the bank's solvency. Frank called his office through the day with more bad news. The Comptroller's Office ordered the bank directors to meet at 8:00 A.M. the next day, February 8. By 2:00 P.M., the OCC formally prohibited the bank from further dealings with WFC and Hernandez-Cartaya. This quick action saved the bank, but it wasn't the end of the fight.

Examiners flooded the bank for a month. But as soon as they started to leave, three very worried independent directors warned the regional administrator that Hernandez-Cartaya was taking over again. Frank sent an examiner back to NBSF, alone, to babysit the "non-Cartaya" directors, and the examiner found he had his own babysitter. One of Hernandez-Cartaya's bodyguards, a heavy-set man with a large bulge under his jacket, dogged his movements. A bank officer warned him about Cartaya's "muscle." After one board meeting, J. M. Baeza, a "non-Cartaya" director came back from the parking lot, visibly shaken. He showed the examiner a bogus newspaper he had found on his windshield. The headline read: "MR. J. M. BAEZA MISSING FROM MIAMI. WHERE ARE YOU?" Director Baeza stated he would never go back to that bank. "Throughout the examination, the examiners and the independent directors were under constant personal fear," testified Robert Serino, director of the OCC Enforcement Division in a later congressional hearing. "I know that personally as I was present in Miami."

Even more unnerving were the hints and clues that NBSF was a new kind of problem bank. Examiners heard tales of large cash deposits that bank officers quickly shipped to Panama in suitcases. One deposit came in a large duffel bag still containing traces of marijuana. The NBSF started keeping its teller windows open late for the purpose, hinted one federal prosecutor, of tapping into the enormous cash flow of the drug trade. "You're not running a bank," a friend said to one of the NBSF directors. "You're running a laundromat."

Some of these hints concerned international intrigue. This one-branch bank in a working class suburb of Miami inexplicably maintained an account with the Moscow Narodny Bank, Ltd., of London. (During this period, Moscow Narodny, a London corporation controlled by the Kremlin, went on a binge of bank buying and loan making from Macao to Panama to northern California. In most cases, the Russian bankers took a bath.) The need for the Narodny account, the OCC examination of NBSF noted dryly, is "subject to question."

This strange connection fed the rumors about Hernandez-Cartaya's contacts with Cuba. Some of Guillermo's old friends from the Vedado Tennis Club had risen in the Cuban government, and mutual acquaintances reported that they kept in touch through Panama. Years later, a Cuban government defector reported seeing Hernandez-Cartaya in Havana in 1976, lunching with General José Abrantes, then head of Cuban intelligence operations in North America. (Abrantes lost his job in June 1989, in the middle of Fidel Castro's purge of senior generals accused of helping the Medellin Cartel smuggle drugs to the United States.) In 1985, a Metro-Dade police wiretap overheard a Hialeah drug lord making the cryptic comment, "all of that grass money Fidel Castro was involved" in the context of the NBSF. The apparent growth of an international money laundering network at the same time as the founding of the Medellin drug cartel might occasion endless speculation. When William Isaac and the Louisville bankers took the NBSF as collateral for their Monomeros loans, they plunged into a bottomless morass. Now it was Isaac's job to sell NBSF in hopes of recouping at least a portion of Louisville's losses.

□ 3 □

AN OPERATION LIKE THE HIALEAH BANK might attract an unusual purchaser, as Isaac soon found out. The first bid for the NBSF came from a local banker named Juan Evelio Pou, and his mysterious partners. Pou was an officer of the Royal Trust Bank of Miami, an offshoot of a Canadian bank with deep roots in pre-Castro Cuba. He had not only fought at the Bay of Pigs; he was past president of the Brigada 2506, the veterans' association for the combatants in that CIA disaster. Pou later earned another distinction. He became the first banker in Miami to be indicted in a money laundering investigation. In 1978, a joint FBI and DEA Task Force called "Group 8" subpoenaed hundreds of accounts from 35 Miami banks suspected of handling funds from drug deals; according to one report 95 percent of the accounts were held by Colombians using fictitious names. The largest block of accounts came from the Royal Trust Bank, and Pou was the fall guy. He pleaded guilty to one of the two money laundering charges then on the books, failing to declare the export of more than $5,000 in currency, and was sentenced to two years on probation. This offense came before his bid for the NBSF. Later he developed a bad habit of trying to take loaded weapons on board commercial airliners. He was arrested twice on that charge over the next two years. (The first case was dismissed; the second resulted in a suspended sentence.)

Pou was a staid Miami businessman compared to his other public partner, Gustavo Villoldo. A shadowy figure who disappeared from Miami for years at a time, Villoldo bragged of serving on the American team that tracked down Che Guevara, Castro's favorite revolutionary, in the jungles of Bolivia. One regulator recalled his impression of Villoldo: "He looked like a hoodlum. He wore a leather jacket before they were popular. He looked very tough."

Villoldo joined the bid for the NBSF during a domestic phase of his career. Between 1974 and 1977, he set himself up in Miami as officer or director of an investment firm, a construction company and a yacht club. He and Pou jointly incorporated an outfit called South East Distributors, Inc. Then, in 1978, all these enterprises lapsed, and Villoldo dropped from sight. He resurfaced in 1986 in the flare of the Iran-Contra controversy. Garbled reports from the Sandinistas placed him in Honduras as a CIA liaison to the Contra supply chain. Investigators for Senator John Kerry developed an intense interest in Villoldo in their attempt to link Contras and drug dealers. The Senate Foreign Relations Committee staffers were especially piqued by a cryptic and unexplained passage in Colonel Oliver North's working diaries. Reporting a call from the Latin American chief for the CIA, it read, "contact indicates that Gustavo is involved with drugs."* Did this refer to Villoldo, or to some other Gustavo? No one can say for sure.

In the bid for the NBSF, a third partner, Gustavo Cachaldora, stayed entirely in the background. Only Pou and Villoldo put their names on the purchase agreements. By mid-August, Pou and Villoldo had worked out terms with Hernandez-Cartaya and the First National Bank of Louisville. Their main worry was getting approval from the Comptroller of the Currency. "The Comptroller has clearly stated that our transaction must be structured in a way so that I have no continuing possibility of regaining or maintaining a stock interest in the bank," Hernandez-Cartaya wrote them.

It took the active help of the Louisville bank to work out this structure. Since Pou and Villoldo had already put a down payment on the bank, Isaac arranged to give First National of Louisville a second lien on the bank, and a call on the first lien it could exercise at will. The First National Bank of Louisville lent Villoldo and Pou $1 million in the form of a promissory note to buy all the NBSF

---

*A later entry read, "Felix Rodriquez close to (White House deletion)—not assoc. W/Villoldo—Bay of Pigs—No drugs"

stock. The two gave the note to Hernandez-Cartaya in part payment for the stock, and he turned around and gave the note back to the Louisville bank to repay the missing money he owed them from the Monomeros notes. So on paper the Monomeros debt was cancelled, and the Louisville bank no longer had an embarrassing case of fraud to explain to the stockholders. At the same time, Villoldo and Pou, its new borrowers, gave Louisville the collateral of "security interest" in "not less than 51 percent" of the NBSF stock. A bailout clause gave Louisville the right to call its note in 60 days if it learned that Pou and Villoldo weren't what they claimed to be. "We didn't know them from Adam," explains Isaac.

It was an ingenious deal. It allowed Pou and Villoldo to take over a \$3.2 million bank while putting up only \$100,000 in cash. The only trouble was that the regulators didn't bite. The OCC wanted money put into the bank, but Pou and Villoldo didn't have it. At the same time, the federal task force was hearing rumors that Villoldo and Pou were fronting for Hernandez-Cartaya. The comptroller's regional office refused to approve the sale, and Isaac invoked the bailout clause. Louisville was back at square one, this time holding the stock in the Hialeah bank.

By contrast, Isaac's next bidder made Pou and Villoldo look like stable, upstanding citizens. Ray Corona, the ambitious younger son of a banking family from pre-Castro Havana, was looking for a bank to call his own. A stocky former Golden Gloves boxer with a sometimes thuggish cast, Ray would erupt in rages and an hour or two later apologize contritely. His flamboyance was becoming legendary. According to a story told by his lawyer, he once tried to go through airport customs wearing a T-shirt emblazoned with the outline of a marijuana plant. His behavior hadn't fully blossomed, however, when he first met Isaac, and he seemed to have the ready cash that Pou and Villoldo had lacked.

In early December 1977, Isaac started negotiating with Corona and his ostensible coinvestor, a young Panamanian woman named Alma Robles Chiari. (Miss Chiari, a cousin of the last two freely elected presidents of Panama, was not all she seemed, but that is a story which we'll return to in Chapter Seven.) During the week of

December 19, the whole cast—Pou, Villoldo and Corona, gathered in Louisville on the eighth floor of the First National Bank building to work out terms. Two days before Christmas, the crew met again in a posh law office on Miami's Brickell Avenue for the closing. But again the Comptroller of the Currency didn't like Isaac's candidate. The meeting stretched into the evening as Lou Frank, the OCC's acting regional administrator, told Isaac from Atlanta that he couldn't approve the sale to Ray Corona. "He did not have a good banking reputation, as far as I was concerned," Frank explained later in court testimony.

Isaac pleaded with Frank over the phone, but Frank refused to change his mind. Frank did offer a compromise. He could grant the approval, "as a nice Christmas present," if Ray would step aside in favor of his father Rafael, who had years of experience as a bank president. But Ray refused. They met again the next week for one more try, this time in the OCC's Atlanta regional office. But the rejection was final. Depressed, angry, and frustrated, Ray stormed from the building and made a long-distance call from a pay phone on the street. This call would return to haunt him, as he would return to haunt Isaac.

By this time, Isaac had a great deal more to think about than the National Bank of South Florida. In mid-August, about the time Isaac seemed to have wrapped up the first attempted sale of the Hialeah bank, word leaked out in Louisville that he was being considered for the FDIC Board. Jimmy Carter made it official on November 7 1977, just as the FBI launched a 60-day special investigation of Hernandez-Cartaya and the WFC. Because of a delay in scheduling the Senate confirmation hearing, Isaac had to sweat it out till the next year. But President Carter renewed the appointment, and in short order the Senate Banking Committee approved it. Isaac was on the FDIC Board of Directors by March 28 1978.

□ 4 □

How did Isaac come to be appointed to the FDIC, largest of the federal deposit insurance funds and supervisor of 13,000 banks?

Although his friends have sometimes tried to minimize the appointment as a minor federal post, it is certainly crucial to the banking industry and to the health of the nation's financial system. As the obscure general counsel for a second-tier regional bank, Isaac was not an obvious choice. He explains that he waged a "long-shot" campaign for the job, with the blessing of First Kentucky's top management. Working through a First Kentucky aide, he enlisted Kentucky Democratic leader Dale Sights, manager of Jimmy Carter's state campaign. "Practically every member of the Carter family had stayed at his home," Isaac says. Sights introduced Isaac to the state's United States senators and to Governor Carroll, who wrote letters for him. The First Kentucky aide asked for help from other regional bankers. "But the key players," says Isaac, "were the top four political leaders from Kentucky." Even so, staff of the Senate Banking Committee were surprised at his nomination. "He came out of nowhere," says one.

He emerged with so much momentum, furthermore, that he wasn't content to be just a member of the board. According to several colleagues and Ray Corona, Isaac was already hoping to become the FDIC chairman. Corona claims that at their Louisville meeting, Isaac told him not to worry about the OCC because "he would be chairman of the Federal Deposit Insurance Corporation in the near future and that he had the ability and influence to get the necessary approvals."

This ambition was quite a stretch, however. Traditionally, the FDIC chairman comes from the same party as the administration in power, and Isaac was a Republican. Carter appointed him as a director, but not as head of the board. The post of chairman remained vacant for 10 months after Isaac joined the board; the reason, said FDIC scuttlebutt, was the backroom struggle over giving the job to Isaac. In the end, he had to wait for the advent of Ronald Reagan to get the title.

In spite of Isaac's undoubted ability and his strong regional ties to Carter, it's hard to escape the thought that his ambitions were immeasurably advanced by his deft handling of the WFC disaster. He had worked hard and successfully to recoup his employer's money and to spare them bad publicity. Had Isaac been pushy?

Frank, head of the OCC's Atlanta office, was asked this question in a later court proceeding. " 'Pushy is not bad,' he replied. "He would call all the time. Not just for Corona but there were others as well. He would give us a strong recommendation toward people. Because they wanted out of the loan. There again he was doing the bidding of the bank, to get out of this problem credit." First Kentucky eventually did get its money back. The Hialeah bank was sold to a turnaround specialist and then back to its original founders, the people from whom Hernandez-Cartaya first bought it.

In a curious parallel, the WFC case appeared to put another First Kentucky employee on the fast track. As an officer in the Louisville bank's International Department, a young Kentucky native named Randall Attkisson sat briefly on the board of directors of Union de Bancos, WFC's Panamanian subsidiary. Fernando Capablanca, WFC's interim president, remembers that Attkisson handled much of the day-to-day relations between Miami and Louisville; he later attended Isaac's meetings with Pou, Villoldo and Corona. Afterward he lingered in Florida to set up a bank consulting firm, dealing, says Capablanca, with bidders for the NBSF. This venture was collapsing when, in September 1980, John Y. Brown of Colonel Sanders fame was elected governor of Kentucky. Brown named Attkisson as his banking commissioner. Attkisson, then 34, was so financially hard-pressed that a member of the state cabinet lent him money for his relocation. The appointment of Attkisson, a struggling consultant based out of state, was unusual on its face. As with Isaac's elevation, it makes sense mainly in the context of the WFC's debacle. One can surmise that the powers at the First National Bank of Louisville were grateful to Isaac and his aide Attkisson for retrieving their investment.

The First Kentucky connection may shed light on another vexed question. Investigators in the WFC case have long felt that their work was mysteriously frustrated. There were prosecutions, to be sure. Six WFC officers were indicted on charges of income tax evasion. Three were acquitted; three were convicted, including Hernandez-Cartaya himself. That charge and a separate conviction for bank fraud at a Texas savings and loan brought him three years in federal prison. But the charges fell far short of the investigative effort and the many lurid leads.

After the initial push, the federal investigation withered. FBI headquarters refused its field office request to continue the extra staffing. Agents complained of lagging interest from Carter's newly appointed United States Attorney for Miami. Assistant United States Attorney R. Jerome Sanford, a mainstay of the strike force, resigned in frustration. "The way we were treated," he said, "I wasn't sure if we were still the good guys."

Even by the prosecutor's account, the strongest charge mysteriously disappeared. At the end of 1978, a Justice Department memo listed the "forged and fraudulently renewed notes" as a prosecutable offense under RICO, the stringent Racketeer Influenced and Corrupt Organization law. These notes included the Monomeros loans that embarrassed First Kentucky. But the charges were never filed.

Something about Monomeros triggered a reaction that still puzzles Isaac. He remembers filing suit against the fertilizer company in a Dade County court, charging it with negligence for allowing the note fraud. "I got a call from the comptroller's office [OCC], of all things," he said, "saying that it was a quasi-governmental entity, and that it would not be regarded as proper for a United States bank to sue a Colombian quasi-governmental agency." The OCC's man said he'd been asked to make the call by the State Department.

"I said if the State Department wants to cancel the debt, it can send us a check for $3 million," Isaac recalls. His joke didn't go over. "There is still a file memo over at the comptroller's office reporting that conversation," says Isaac. "It says that this fellow Isaac is a loose cannon."

The Monomeros incident expands the mystery. The WFC case has attracted a small group of journalist buffs who blame the meager results on the interference of the Central Intelligence Agency. Their argument rests on the number of WFC personnel with some CIA background. But the same case could be made about nearly every Cuban enterprise in Miami. Another possible influence was the First National Bank of Louisville. The WFC was already an intense embarrassment, and a prosecution of the Monomeros fraud would expose it to public scrutiny. During most of this time, almost nothing about the case had appeared in the Louisville papers. Nothing indicates that Isaac personally tried to influence the WFC investigations. But if anyone compared the domestic political clout of a regional bank against that of the CIA, the bank would win every time.

Yet Isaac and First National of Louisville were willing to pursue Monomeros in open court, over some opposition from Washington, D.C. A third hypothesis could point to a political connection in the nation's capital, for which WFC had become a heavy albatross. Such connections existed. (See Chapter Ten, "The Seamless Web (I)"). But even now, after more than a decade, the record remains too murky to support a definitive answer. It seems reasonable to surmise, however, that this strange affair played some role in the elevation of William Isaac. His superiors at First National of Louisville certainly had cause to reward him for outstanding service. If they chose to do so by the FDIC appointment, did they have the political clout to deliver? We shall see that they did. More important, if this explains how Isaac got his appointment, did it place him under undue influence? Judge for yourself from the pages to follow.

CHAPTER FIVE

□□□

The Butcher Revels

□ 1 □

THE FEDERAL PRISON CAMP IN ATLANTA, Georgia, holds one answer to the mystery of William Isaac's emergence. A chain link fence along a black residential street marks the camp's perimeter. The Pentecostal Church of Repentance stands guard by the visitor's entrance. The camp's low gray buildings spread over the meadow like the campus of an agriculture school. The khaki-clad inmates of the minimum security camp meet with their families on a lawn dotted with picnic tables, shielded from the unblinking sun by bright blue beach umbrellas. There is an invisible line several yards from the fence. If crossed by an inmate, it makes him an attempted escapee. This is the boundary of Jake Butcher's world.

Ten years ago, Jacob F. Butcher was one of the richest, most powerful men in Tennessee. With his brother, Cecil H., Jr., he controlled a chain of nearly 30 rapidly growing banks and thrifts, with $3 billion in assets. He ran twice for governor and a third time delivered the Democratic nomination to a henchman. He was a close friend of President Jimmy Carter and Carter's confidant, the Georgia banker Bert Lance. He and his brother also had the confidence of the First National Bank of Louisville, Isaac's employer, which loaned them $26 million to build their empire.

Jake is now serving a 20-year sentence for bank fraud, but he still retains his charm and expansiveness. He has many unfriendly things to say about Isaac, spoken like a victim of ingratitude. I asked him how Isaac came to be appointed in the first place.

"You know a hell of a lot more than you're telling me," he said with a laugh. Then, leaning back in his plastic chair, he exclaimed, "We recommended him! We recommended to Jimmy Carter to appoint him FDIC director! All of our Kentucky friends recommended him highly!"

The Butchers used to get on well with Isaac. As general counsel at the First National Bank of Louisville, Isaac helped C. H. with some legal work, a courtesy extended to a good client. Jake and C. H. could claim that they literally brought Isaac to Washington. Jake says that when Isaac was being considered for the FDIC, they flew him down on their corporate jet to meet with President Carter. They provided the jet again to take him to his confirmation hearings before the Senate Banking Committee. As director, Isaac invited Jake to lunch in the FDIC dining hall. The third man at that lunch was the president of Jake's United American Bank, a friend and former colleague of Isaac at the First National Bank of Louisville.

"It was a social occasion," says Jake. "We talked about this and that."

Isaac acknowledges some support from the Butchers. His aide at First Kentucky, a veteran staffer named Leonard Kernen, asked them for help in the campaign for the FDIC post. C. H., Jr. invited Isaac to Atlanta in mid-1977 to meet the top management of Citizens and Southern Bank, which had supported Carter since his days as governor of Georgia. Late that summer, Isaac received another invitation through Kernen to a dinner party at Jake Butcher's mansion, "Whirlwind," where Bert Lance would be guest of honor. "I was tempted," said Isaac, "but decided to decline. To this day I have not met or spoken with Bert Lance." Isaac says he can't recall any other contact with the Butchers until they were summoned to a meeting at FDIC headquarters in January 1983.

Isaac was later much more seriously embarrassed by Jake Butcher than by any of the Miami crew, whom he had dealt with as a lawyer representing a client. More than a client, Jake could claim to be Isaac's benefactor and friend; he was also a cause of the FDIC's biggest bank fraud. The Butchers' empire may have been based on crooked books since 1977, but it survived until November 1982, a full five years after Isaac's nomination. Its slow collapse included the biggest series of bank closings since the Great Depression. It ultimately cost the federal insurance fund around $1 billion. None of these misdeeds were publicly apparent when Isaac knew the Butchers. The question is whether they should have been apparent to the FDIC examiners.

When I first met Butcher, his hair was whiter and his face more deeply lined than in his pictures. But, even after two years in prison, with 18 more to go, he retained the upbeat charm that made him hard not to like. "It's a lot like the Marine Corps," he said of his daily prison routine, "except with a longer tenure."

Jake is still perplexed by the suddenness with which his luck had turned. One day he had clear sailing; the next the full force of the United States government crashed on his head. At one point, the regulators were approving his requests; at the next they were attacking the heart of his empire. "I thought I had a green light," he complained.

□ 2 □

THE GREEN LIGHT HAD BEEN ON FROM THE BEGINNING of the Butchers' careers, in the east Tennessee town of Maynardville, located in the mountains 15 miles north of Knoxville. The dominant figure at the start was patriarch Cecil Hilgie Butcher, Sr., born in 1903. A strapping figure in a white three-piece suit, he stands in one picture with a lopsided grin and a big cigar behind a table of homecooked vegetables, casseroles and cold cuts that his bank used to serve at the Friday lunch hour to all comers.

This country hospitality helped make C. H., Sr., a business and civic leader in his corner of the hills for more than 50 years. In 1924, Cecil quit teaching school to peddle local produce from the back of a truck. His enterprise soon grew into a general store, still in operation. In 1929, he and two partners incorporated the Southern Industrial Banking Corp. Not a bank, in spite of the name, it helped out the store by financing customers' purchases of major appliances, cars, and farm equipment.

Cecil's foray into banking began in 1950, when he and three Maynardville friends decided that local farmers needed their own financial outlet. Together they chartered the Union County Bank with a capitalization of $37,500. For years it was the only bank in the county. Here Jake and C. H., Jr. learned the rudiments of the business.

Jacob Franklin Butcher was born in 1936; Cecil Hilgie, Jr. a year later. To their friends, it seemed that the two competed all their lives for their father's approval. Jesse Barr, Jake's right-hand man, tells a revealing story. In the brothers' heyday, C. H. Jr. sold his interest in a Denver, Colorado, cable television company for $1.2 million. Flying back overnight on the corporate jet, he and an aide arrived in Knoxville "good and drunk." He took the check to his bank and decided he wanted to cash it. It was 9:30 A.M., and Barr, C. H. Jr. and C. H.'s aide, David Crabtree, sipped Bloody Marys and stared at the cash piled on the conference table.

"Then" says Barr, "C. H. wanted to take the cash to his Daddy's bank and make a deposit. We followed him up there riding shotgun and let him set it down on his Daddy's counter and make out a deposit slip. It's all he did. C. H. wanted to show off before his Daddy."

In spite of their father's local prominence, both the charismatic Jake and the businesslike but forceful C. H., Jr. had to work hard to make their way. During their school vacations, they helped out as tellers in the Union County Bank. After a stint in the Marine Corps at the age of 19, Jake earned a degree in business finance at the University of Tennessee. He started out as a gasoline and heating oil jobber, often driving the delivery trucks himself over the steep mountain roads. He recalls that in 1968, "I found a man over in the other county that wanted to sell his bank. I bought it. I went into banking in 1968."

Unlike Jake, C. H. tied himself down early, marrying his cheerleader sweetheart right after high school graduation. While he continued in nearby Lincoln Memorial College, his wife, Shirley, worked as a secretary in Knoxville. His college degree in hand, C. H. started his own insurance agency and joined his father's bank. By 1967, he held the title of executive vice president of the Union County Bank. It was then that the brothers had their first run-in with the regulators. A card on file in the FDIC's "Intelligence Section" reports that Cecil H. Butcher, Jr., "aided by Director Jake F. Butcher," was involved in "falsification of cash records, kiting, and misapplication of bank funds" in the amount of more than $70 million.* The kite was made good. "Any other reimbursement," notes the card, was "unknown." The affair went into the files, apparently to be forgotten.

Undaunted, C. H. stepped up his pace. He began to gobble up small country banks in east Tennessee and southeast Kentucky. In 1971 he moved into Knoxville, acquiring his own flagship, the City and County Bank of Knox County. The C&C-Knox became the heart and brain of C. H., Jr.'s network. By 1981 it had grown into a "multistate financial organization" with 21 separate banks and $1.5 billion in assets.

Jake was buying banks too, although on a smaller scale. "I'd go to a county, and to the most remote part of the county," he explained in the Atlanta visitor's room. "I'd find a small bank owned by an individual and I'd buy it from him. After I bought it, I'd branch into the county seat. I did that several times. I made a lot of money from it. My business was buying, selling, trading banks."

Jake's turning point came in 1974. In his first foray into statewide politics, he missed election as state treasurer by one vote. And he bought his first major bank, the ailing Hamilton National Bank in Knoxville. The Hamilton, chartered and regulated by the Comptroller of the Currency, came with a bag full of bad loans that grew

---

*This figure seems extraordinary for a small country bank. Possibly the FDIC typist misread the bank examiner's notation "m" for million, when it actually signifies thousand. (So "$70m" would mean $70,000.)

even fuller in the next nine years. But Jake changed its name to the United American Bank of Knoxville (UAB-Knoxville) and made it the flagship of his convoy.

It was also in 1974 that Jake succumbed to political fever. After failing to win the treasurer's post from the legislature, he decided to run for governor. There were 12 Democrats in the primary that year, the "Watergate election" in which the favorite speech denounced corruption in high places. Jake recalls that he was ahead of the pack on Labor Day. But when the polls closed, he finished 20,000 votes behind a former congressman from the West Tennessee flatlands named Ray Blanton. In November, Blanton beat Republican Lamar Alexander, and the state embarked on its most disastrous administration in memory. For the next four years, according to the later convictions of Blanton's cronies, pardon could be bought for $20,000, and special deals on liquor licenses went for 20 percent of the stores' profits. Blanton himself was convicted on numerous counts of official misconduct, but most were later overturned by the United States Supreme Court. One can't help thinking that both Jake Butcher and Tennessee would have been better off if he had won that election and quit banking.

"That should have been my last race," Jake reminisces. "My heart was in it then." But even in losing, Jake cemented political friendships that made campaigning hard to stop. "Jake Butcher and I share something in common," Bert Lance explained to the Senate Governmental Affairs Committee in 1977. "We both lost the governor's race in 1974—his was for governor of Tennessee and mine was for the governorship of Georgia. . . . He and I have been friends. It is a relationship that comes I guess from the mutuality of having gotten beat in a political contest." Jake echoed the regard in his Atlanta interview. "Bert Lance and I were friends," he said. "Bert always banked with us. I loaned him a lot of money."

Friendship with Bert Lance carried entry into Jimmy Carter's inner circle. Carter received at least $5,000 from the Butcher clan for his 1976 presidential primary campaign, and his finance committee maintained an account at Jake's United American Bank. President Carter's backing was too much to forego. Jake won the gubernatorial primary in 1978. Carter campaigned for him, calling him a "true treasure" in a mid-October rally in Nashville. Jake's campaign warchest topped $4.6 million, making it one of the most lavish in the nation. He so saturated the airwaves that the *Knoxville Journal* ran a cartoon with the caption, "We interrupt this Jake Butcher political ad to bring you a Jake Butcher political ad." Around $3 million may have come from Jake's United American Bank, using his father's Southern Industrial Banking Corp. as a conduit.

In his campaign, Jake took a tough stand against pardons. One of his ads brandished the headline, "I am against reduced sentences and political pardons. I will keep criminals in their place." But as a Democrat, Jake still carried the weight of the Blanton scandal.

When the returns were in on election night, Republican Lamar Alexander had beaten Jake by 180,000 votes. Jake's electoral career was over. But both Butchers stayed busy behind the scenes. They contributed lavishly to out-of-state politicians such as Senator Joseph Biden. Their banks gave large loans to elected officials in Tennessee, some of whom were also direct or indirect business partners. The Butchers were mainstays of the National Democratic Finance Committee, giving it $ 17,000 during the 1977–78 campaign season. According to Jesse Barr, national party circles were so grateful for Jake's fund raising that they considered him for Democratic National Chairman.

After Jake's electoral defeat, however, he focused his energies on the 1982 Knoxville World's Fair. Officially called the Knoxville International Energy Exposition, it was Jake's show from day one. As chairman of the Expo, he hustled up seed money and cajoled foreign governments into sending exhibits. He flew to Cairo with Bert Lance to arrange a display of Egyptian antiquities. When the United States Department of Housing and Urban Development refused its support, he pulled strings with President Carter to land a $12.45 million grant. Jake had been lobbying Carter for support since three weeks after the presidential inauguration. When HUD objected that Knoxville wasn't eligible for a grant, Carter assigned the project to his Interagency Coordinating Council, answerable only to the White House. His staff pulled together a package of loans from four agencies, two of which hadn't even been approached by Knoxville. In early October 1978, Butcher interrupted his campaigning to fly to Washington. Along with Senator James Sasser, a Democrat from Tennessee and another taker of Butcher campaign money, he stood by as President Carter announced the grant.

The World's Fair was Jake Butcher's final act of hubris. He had filled a 30-acre abandoned railway siding with monuments such as the United States Pavilion, a six-story replica of a solar panel, and the 266-foot tall Sunsphere, a gold-tinted glass globe resembling a ballroom chandelier perched on an erector set. He had turned a garbage-strewn creek into a four-acre landscaped lagoon (called alternately Waters of the World or Jake's Lake.) He provided extravagant entertainment for a stream of distinguished guests, in line with his already lavish lifestyle. The bank's helicopter would waft visiting dignitaries over the hills to Jake's mansion, Whirlwind, perched on a ridge overlooking the Clinch River in his hometown of Clinton. Jake would entertain them with banquets in his huge dining hall, complemented by the best private wine cellar in the state.

On November 1, 1982, the day after the fair closed, 200 bank examiners moved into banks owned or influenced by Jake and C. H., Jr. throughout Tennessee and Kentucky. The examiners would eventually discover that the prosperity of the Butcher clan was built on fraud, that they were living high on other people's money.

□ 3 □

NO ONE SEEMS ENTIRELY SURE when the banks began to lose money and the Butchers crossed the line into deceit and swindling. It may have been right at the start, when they took over troubled banks they simply couldn't turn around. Knoxville's Hamilton National Bank was declining rapidly when Jake moved into control in 1975. He still claims that he saved it, and his first year did show a near fourfold increase in its return on assets. But this figure deteriorated sharply in the following years. The FDIC later concluded that losses in real estate loans "were concealed almost from the very beginning."

Other losses hit in 1980. One report mentions disasters in government securities trading, always a treacherous market. If the Butchers weren't totally lost by 1980, their doom was sealed when interest rates soared to exotic levels. Like many banks and thrifts from 1980 to 1982, to get money in, they had to spend more in high interest rates on deposits than they were making on their fixed interest loans. Unlike most banks, the Butchers relied on fraud to mask the deficit.

In 1980, as they found themselves nearing a dead end, Jake and C. H., Jr. decided to split their empire. In the past, they had both joined the board of directors of their acquisitions. But from that point, they rigorously avoided any public overlap of their interests. Jesse Barr says that C. H. emerged from his older brother's shadow and started empire building in his own right. Jake still insists he had no role in his brother's banks.

Whether or not the two planned this split as part of their fraud, it certainly helped further it. With separate but coordinated banking chains, they could now shift bad loans back and forth without undue fear that examiners would follow the trail. Coordination was left to a few trusted lieutenants attached to either Jake or C. H. The "financial wizard" behind C. H., Jr. was David Allen Crabtree, a wiry accountant with a bandido moustache and a three-piece suit. An alumnus of the Big Eight accounting firm Ernst & Whinney, which gave the Butcher banks clean audits right up to the end, Crabtree ran the Butchers' nonbank businesses from Suite 2136 of the United American Bank Building. Some 60 companies shared this address: investment trusts, real estate developers, coal traders, and an aviation company that handled the Butchers' fleet of leased planes and helicopters.

Suite 2136 pops up throughout the federal civil court records, in suits calling its companies "sham and shell" corporations formed as a "fraud upon creditors," chief of which were the Butcher banks. A Suite 2136 shell would borrow from the bank and then channel the loan money to an insider or to another shell that had to tidy up an overdue payment at a bank where the examiners were knocking at the door. For instance, one of C. H., Jr.'s bigger entities, a mortgage and lending firm called Tennesco, Inc., received over $10 million from Jake's UAB-Knoxville and the C&C banks of Knox and Anderson County. The FDIC charged that some of the money went to a Butcher crony and his company so that he could pay "otherwise uncollectible debts" to the C&C banks in Union and (again) Anderson County. This round robin, said the government, was to give "the appearance that [the crony] was a performing borrower."

The master of the round-robin loan, however, was Jake's alter ego, the defrocked banker named Jesse Barr. Now serving his second prison term for bank fraud, Barr enjoys somewhat less luxury than Jake. I met him when his address was the Renaissance Unit, Lexington Federal Correctional Institution, converted from a federal hospital for alcoholics. At the top of rolling hills divided by the whitewashed fencing of the Kentucky horse farms, it sits behind a twenty-foot high fence crowned with accordion wire. Jesse was sent here on an 18-year sentence. I talked to him in a visitors' room smaller, noisier and much more crowded than the one in Atlanta. He was relaxed, genial, expansive. Shuffling plastic chairs among the Formica tables, he pointed out Colombian drug lords and Mafia lieutenants as if he were guiding a tour. He was as nice a guy as Jake Butcher was charismatic.

Barr's particular talents deserve much of the credit for giving the Butcher empire as long a run as it had. Barr possessed the fortunately rare combination of financial ability and amoral loyalty needed to keep the game going. There is a misconception that criminals are lazy. On the contrary, the greatest business criminals are hyperactive. They seem to lack a moral flywheel to regulate their energy. Sometimes they care less about the money than about the thrill of deception and the excitement of manipulation. Their most socially useful outlet seems to be prison, where they are the heart and soul of the adult education program. This, it occurred to me, was Jesse Barr's ilk.

The native of a small Mississippi delta town, Jesse first met Jake in the late 1960s in Memphis. Jesse was rising through the ranks at the Union Planters Bank. Among his accounts as loan officer was Jake Butcher's oil distributorship. Their friendship grew closer as Jesse financed the Butcher brothers' first attempt to expand their banking empire. Barr served on the finance committee for Jake's 1974 campaign for governor. In 1975, the Butchers made a play for control of Union Planters. Barr, by that time the bank's executive vice president, was their inside ally.

Union Planters Chairman William Matthews faced down the bid, telling the Butchers in a personal meeting that a federal grand jury was examining Jesse Barr's banking habits. Barr resigned and was indicted twice on more than 40 counts of conspiracy, fraud, and embezzlement. He served a year in the federal prison at Eglin Air Force Base, Florida. Even before his conviction, Jesse had begun to work for the Butchers. Moving to Knoxville, he acted as consultant in Jake's purchase of the troubled Hamilton National Bank which, as the United American Bank-Knoxville, became the hub of Jake's network. After his release from Eglin and a stint in Jake's 1978 campaign, Barr settled down as eminence grise of the Butcher empire.

As a convicted bank felon, Barr had no hope of a formal position with UAB or any other bank, but his word had total authority throughout Butcher's system. Loans and fund transfers were executed on the strength of his initials, "J B.," which UAB bank officers now say they thought stood for Jake Butcher. Working from the 23rd floor of UAB-Knoxville's rectangular glass tower, Jesse held the title of consultant to both Jake and C. H. Butcher's banks, but he worried most about Jake's spending.

Toward the end, Jake was running through $2 million a month, an astounding sum even for a world-class embezzler. Most of the money went for interest on loans; Jake had mortgaged himself to the hilt to buy up his banks. "Back in 1981, before he bought the bank in Lexington," Jesse recalled amid the babble of the prison visiting room, "his monthly living expenses and his monthly interest payments were about $500,000. When he bought the two other banks, his debt went to $20 million, and his interest and living costs went to $2 million." (Jake himself explained that he bought the banks in Lexington and Chattanooga in hopes that he could resell at a tidy profit when Congress approved interstate banking.) But finding $2 million a month, $24 million a year, isn't easy, even if you have a $3 billion bank network to dip into, and Jake made things harder by his lavish, unpredictable spending sprees.

"He once bought a $600,000 yacht and didn't tell me about it," complained Barr, exasperation lining his forehead.

Jesse tried to put Jake on a budget. Jake agreed, for a while. "We stuck to it for a month," Jesse said. "That was the smoothest month we ever had. Everything went slick. Then Jake said, 'I don't have time to fool with that shit.' "

So Jessee went back to "calling up" cash whenever Jake drained his checkbook. Judy Franklin, Jake's secretary, kept a drawer full of blank loan notes in her office, some from each of the banks in the system. Whenever Jake needed more money, said Jesse, "she'd pull one out." Jake's staff would fabricate a loan to a friend or a dummy corporation, and he would take another dip into his bank.

At the end these phony loans ran to the hundreds of millions. The money flowed to Jake, to C. H., Jr., to in-laws, friends, business buddies, to flaky investments, and political campaigns. It was Jesse's job and genius to keep the fraud afloat and to hide it from the bank examiners. It would have been a crushing task for an ordinary man, but Jesse revelled in it.

"Every day was a new world for me," said Barr. Office hours were a constant series of crises. Barr tried to keep them to a schedule. In the first hour, he would raise the cash to keep the system afloat, usually by selling loan participations. Barr would sell portions of the banks' loans to their "upstream" or "downstream" correspondent banks, usually promising to buy them back if they got too hot to handle.

"In the second hour," said Barr, "the overdrafts would come in." The Butchers' constant drain on their banks would show up first in one account, then in another. "One day we might have $500,000 at Nashville, or $800,000 at Knoxville," he said. "So I would worry about them for the next hour." Later on he'd give advice to a loan officer or listen to a teller or guard "complain that somebody's been ugly to them." But one part of the day never varied. "At 2:00, wherever I was," he said, "I'd check with the computer on the Fed Fund balance." The banks had to keep up the front of liquidity, of meeting the Federal Reserve's requirements for keeping cash reserves on hand. If a bank was temporarily short of cash, it could borrow from the Fed Funds market, in which other banks would lend out their excess reserves. Constant borrowing from the Fed Funds market would be a "red flag," said Jesse, "especially the amounts that we were borrowing." But no one called them on it, until the very end.

During the day, Barr kept track of problems on little cards. In the evening, he would ride home with Jake, flipping through his cards while Jake drove. The next day, he would carry out Jake's decisions and start on a new stack of problems. It was a life of constant crises, many of which never came to Butcher's attention. "Jake was a P.R. man, a front man," said Jesse. "He didn't want to hear about a lot of problems." But Barr reveled in the tumult. "I thrive on problems," he boasted. "It was wild out there."

The biggest crisis of all was the annual bank examination. This Barr handled smoothly, so smoothly that many believed that someone in the FDIC was leaking advance word of these supposedly surprise visits. Barr gave another version. The tipoff, he said, came automatically from the examiners' own procedures.

Before each examination, the FDIC would ask for a computer printout of the bank's loans. All the computer work for the Butchers' empire went out to the UAB Service Center, which the Butchers owned. Every time the examiners asked for something, the computer center notified Barr. "It didn't take me long to figure out who got the printout," he said.

By 2:00 P.M. on Friday, Barr would know where the examiners were going to show up on Monday morning. And he would start on his most important job, purging the target bank of all the shaky, suspect loans, the insider dealing, the nominal borrowing that covered the Butcher brothers' looting, and moving them into other parts of the system.

"I had a printout of all of the loans related to Jake and C. H.," Barr said, describing one of the century's greatest bank frauds as calmly as if it were a routine mortgage. This list covered what they called the "family loans," not only the brothers' own borrowing, but their delinquent loans to friends and the notes in the sometimes forged names of front men, covering funds that went to the Butchers' personal use. Barr also kept a card file of the loans. On Friday afternoon, his desk would be the center of the Butcher domain, as he made a telephone call for each card, transferring the loan to a bank where the examiners were not going. When the loans were reassigned, he would send couriers to deliver the files. "There were some where we didn't have the paperwork," he said, "so I'd pay them off."

When the examiners came into the ground floor offices on Monday and started totting up the cash balances, the bank would look clean, if not exactly healthy, thanks to the frenetic activity 23 stories up. The field examiners never questioned Barr during their visits.But after the FDIC inspections of UAB-Knoxville, he recalled that an examiner friend would drop by his office for a drink of Old Charter Scotch.

□ 4 □

DID ANYONE HAVE A CLUE as to what was going on? During all this time the Butchers were borrowing heavily from major regional banks. There were unrefuted reports that they received $26 million from the First National Bank of Louisville. Jake personally borrowed $8 million from the Mercantile National Bank of Dallas (later MBank), where his fellow Democratic fund raiser Jess Hay sat on the board. Mercantile National had to sue Jake for its money, but First National of Louisville claimed not to have lost anything. It managed to retrieve its loans and send back its loan participations before the crash.

What did the Louisville bankers know about the Butchers? I went there several summers ago to ask. A. Stevens Miles, the smooth-as-silk chairman of First Kentucky National Corp., proclaimed his ignorance and referred me to Executive Vice President Leonard V.

Hardin, the officer in charge of hot potatoes. I found Hardin at a Rotary luncheon in the renovated Brown Hotel. Sitting under a potted plant in the ornate, wood-panelled lobby, he gave ready, practiced explanations. First National was one of several big regional banks to finance the Butchers. They had been excellent clients for 12 years. They paid their loans on time. There was absolutely no improper influence on William Isaac.

I watched Hardin's hands as I scribbled notes. He turned his keychain over and over. Then I asked him about Guillermo Hernandez-Cartaya. He gave his keys an involuntary shake, but his face was perfectly composed. That connection, he said, was handled by a long-gone bank officer, current whereabouts unknown. He was still smiling, with an affable, inscrutable midwestern bonhomie.

William Isaac himself had two shots at guessing the Butchers' game. As general counsel for the First National Bank of Louisville, he dealt with them personally, although back then they were considered respectable, if aggressive and somewhat flamboyant. His second contact came as director and then chairman of the FDIC. Isaac may have excused himself from their case because of his personal involvement, but he could not escape his role as the man ultimately in charge of examining their banks and insuring their deposits. At best, his conduct raised questions about appearances. From any less charitable view, it revealed serious weakness in federal supervision and foreshadowed the total collapse of the system in the savings and loan disaster.

CHAPTER SIX

□□□

"I Think We Had Them"

□ 1 □

"I THINK WE HAD THEM. I think Jim and I were on the right track, and I believe if they had let Jim and I alone, we could have saved the banks. I really think that," stated George M. Little, Jr. a former Tennessee state bank examiner, speaking under oath. One can almost see him grow more excited and agitated, his words tumbling out faster and faster, as he finally told the story that had been gnawing at him for years. Little was describing his examination of the United American Bank of Knoxville, Jake Butcher's flagship, in 1979. His partner Jim, "a very fine examiner," was James L. Sexton from the FDIC. A witness in a civil suit against the FDIC, Little told of sterling detective work cut short by strange orders from his superiors. His deposition reads like a film noir.

Little came from the hollows and mountains of far eastern Tennessee, where he started out as teller, chauffeur, and factotum for Mrs. Raise, owner of a small town bank. When she sold the bank, he drifted into a job with the Tennessee Banking Department. Starting in 1969, he learned the trade of examiner on the job, through "hand-me-down information," and rose steadily through the ranks. In 1979, he took the post of division supervisor, the chief of state examiners in eastern Tennessee. The state banking commissioner made the appointment directly. "It put me off of civil service," Little recalled. "Worst job I ever had with the state."

Along the way, Little had become the bane of the Butcher system. In late 1978, while examining a bank run by Jake's brother-in-law, Lionel Wilde, he had stumbled on a trace of the Butcher loan shuffle. Little noticed that large volumes of checks from Jake's Publix Oil Company flowed daily through Wilde's bank. "I thought I had him caught on a big check kite," Little said.

Little and his assistant tracked these checks to accounts in UAB-Knoxville and C&C-Knox. Thinking "we would make pretty good detectives," they decided to get a firsthand look. A friend let them into UAB after hours. "We get in there confidentially and nobody knows what we're doing and get Lionel's Publix Oil records and his personal records and make copies of all that stuff, see," Little told the lawyers. "They didn't know what we were doing and they was suspicious, but they didn't know what we were up to." But at C&C Knox, "We run into a stumbling block because we get too many helpful hands in the pie and they saw who we was looking at." Somebody made a phone call to the Butchers. "Anyway," continued Little, "I was told from Nashville, I was called and told specifically that I better watch out." Little's superior from the Banking Department warned him "that I better know what I'm doing." Blanton was in office, Jake was running for Governor, and Little's boss in the state capital said, "You know what this could do to the election."

Jake also applied sweet reason. He had Wilde meet with the examiners, bringing along "five lawyers or five accountants . . . and some kind of story." Butcher's men gave a plausible explanation of the transaction, and the examiners dropped the case. "To be honest with you," said Little, "I got conned out of a big kite, over a million dollars that he had going."

Little kept worrying about what he'd seen, however, and brought it up later in a Nashville meeting of the district supervisors. State Banking Commissioner Tom Mottern and his deputy Talmadge Gilley were presiding.

"Look, we've got a big problem," Little said. But his superiors weren't impressed. "Tom and Talmadge laughed at me," Little recalled, "and said, 'George, how come it seems like every time we have a meeting, you have more problems in east Tennessee than anyone else?' " Little says he stood his ground on the issue of "interlocking loans." ("Say you have a bank and I have a bank," he explained. "You lend me $100,000; I'll lend you $100,000.") Under his nagging, the department made a half-hearted stab at watching for them. This conversation occurred in late 1979, and Little thinks the department could have stopped the Butchers then, "if we had continued and kept on this track." But something intervened.

"I think somebody higher than me was gotten to and pulled me," he surmised. "I think that they didn't want me examining their banks, and they went to the office and said, 'George has got a vendetta against us; get him off of us.' That's what I think happened.

"I don't know, for some reason or another, I didn't get to work too many Butcher banks after that happened," he mused. "I think I got close to them, and I believe they conned some people above me into thinking that I was after them, you know."

Little wasn't asked to follow up on UAB-Knoxville. "I wasn't allowed to," he said. "Mr. Mottern or Mr. Gilley, one said this bank is big, and they used the excuse Mr. Sexton worked it last year, we're going to send Mr. Gilley down to do it. And they just took it away from me."

Instead, in November 1979, Little visited a smaller Butcher bank in the mountainous outpost of Johnson City. His report proved him incorrigible. "Management is considered to be very unsatisfactory," he wrote, "and should be removed as soon as possible before they loan the whole bank to insiders, friends, and partners." He called specifically for the ouster of bank chairman C. H. Butcher, Jr., and sent a file on the president to the state attorney, "for possible indictments."

"It really hit the fan then when I did the Johnson City bank," Little said. The Butchers, he said, "went down to the office and convinced the people down there that I was out to get them." Little did draw one more Butcher assignment. In 1980, he was nominally in charge of the examination of C. H. Butcher's City and County Bank of Knox County. But he fell sick and turned it over to another examiner. He recovered enough to join the team on the day of discussion with bank officers, which caused the bank president to start "eating Rolaids like they was going out of style." Little rated C&C-Knox a problem bank but ironically missed the most severe problems. "I have an idea that they had shifted some loans," he said. For two more years, Little sat out the Butcher exams, offering his expertise once more only at the very end. In the spring of 1983, he was part of the state team working on the FDIC's massive, multibank audit of the Butchers. Vindication was short-lived. The incoming state banking commissioner didn't like him, and in June 1983 he was fired.

□ 2 □

JAMES L. SEXTON, the examiner from the FDIC, had followed a different career path. By the time Sexton joined Little in the 1979 visit to UAB-Knoxville, the lanky Texan was already known as a rising star in the FDIC. Universally praised as one of the best and the brightest of the corporation's examiners, he had already been promoted to assistant regional director when he went back into the field with Little. As Little said, it was an eye-opening examination. "Jim and I were on pretty strong onto them," Little said in his deposition. Looking at an FDIC document from the 1983 exam that closed the UAB-Knoxville, Little ticked off the names for the lawyers. "We classified a lot of these banker loans in that UAB '79 report. These loans that we had on this spread sheet a minute ago, we classified all of these."

It emerged years later that Sexton wasn't content with merely filing his report. After the examination, he wrote to the chairman of the FDIC and to the United States Attorney in Knoxville, recommending criminal prosecution. These letters are still sealed documents. Their existence wasn't known outside of the FDIC until mid-1987, and the current United States Attorney in Knoxville, John W. Gill, Jr., who prosecuted the Butchers, said he hasn't seen them. I learned about them from Jake Butcher himself. His lawyers had unearthed them just weeks before our Atlanta interview. "I didn't know [Sexton] had that vindictiveness out for me," Jake complained. "I didn't know that as he got promoted and went to Washington, that eventually he'd be going to try to prove his point right and come back in my days of vulnerability, with me being gone on the World's Fair for two years, and take the fort while I was away.

"In 1980, '81, '82, I thought I had a good rapport with [Sexton] because he approved me buying these large banks in Chattanooga and Lexington. He led this lamb to slaughter."

After Sexton finished the UAB-Knoxville exam, he was very quickly transferred to the Philadelphia office. Sexton considered the move a promotion. He said he was called away to help handle the collapse of the First Pennsylvania Bank, at the time the FDIC's largest problem. But the move demoralized his co-workers on the Butcher case. "I think they might have gone all the way to Washington to get Mr. Sexton and me away from them," says George Little. The deposition does not specify who "they" were, but rightly or wrongly, Little was not the only state regulator to see the Butchers' hand in Sexton's transfer.

Little may have received a false impression, but one can hardly blame him. Even though the entire Butcher episode had been scrutinized by lawyers in myriads of suits and by a congressional subcommittee, much of the record remained shrouded in the regulators' obsessive secrecy. Little's testimony came to light only after a *Knoxville News-Sentinel* reporter followed an obscure civil suit in the federal courthouse in London, Kentucky. FDIC lawyers responded to the story by attempting to seal the entire case file. Little himself received a warning from the State Attorney General's office against talking publicly about his examinations. Normally loquacious, he is still bound by this gag order.

The two main sources of information on the regulators' performance remain, first, a two-day congressional hearing by Congressman Barnard's subcommittee plus a scathing report by his Staff Director Peter Barash, and, second, about 30 lawsuits accusing the FDIC of negligence. These documents show that Sexton and Little weren't the first to worry about the Butchers. Before 1978 the brothers had aroused the intense suspicion of every federal bank agency. As early as April 1971, the Federal Reserve System rejected a membership application from the City and County Bank of Powell, Tennessee, because Jake and C. H., Jr. were its controlling officers. These two, said a letter from the Federal Reserve Bank of Atlanta, "were not regarded as satisfactory management."

Later, only one of the Butchers' major banks fell under Federal Reserve jurisdiction: the United Southern Bank of Nashville (called the United American Bank until January 1981), which catered to the country music industry. It was already troubled when the Butchers took it over in 1976, and in July 1977, the Fed started a crackdown on its management. In May 1978, Fed supervisors issued a cease and desist order, alleging "serious banking abuses and possible criminal misconduct." The Federal Reserve Board of Governors notified the Justice Department of a possible criminal case in the bookkeeping on a $6.7 million Federal Funds purchase. But the charge dropped from sight. The cease and desist order stayed in effect for the next four years, with diminishing impact, while Jake severed his ties with the bank. C. H., Jr. stayed in the background.

The Office of the Comptroller of the Currency (OCC) dealt briefly with the Butchers, but it was a memorable encounter. In February 1975, when Jake took control of the federally chartered Hamilton National Bank of Knoxville (later the UAB-Knoxville), he inherited supervision by the OCC. The OCC examined the bank three times in that first year, a sure sign that it expected trouble from Jake's management. The OCC's examiners found some signs of improvement, but Jake's high compensation bothered the agency. In June 1976, it scheduled a meeting with UAB's board of directors. Jake responded with his usual dash. He asked for a postponement of the meeting and then announced that he was converting to a state charter.

The move placed Jake's UAB-Knoxville under the control of the Tennessee Banking Department and the federal insurer, the FDIC. Much later, FDIC Chairman Isaac denied the plausible conclusion that Jake was shopping for more lenient regulators. The switch to state supervision, he told the Barnard subcommittee, was an attempt by the Butchers to escape Federal Reserve requirements for higher cash reserves. More than 600 banks had moved from the Federal Reserve System to more lenient state charters between 1970 and 1980, he argued. At the time, however, regulators weren't so complaisant. Former Comptroller of the Currency John G. Heimann described his staff's reaction to the switch, "They were so mad they couldn't see straight."

Within two weeks of Jake's announcement, senior officials of the FDIC, the Federal Reserve Board, and the OCC were meeting about the Butcher banks. In a July 6 conference, they decided to launch a simultaneous examination of all the Butcher-controlled banks. The agenda was broad and prophetic. One of the main goals, according to the OCC, was to uncover "the interrelationships among the banks, including participations purchased or sold." A memo from the Memphis office of the FDIC told examiners about previous problems in evaluating "the extent of the Butcher indebtedness, and the resulting debt service requirements and its effect on the individual banks." The examiners received a separate form to list "breakdown of loans to the Butchers, their families, their corporate interests and close associates." Another form cast the net even wider:

> Inasmuch as the listing of Butcher associates and interests may be far from complete, a listing of all out-of-territory credits of significant amounts should be provided on this schedule.

So when the multibank joint exam started on November 1, 1976, the regulators were looking for the pattern of insider lending, family deals, and loan shuffles that finally sank the Butcher banks seven years later. After spending the better part of a year digesting the results, the examiners had learned a lesson strikingly similar to the lesson they relearned in 1983, at a much higher price.

Since the Federal Reserve and the Comptroller of the Currency now had limited jurisdiction, it fell to the FDIC to act on the evidence. Two papers, one only recently released, show just what the FDIC knew as of mid-1978, and what it planned to do about it. The Federal Court files in Knoxville recently yielded an October 1977 memo from Roy E. Jackson, head of the FDIC regional office in Memphis, addressed to John J. Early, director of the FDIC's Division of Bank Supervision and the man in charge of all examinations.

Jackson told the Washington headquarters that his examiners were up against "an informal organization, involving numerous associates," that influenced 27 banks. This group operated in regulatory loopholes. Reported Jackson, "My examiners have had no success in establishing legal affiliations . . . , since the group obviously knows the law and its restrictions quite well." But Jackson's examiners tracked the insider network, and Jackson provided a list of 79 names and businesses fated to become very familiar a half-decade later.

Even in 1977, it was clear that the Butchers and associates had loaned themselves significantly more than they had invested in the banks. Their loans were highly vulnerable; they had used 30 percent of their borrowing to buy stock in the banking network. This self-financing had puffed up the balance sheets to make the banks look far more liquid than they really were. One pin could burst the balloon. As Regional Director Jackson dryly said, "The welfare of a significant number of banks appears unduly dependent upon the personal fortunes of the Butchers and a close group of associates."

What to do was a problem. The Butchers had cleverly exploited the loopholes in existing law, depriving the FDIC of an easy legal response. Complained Jackson:

> Although the most casual observer can easily determine that there exists a huge amount of insider debt through accommodation and reciprocal arrangements among the banks, the effectiveness of [the applicable law] in dealing with this situation is almost totally subverted by the loose organizational structure.

Jackson didn't think he would get far with words alone. "C. H. Butcher, Jr.," he wrote, "is a resourceful individual who is not likely to be impressed with our philosophies about sound banking." The best Jackson could recommend was to meet with the Butchers for a "conversation," and, if that failed, to begin the laborious procedure of bringing cease and desist orders against each of their banks.

Jackson, along with James Sexton, held this conversation with the Butchers in the Memphis regional office on November 17, 1977. Sexton drafted the official memo to the files. Sexton and Jackson made six points, drawn from the examinations. The banks (1) carried too many questionable loans, (2) made too many loans out of their trade area, and (3) booked a "dangerously high" level of "official family debt." (4) The banks were capitalized by debt rather than "commitment of personal worth." (5) "Round-robin" deposits, "for the purpose of funding out-of-territory loans" inflated the system. (Wholesale banks such as UAB-Knoxville would sell participations to the smaller banks "downstream" and then lend them the money to cover the purchase.) So far, the supervisors had their sights on the flow of loans and funds within the Butchers' system, and they saw how it operated as an organic whole. Red flags flew everywhere.

Item number six was more a matter of the Butchers' personal finances. The brothers pocketed the commissions on credit life insurance, the policies on the mortality of the banks' big borrowers, instead of turning them over to the banks. According to the regulators, the Butchers snagged more than $500,000 from this abuse.

Sexton and Jackson ended their conversation feeling satisfied. Wrote Sexton, "C. H. Butcher, Jr., considered the 'brains' of the group, understood our concerns fully." As far as the "big problems," listed as one through five, Sexton said, "we gained the impression that correction will be forthcoming." But Jake and C. H. came through only on item number six, the credit life commissions. (They may have hastened their compliance when the commissions became an issue in Jake's 1978 campaign.) Official attention focused on this one success, at the expense of the larger problems on Sexton's agenda, problems that cut to the structure of the Butchers' operation.

At the congressional hearings years later, FDIC Chairman Isaac defended the follow-up to the 1976-77 examination and the Butchers' switch from the Comptroller of the Currency to his own jurisdiction. Seated next to Mr. Sexton, he blandly told the Barnard subcommittee:

The Comptroller had expressed concerns about some of the bank's practices. The FDIC expressed the same concerns and obtained corrections following the conversion. It is important to recognize that none of those items—executive compensation, credit life commissions and dividend policies—played the slightest role in the bank's failure.

□ 3 □

THE MEMPHIS OFFICE SCHEDULED ANOTHER MEETING with Jake in February 1978, and Regional Director Jackson received the complete Butcher treatment. Butcher began with a full-blown challenge, telling Jackson he was thinking of running for governor. "I have no interest in politics," Jackson replied stiffly and tried to press on with the business at hand. In spite of the clear message of the November meeting, Jackson told Butcher that they "were a little disappointed with the response to date." Jake strongly hinted that he would holler "politics" at any pressure from the regulators. He mentioned a possible enforcement action against one of his brother's banks and asked if the FDIC meant to make "adverse publicity" during his campaign. The bluster alternated with an effusive display of cooperation. Jackson complained about the guidelines the UAB had adopted after their November showdown. Said Jackson, they "left loopholes which suggest a potential for major deviations." Jake agreed immediately, promising to close the loopholes. Then he told Jackson not to worry about the other complaints, because he would revise the guidelines to take care of them, too.

The Butchers perfected this type of response, to the constant frustration of the examiners. According to one supervisor, they would make a big show of compliance on some minor point. But on the main issues, nothing solid ever seemed to happen.

The Memphis team of Jackson and Sexton took one last stab at controlling the Butchers. On January 15, 1979, Sexton went to Knoxville to conduct the UAB examination, working with George

Little from the state. As Little said, they came close. Sexton wrote a tough report, noting "adverse trends . . . in almost all areas of the bank's operations." But his chance to follow up was much delayed. Shortly after the report, the FDIC headquarters transferred Jackson to Dallas, and Sexton to Philadelphia.

By this time, the Butcher case had become involved in the higher politics of the FDIC board of directors. For most of 1978, the FDIC had limped along with a two-man Board: Comptroller of the Currency John Heimann and William Isaac. After the resignation of the previous chairman in mid-August, Heimann, an ex-officio director by virtue of his position as comptroller, also held the post of acting FDIC chairman. He found the double appointment a great embarrassment. "Nothing is more difficult than trying to run two agencies simultaneously," he explained, "especially when they have different traditions and patterns of operation." So Heimann delegated supervision of day-to-day affairs to Isaac. This position put Isaac in a quandary. By Isaac's own account, he felt he should stay away from anything dealing with the Butchers. But in the fall of 1978, he read a highly critical article in the *Memphis Commercial Appeal* about Jake's insider loans. Isaac said he decided to risk an impropriety, and he asked his director of supervision what was being done about the Butcher banks. The supervisor's weak reply provoked a blast from Heimann about the passivity of the office. This high-level interest, said Isaac, led Sexton, the Memphis assistant regional director, to take personal charge of the next Butcher examination in January 1979.

This apparent resolve ended in a bout of finger-pointing. In February 1979, the White House ended a prolonged stalemate by naming Irvine H. Sprague as the new chairman. A veteran lobbyist and insider with the bluntness of an old newsman, Sprague had already served a six-year term on the FDIC board as an appointee of Lyndon Johnson. Isaac stated that he was reduced to a minority board member with no operating authority. "My ability to get things done," he said, "was extremely limited." He said that he did tell Sprague about his worries over the Butcher banks, a conversation Sprague does not remember at all. Sprague does, however, recall an incident involving

James Sexton. Taking charge of the FDIC, he decided to stiffen its division of bank supervision by bringing in Quinton Thompson as its head. Thompson, a Texan with a reputation for tough examinations, asked for Sexton, his fellow tough Texan, as his deputy.

William Isaac opposed the appointment. "He said Thompson was the meanest man in the organization, and Sexton was the second meanest," recalled Sprague. "He said it would make the office unbalanced." But Thompson refused to come to Washington without Sexton, and Isaac backed down. "He later said, 'How wrong I was. Sexton was a real gem,' " Sprague reported.

Isaac finally became FDIC chairman in mid-1981, with the advent of a Republican administration. (The Reagan White House held Sprague over for so many months that he became embarrassed. Finally, Isaac's friends in Congress forced the transition.) Thompson, who acknowledged "philosophic differences" with Isaac, resigned soon after, and James Sexton became director of bank supervision.

In the meantime, attempts in the Memphis office to discipline the Butchers were turning into mush. David Meadows replaced Jackson as regional director and found himself baffled by the Butchers' tactics of wheedle and bluster. The constant nagging from Memphis quickly lost its impact. The Barnard subcommittee report written by Peter Barash counted a minimum of 44 exchanges of official letters and 17 top-level meetings between the Butchers and the Memphis office from 1978 to 1982. This "regulatory sound and fury" signified so little that Jake Butcher refused to let the Memphis supervisors attend his April 1982 UAB board of directors meeting to discuss the 1981 examination report. Instead, the UAB board spent its time deciding to sponsor a celebrity tennis tournament at the upcoming World's Fair.

The regional FDIC office had little support from Washington. At the time of the April rebuff, Regional Director Meadows was telling Jake that he had "difficulties" approving an application for a UAB branch at the World's Fair because of his "concern for the bank." Yet FDIC headquarters approved the branch shortly after on delegated authority. The Barash report sharply attacked the FDIC's "failure to use Butcher applications for mergers and branches as leverage against continuing unsafe practices." From 1978 on, the FDIC approved 16 UAB requests for remote service machines. In May 1980, it approved an off-shore branch in the free-wheeling bank haven of the Cayman Islands. Most curiously, the FDIC Board voted in 1982 to allow a significant merger at Jake's Chattanooga bank.

At first this merger met stiff resistance. After the application languished for six months, Jake led a delegation to Washington to meet his old critic James Sexton, by now the FDIC's director of bank supervision. Jake's lawyers made the strange argument that the merger delay kept Jake from paying for the stock he had bought in pursuing the takeover. Sexton and Meadows instead hammered on the condition of UAB-Knoxville. But their message was considerably diluted on August 20, when the FDIC board, after five meetings, voted for the merger. Jake Butcher thought he had the go-ahead.

Isaac claimed, to the contrary, that the August 20 meeting sharply changed the signals. In approving the merger, he said, he also ordered a comprehensive examination of the Butchers' empire. The Memphis office had been brewing plans for an across-the-board exam for some time. Since the December 1981 exam, which raised an alarm, and certainly since the humiliation of taking second place to a celebrity tennis tournament, Meadows had been talking about the need to visit the Butcher banks simultaneously. His new second-in-command was well briefed on the problem. George Muraco, who took up the post of assistant regional director in July, had worked in Dallas with the Butchers' old critic, Roy Jackson, director of the 1976 multibank examination. Jackson had told Muraco how the Butchers had "caused him some consternation on occasion." While making plans, said Meadows, "We had informal conversations with James Sexton." But Meadows insists that the impetus came from the field, not from Washington.

High-level approval was helpful for such a massive deployment of resources, however, and the August 20 board meeting appeared to have set things in motion. "By certainly the first week or two in September," Muraco recalled, the decision was made. Memphis brought in the Columbus, Ohio office, which supervised the Butchers' Kentucky banks. On learning that the Federal Reserve Bank of Atlanta was planning to move against the Butchers' bank in Nashville, Muraco phoned to bring it on board. Memphis asked for additional manpower from the FDIC Atlanta region and coordinated visits with the Kentucky Banking Department. But the Tennessee regulators backed off, saying that the on going campaign for governor had made the Butchers too hot an issue.

The visits to the banks started on November 1, 1982, the day after the World's Fair ended and the Knoxville hotels had emptied. Some 150 FDIC staff fanned out across the two states. Fifty descended on the Butchers' two Knoxville headquarters. Orders were given on a "need-to-know" basis. For the first time in years, there was no advance request for the banks' computer printouts.

The surprise tactics worked. Former FDIC examiner Robert Shober, one of 25 who worked UAB-Knoxville, recalled getting a normal reception from the bank staff. By the third week, things didn't add up. "We started to see that the loans were structured rather unusually," said Shober. "We were starting to get into discussions of the loans with some of the officers, and they weren't giving us real good answers to some of our questions.

"We got to sharing information with the people in the other banks, and we realized that the amount of loans, the concentration of loans to certain borrowers, was a lot more enormous than what we saw."

In a series of informal meetings through December, the examiners coordinated information through George Muraco. By January the Memphis office had pieced together enough of the picture to understand what the Butchers were doing. As the examinations wound down in the bigger banks, field staff were reassigned to a second round of visits, this time to the rest of the system. The Memphis staff drafted cease and desist orders to bring the banks under control.

These orders led to one of the stranger episodes in this saga. On January 3, 1983, Memphis sent Washington the draft of a Section 8(c) temporary cease and desist order, an emergency measure to keep UAB-Knoxville from shuffling bad loans through the system.

Two days later, the Board of Review in D.C. approved the order, with two dissenters urging "more stringent" action. Expecting the full FDIC board to make the order final on January 6, Thursday morning, Regional Director Meadows prepared to serve it on the Butchers in Knoxville. But at 8:00 A.M., James Sexton called from headquarters. Washington wanted to table the order. Instead, Sexton was coming to Memphis the next day for a high-level meeting with Jake and C. H.

The meeting started with a warning from Meadows that he had asked for a temporary cease and desist order, but it ended with considerably less. After confronting Jake and C. H. with evidence of their loan shifting, Sexton and Meadows offered to let them sign an informal agreement; they would suspend the verbal commitments they had made to their "downstream" banks to repurchase the bad loans they had parcelled out, if trouble ever came up. Sexton defended the letter as a necessary tool to allow the examiners to finish their work. Millions of dollars in shaky credits were flooding back to the Knoxville banks, constantly increasing their losses. This flood also happened to increase the potential charge on the FDIC fund. Relatively healthy downstream banks were trying to save themselves from heavy losses by sending back the Butchers' garbage. They were understandably bitter at Sexton's letter. In addition, it was a major breach in FDIC procedure.

When the regulators uncovered a problem bank, they would normally start by negotiating a Memorandum of Understanding for voluntary steps to correct problems. In serious cases of "unsafe and unsound practices," the FDIC could issue cease and desist orders, forbidding the abuses. A regular Section 8(b) order would take effect after an administrative hearing. In a real emergency that threatened to put a bank under or hurt its depositors, they could issue a temporary 8(c) order to take effect immediately. To protest, the bank officers would have to ask a Federal Court to lift the order. The FDIC also had the power to remove unsafe and unsound bank officers. These powers were long-standing, but they had been strengthened by the so-called Bert Lance Act of 1978, passed in reaction to the alleged banking abuses of President Carter's confidant (and the

Butchers' friend). Even though the group examination gave the worst possible ratings to the Butchers' flagship banks, Sexton's letter used none of this apparatus. As one critic said, it "did not even rise to the level of a Memorandum of Understanding."

Even worse, the letter was legally shaky. As the FDIC well knew, the responsibility for a bank's policy lies with its management and its board of directors. (A binding Memorandum of Understanding would be signed by bank directors.) But in much of their system, the Butchers were neither officer nor director. The letter was a legal shortcut. Sexton and Meadows defended the measure, ironically, on the grounds that the Butchers were known for keeping their word.

□ 4 □

THE BUTCHERS DID HONOR THE LETTER, freezing their loans in place. But Sexton's agreement was swamped by events. The numbers from the examination worsened rapidly. The Comptroller of the Currency slapped its own cease and desist order on the one Butcher bank still in its jurisdiction. Within two weeks the FDIC was forced to go ahead with its original temporary cease and desist order. On January 25, Regional Director Meadows delivered the results of the examination to a UAB-Knoxville board meeting, "the most important board meeting," he said, "that he had conducted or attended in the State of Tennessee."

"Almost beyond comprehension," exclaimed Chief Examiner Ronny Parham about the bad loans. "I'm not used to seeing this much wrong." It was a grueling meeting. The regulators at last hammered on the deceptive loan shuffle, and they focused on apparent law breaking in such detail that it made Jake squirm. Meadows said he would recommend pulling the FDIC insurance. "If you haven't taken us seriously before," he said, "now is the time to do it."

But Jake thought he still had some cards to play. Tennessee Banking Commissioner W. C. "Billy" Adams, the only official with authority to close the bank, was willing to keep UAB open if Jake would put in another $40 million. In the meantime, Adams called his own Butcher expert, George Little, now back in favor, to get his own figures. "Commissioner Adams called me at home and told me to schedule the examination and go in there with as few people as I could," Little recalled. But as Little worked, the job got bigger and bigger. Little finally gave Adams the unwelcome news that the bank was deeply insolvent. "The more you checked," said Little, "the worse it looked."

Oblivious to this erosion, Jake overplayed his hand. UAB was due to issue its year-end financial statement right after the board met with Regional Director Meadows. The release came out with figures so extravagantly rosy that the FDIC blew its top. The FDIC board in Washington voted a new temporary cease and desist order prohibiting the release of "false and misleading" financial reports. Sexton handed the order to Jake at the end of their February 4 meeting in D.C. Jake decided to fight back and applied to the Federal Court in Knoxville for an injunction to stay the FDIC's order. The move was suicidal.

Rumors about the examination had already been flying through Knoxville. Jake said the leak was inevitable with all the examiners in town; their presence was bound to be noted in the bars and restaurants. The FDIC retorted that Jake's lawsuit confirmed his depositors' worst fears. Jake went to court on Tuesday, February 8, complaining that the new order "would lead to a very severe liquidity crisis." By Thursday, his bank was hit by a run. "Upstream" creditors, large banks such as the First National Bank of Louisville, pulled their loans. Some stores posted notice that they wouldn't accept UAB checks. Small depositors lined up at the doors of one branch. Through the week, Jake had been turning to his lender of last resort, the Federal Reserve Bank of Atlanta. By the weekend, he had drawn $80 million.

In a marathon that ran through Saturday, Sunday, and Monday night, the nation's senior regulators huddled in sweaty, ill-tempered conference. Jake remembered that he and his board met with Tennessee Banking Commissioner Adams on Sunday to save his bank. Jake asked Adams how much new capital he needed. Adams estimated $40 million, and UAB Director B. Ray Thompson, "the richest man in Tennessee," offered to supply it by February 18. Then Adams went to Atlanta for the fateful meeting with the Federal regulators. The FDIC and the Federal Reserve Bank warned of a massive run the next day, noting that "television cameras and newspaper reporters were camped around the UAB offices." Adams proposed calming them with a press release about the new capital. Not enough, said the Atlanta Fed. The UAB probably won't survive until February 18 without an "enormous escalation" of Federal Reserve lending, said Atlanta Fed President William Ford. The Fed didn't want to throw good money after bad. That statement sealed Butcher's fate. Adams bowed to the inevitable and ordered the UAB to close, as only he could do.

Back home, an embarrassed Commissioner Adams broke the news to Jake. "He called and said I'm not able to do what I promised," Butcher remembered. "He said I've got to welch on my commitment. I've got to reneg because the FDIC won't let me do it."

In the meantime, the FDIC board met in Washington to figure out what to do with the UAB. "It was the longest, most contentious board meeting in all my service at FDIC," said two-time Director Irvine Sprague. All through Sunday, the board worked to save UAB with an "open-bank" merger. By 5:00 A.M., First Tennessee National Corporation of Memphis came up with a "generally acceptable" offer. But time was up. According to the official FDIC account, "It was simply not possible in the few hours remaining prior to the bank's opening to put together the merger."

So the UAB closed its doors on February 14, in what the folks in Knoxville call the "Valentine's Day Massacre." The FDIC's job now was to sell the remains as quickly as possible. Already frazzled by a sleepless weekend, the board found itself working under the previously untested provisions of the new Garn-St Germain Act, allowing out-of-state bids on failed banks. The bidding pitted the flamboyant Citizens and Southern Bank of Atlanta against First Tennessee. FDIC Chairman Isaac wanted to stick with the deal he had negotiated with First Tennessee Chairman Ronald Terry, but it was a "nonconforming bid," and a majority of the board voted for C&S. Then, at 8:50 P.M., a hitch developed in the C&S bid. The board reversed itself, and First Tennessee took the prize. The anger of the conference call meeting still rankles. "They didn't get near what the bank was worth," complained Jake Butcher. He claimed that Ron Terry's political ties with Governor Lamar Alexander and United States Senator Howard Baker gave First Tennessee the inside track.

Sprague, who has written the book *Bailout*, an insider's history of FDIC bailouts, concurred with brutal frankness. "Isaac was campaigning for reappointment as FDIC chairman," he said. "He hoped fervently for a second term." The price was high, both for the FDIC and for First Tennessee. The principle of the nonconforming bid had merit, since it placed the task of disposing of bad assets on the bank rather than on a government bureaucracy. (With its own profit at stake, the bank presumably would strike a better deal.) But the bad loans were more crushing than First Tennessee expected, and it returned repeatedly to the FDIC for help. The extra bill eventually totalled $35 million.

The day after UAB-Knoxville reopened as the First Tennessee, a bleary William Isaac told the *Knoxville Journal*, "All of the banks were solvent except United American Bank." C. H., Jr. held out for three more months, selling his smaller banks and trying desperately to consolidate the rest. Almost daily, C. H. put through calls to United States Senator James Sasser, a member of the Senate Banking Committee, and Sasser vouched for him with the FDIC. Said Sprague, "Jim would call and say, 'I wouldn't tell you anything on Jake Butcher, but C. H. is pure as the driven snow.' Jim Sexton gave me the same report." But as Jake said later, the brothers knew that Valentine's Day was the end. "They might as well have closed C. H.'s bank on the same day," he said. On May 27, the City and County Bank of Knox County shut its doors, along with the United Southern Bank in Nashville and three others in the chain. It was the largest single day of closures since the Bank Holiday of 1933.

□ 5 □

THE BACKROOM POLITICS IN THE BUTCHER CRISIS came closest to daylight in Kentucky, under a different set of regulators. "The worst

Butcher bank in Kentucky was better than the best Butcher bank in Tennessee," said the FDIC's Sandra Waldrop, who had jurisdiction in the state as regional director of the FDIC's Columbus, Ohio office. Kentucky was able to sell these banks rather than close them, but as the powerful regional banks that had financed the Butchers scrambled to save the situation, an illuminating power play intervened.

Governor John Y. Brown, the Kentucky Fried Chicken franchiser, was a close friend of the Butchers. He called on them for national Democratic party fund raising through his Lexington Group, a political networking organization. With Jake bankrupt and C. H. teetering, he appointed two political cronies to manage the crisis. But his Banking Department was hard to control. By something of an accident, the acting bank commissioner was Neil Welch, a gruff former agent of the FBI, who as head of its New York office was once a candidate for J. Edgar Hoover's job. Governor Brown had recruited him as Secretary of Justice to help clean up Kentucky politics. But Welch showed discomfiting vigor. When he started to investigate the governor's close friends and wiretap illicit deals involving state cabinet members, Brown reassigned him to the Public Protection and Regulation Cabinet, which happened to include the Banking Department. Welch was in no mood to take dictation from the governor's political buddies.

Governor Brown's crisis managers moved in with a notable lack of subtlety. His point man, R. Gene Smith, the vice chairman of the cabinet, went directly to the FDIC suggesting "regulatory forbearance," meaning a break from the supervisors, to help sell the banks. His interjections drew a stiff reply. The FDIC's Jim Sexton wrote back:

> I see no reason for us to confer. In the first place, I am uncomfortable in dealing with the governor's office on bank regulatory matters as opposed to the Kentucky Banking Department, with which we enjoy a good and legally permissible regulatory relationship. In the second place, I do not see that we have anything to talk about.

Leonard V. Hardin, executive vice president of the First National Bank of Louisville, sent Smith proposals for a cease and desist order

tracking his bank's own steps "to shore up our loan agreements."
The letter addressed Smith as "Acting Banking Commissioner,"
which was news to Welch and the Banking Department. But the last
straw came when the counsel at First National complained to the
FDIC that Gene Smith had been left out of a regulators' meeting
with the Butchers. When Welch heard this, he erupted.

"I immediately called Leonard Hardin," he wrote to his files,
"and asked him to please pay close attention to the message I had
for him." The memo continues in capital letters:

GENE SMITH, WHATEVER THEY MAY HAVE PREVIOUSLY PERCEIVED
TO BE HIS ROLE, THAT I WANTED IT TO BE CLEAR IN THEIR MINDS
THAT GENE SMITH HAS NO AUTHORITY IN THE DEPARTMENT OF
BANKING, HE HAS NO DECISION MAKING ROLE HERE, HE HAS NO
OFFICIAL INPUT HERE, HE DID NOT SPEAK FOR THE DEPARTMENT
OF BANKING AND THEY SHOULD BE GUIDED ACCORDINGLY. AND
FURTHERMORE, MR. SMITH, AS LONG AS I WAS COMMISSIONER,
WOULD NEVER HAVE AN OFFICIAL RELATIONSHIP WITH THE DE-
PARTMENT OF BANKING.

The next day, Welch was no longer the commissioner.

As the pace of events in April accelerated, Brown quickly appointed a respected professional banker, Leonard Marshall, as commissioner. The crisis managers departed the scene, and Marshall
turned to the serious business of selling C. H. Butcher, Jr.'s Kentucky banks. The deal revealed a new side of the Butchers' network.

The buyers turned out to be a group from Longview, Texas, who
knew C. H., Jr. from his hobby of breeding quarterhorses. (The lead
investor, Jack Strong, was a former state senator who had introduced
a pivotal bill in the notorious Sharpstown scandal in Texas more
than a decade earlier. See Chapter Thirteen.) The sale went through
in May one step ahead of a bank run, in a marathon session that
lasted from Thursday to the next Tuesday. The Louisville law firm
on the closing kept a full staff working 24 hours a day through the
weekend. "At two o'clock on Sunday morning," said the lawyer, "it
looked like high noon here." The financing pivotted on First National Bank of Louisville, which provided more than $9 million to
the buyers.

C. H., Jr. stayed the course, negotiating, signing papers and bantering with the Texans. One of the lawyers said, "I heard him tell Jack Strong in the middle of the night, 'You don't know what a big favor I did you.' "

Not many did know the details of this favor, it turned out. On the last day of the closing, C. H., Jr. and Jack Strong made a side agreement leaving C. H., Jr. a financial toehold in the banks. Neither the state nor the FDIC field office regulators knew about it until three years later, when the bankruptcy trustee began to ask if it had any value. It also turned out that the three Longview millionaires weren't simply acting for themselves. A group of 21 other Texans, including prominent politicians and a state supreme court justice, had also kicked in money. The FDIC Columbus office started to fuss about the secrecy of these names, muttering about violation of the Change in Bank Control Act.

But the Texans were masters at facing down the regional staff. The structure of the deal, they said, had been cleared in conversations with Bill Isaac and Jim Sexton. Impressed by this endorsement, the field office dropped the matter, leaving others to wonder at the apparent failure to comply with the laws on full public disclosure.

To the amazement of less involved staffers, the Butcher debacle didn't seem to hurt the careers of the FDIC supervisors who were directly in charge. Months after the closings, in November, 1983, James Sexton left the FDIC to assume the post of bank commissioner of his native Texas. Memphis Regional Director David Meadows went to Washington as assistant to Sexton and then became his successor. Isaac himself weathered the embarrassing questions raised by the Barash report. The Barnard subcommittee confined its political insinuations to the thought that a Republican administration was somehow trying to embarrass prominent Democrats. No one outside of Kentucky and Tennessee had a hint that Isaac might have been beholden to those Democrats.

Unlike FSLIC's meetings with Speaker Wright, no direct evidence has surfaced of political pressure on Isaac or the FDIC staff. Perhaps the episode was an accumulation of innocent but simply awful appearances, compounded by a foolish doctrine of forbearance. (As Isaac explained it, the supervisors preferred to give troubled banks some leeway, in the hope they could manage a recovery.) Perhaps that explanation is remotely possible. But the circumstantial evidence portrays the Butcher debacle as the first costly product of political interference with supervision, a habit that grew uncontrolled in the savings and loan disaster.

The last word belongs to Jake Butcher. "I made some grave errors," he said after four years of reflection, "leaving the bank for the World's Fair, running for governor the second time, delegating to people who didn't have the ability to do it." But the greatest mistake of all, he said, was "losing a line of communication with the regulators. That was my grave error. It was the thing that finished me up."

CHAPTER SEVEN

□□□

Darkness at Sunshine State

□ 1 □

WHILE ISAAC TRIED TO DETACH HIMSELF from the Butchers, another ghost from his past returned to haunt him and the FDIC. This ghost thought he knew a secret that would scare Isaac away from his case. When the FDIC took him on in a long and bitter fight, he threatened to reveal that secret. But Isaac stood his ground.

The ghost was Ray Corona, to whom Isaac once tried to sell a bank in his days at the First National Bank of Louisville. After Isaac left for Washington, Ray did buy his own bank, the Sunshine State Bank of South Miami. It took years for the FDIC to close down this bank, even after a federal indictment called it "part of a vertically integrated drug conspiracy," and Ray and his father were convicted. But in this struggle, the FDIC wore the white hat. Whatever the ambiguity surrounding the Butchers' case, Isaac did not allow the appearance of compromise here. The interference this time came from another set of regulators.

□ 2 □

WE LEFT RAY CORONA AT A STREET PHONE near the Atlanta regional office of the United States Comptroller of the Currency. It was the week after Christmas in 1977. The comptroller's office had just vetoed his deal with William Isaac to buy the Hialeah drug bank that had been dumped in the lap of Isaac's Louisville employer. Ray stormed out of the meeting to call his financial backer, a Miami drug lord named José Antonio Fernandez.

As the government later proved in two protracted trials, Tony Fernandez provided the funds for Ray Corona's bank ventures. But the two men, in a sense, inherited a connection that existed before them and will persist as long as the drug trade generates fabulous profits. The cash flow from narcotics may reach $150 billion a year. But cash has only limited value until it enters the legitimate economy, where it can be booked, audited and plausibly explained to the Internal Revenue Service. That is where the banks come in. The drug dealers need quasi-legitimate financial services to handle their cash transfers and their investments. Bankers are tempted by the huge volume of funds, the high profit, and the loyalty of the depositor. But the tainted money invites a surprising range of corruption. If tolerated, it subverts the bank, the regulator, and ultimately the government.

Tony Fernandez fled to the United States from Cuba in 1962 and survived for the next 14 years through low-paying odd jobs. He measured drapes, stamped circuit boards for personal computers and, for two years, did contract assignments for the Central Intelligence Agency. In 1976, a friend brought him to meet a sinister figure named José Alvero-Cruz, and Tony's fortunes took a dramatic turn. Alvero-Cruz was considered the largest marijuana smuggler in Miami; he was called the "King of the River" for his control of the Cuban fishermen docked along the waterway that bisects the city. Alvero-Cruz hired Tony as a lookout and truck driver. Tony had useful assets. He spoke English well, with an accent, and he had a sense of humor. He was engaging, sometimes buffoonish, and his colleagues often failed to see how sharp he could be. His ability to recall the dates, quantities, and costs of drug shipments amazed federal prosecutors years later. He gave such an accurate time for Ray Corona's call from Atlanta that the FBI was able to corroborate it from the records of the phone company.

More and more often, Alvero-Cruz asked Tony to babysit their good ol' boy Anglo distributors. In mid-1976, with the feds bearing down, the King of the River took an extended vacation in Spain, the drug dealer's haven for rest and recreation. Tony moved into the vacuum. He described himself as a broker between the Yankee-hating Colombians and the red-neck buyers, like a "broker of avocados." In the next four years he moved one and a half million pounds of marijuana. He made a profit of more than $20 million and remitted almost ten times that amount to his Colombian suppliers. Like Tony Montana in "Scarface," his biggest problem was what to do with the money.

Tony said he first met Ray Corona through Alvero-Cruz. Ray was working with his father Rafael and his three brothers in a rapidly growing institution called Totalbank, which had started out in a trailer two years earlier and now had its own building. After a career as senior executive at banks in Havana and Miami, Rafael was now president and chairman of Totalbank. Ray was second in the hierarchy. Toward the end of 1977, after Alvero-Cruz's return from Spain, Ray invited the two drug dealers to a clients' lunch in honor of their role as major customers. As they sat around the table in the bank's dining room, Tony later recalled at the Coronas' trial, "some gentleman from the bank asked what was my business." Tony had brought his lawyer to cover any faux pas, and his mouthpiece answered, "Mr. Fernandez is an entrepreneur.' "

"It is the first time I heard that word," Tony said. "I said 'Jesus, who knows what he called me.' "

After the lunch, Fernandez and Alvero-Cruz sat with Ray Corona in his private office. As Ray brought out his favorite Cuban cigars, the three started talking about buying their own bank. Tony had already discussed financing with Alvero-Cruz, meeting in the back of Alvero-Cruz's beauty parlor as a manicurist did the kingpin's nails. But Tony had his doubts about a partnership with his former boss. When Tony bought a 50,000-pound shipment of marijuana from Alvero-Cruz in December, the former King of the River tried to short him by 5,000 pounds. Tony caught the trick, weighing the load with his own scales. But Alvero-Cruz told the suppliers, a Colombian family named Cotes, that Fernandez's payment was $1 million short.

"You do not want to make the Colombians mad," Tony remarked. He met with the Colombian chief, bringing detailed receipts to bolster his case. The Colombian invited Tony to a New Year's celebration hosted by Alvero-Cruz. When Tony showed up and Alvero-Cruz slipped out the back, the signal was given that Tony had won the dispute. But Alvero-Cruz extracted a minor revenge. One of Tony's men had lent Alvero-Cruz a Buick Rivera. When the car was returned the next day, the floor mats were missing.

Alvero-Cruz's cheapness showed up after the meeting in Ray Corona's office. As the two dealers headed out to the bank's parking lot, Alvero-Cruz said to Tony Fernandez, "I am a little short of money at this time. So if any money is needed right away, you go ahead and give it, and I will fix it up with you later on."

Fernandez dropped Alvero-Cruz from the deal. Shortly afterward, Ray called Fernandez at his farm in Ocala and asked for $500,000 in a hurry. The Hialeah bank was available. One of Ray's brothers flew up in a Lear jet, and Fernandez gave him a suitcase full of cash. Ray called several more times as negotiations dragged on, and when they collapsed, sent back the cash.

By this time, Fernandez was relieved that the deal had fallen through. He didn't know much about the National Bank of South Florida or Guillermo Hernandez-Cartaya, its owner, who had a murky relationship with Alvero-Cruz dating back to the Bay of Pigs. Another associate berated Tony for getting involved in a bank under heavy federal investigation. As Tony learned about the "wrongdoing with Arabs and American passports and all this," he said, "I saw where he was right. Who wants to get in a place that is already had?"

Tony was getting this contrary advice from a slick, silver-haired Hungarian refugee turned United States citizen turned Panamanian businessman named Steven Sandor Samos, who handled his off-shore investments. In the late 1960s, Samos had helped establish the Miami Free Trade Zone, serving briefly as its president. He now specialized in setting up Panamanian dummy corporations for foreigners, a service that included the recruitment of Panamanian citizens to serve as officers and directors. "You had better not complain," he once told a client who had been splattered with coffee by a clumsy messenger. "He is the president of your company." His clients included an alleged New York Mafia capo named Lawrence Iorizzo, now serving a federal sentence for mail fraud.

Samos handled the laundering of Tony Fernandez's marijuana money, channelling it through shell corporations in St. Vincent and Cayman islands to his own Panama company. From there, he disbursed it to the Colombian suppliers or Fernandez's own Swiss bank accounts. Samos was married to Alma Robles Chiari, the relative of Panamanian presidents, who acted as the front for the drug money behind Ray Corona's bank buying. Samos nonetheless opposed Tony's plans to buy a Miami bank.

"He always says that buying a bank in the United States is like being a fish in a big tank," said Fernandez. "You are there to be observed all the time moving around by authorities. He was not in favor of buying the bank, but I was, and so he provide his services because he earn some money on that."

Tony's friend, Ray Corona, also had his heart set on running a bank. When the office of Comptroller of the Currency gave Ray his final veto at that meeting in Atlanta, the acting regional director, still Lou Frank, tried to soften the blow with some fatherly advice. He said that the office felt Ray was too inexperienced to handle a bank as deeply troubled as the National Bank of South Florida. "Look," he said, "find another bank not in trouble, maybe even a smaller bank, and try again."

□ 3 □

RAY'S FATHER, RAFAEL, KNEW OF ANOTHER BANK, the Sunshine State Bank in South Miami. By May 1978, Ray Corona and Steven Samos acting as Fernandez's agents, had completed the deal. They took a Lear jet to Ocala to tell Tony the good news. Ray came into his family room, Tony recalls, "and embraced me and jumping and all of that, and Samos was laughing and [Ray] said, 'We made it. We got the bank.' " Over a bottle of Dom Perignon, Samos added that they needed another $1.1 million to complete the purchase.

Tony brought the two into his master bedroom and opened a safe. He started stacking bundles of bills on his bed until the three had counted out the million plus. They quickly filled a suitcase with the wads of twenties and hundreds and had a mound left over. (The drug world considers that a full-sized Samsonite suitcase will hold half a million dollars in twenties.) Tony went to the kitchen and returned with a cardboard box. The rest of the money filled this box.

But what was the most remarkable about the purchase was the lack of trouble with the regulators. "I talked to Ray several times," Fernandez told the court. "He told me everything was going fine in Tallahassee. Not to worry about that. That part he got control.

"Really we had a conversation, he got somebody there that was to make sure it happened. He was using some kind of attorney or something, somebody who has some kind of power in politics. He was very sure it would be approved."

These connections became even more important as the bank went steadily downhill. Ray Corona installed his father as chairman and himself as president, but the family banking tradition didn't sit comfortably on his stocky shoulders. After Ray's divorce in mid-1978, his behavior started to worry his silent partner, Tony Fernandez. Said Fernandez, "People were telling me rumors he was being disorderly and doing strange things and driving Rolls Royces, using mink coats and making big fights at the Mutiny." The plush bar at the Mutiny Hotel in Coconut Grove used to be a big hang-out for drug dealers until they were crowded out by tourists, and Ray provoked a dispute with one of Fernandez's toughest drug smuggling partners over one of its sparsely clad waitresses. Fernandez claims he had to use all of his diplomacy to keep Ray from getting killed. As much of Miami soon guessed, Ray had become a cocaine addict.

But Ray Corona outlasted Tony Fernandez. As the DEA infiltrated Tony's operations, he began to lose more and more of his consignments. His Colombian suppliers grew restive. Finally, claiming he owed them $8 million, they kidnapped him. Tony was taken to a farm near Barranquilla in March 1981, and he spent the next four months liquidating his property to pay his captors. Following standard practice, they presented him with a bill for the cost of the kidnapping, including purchase of the guns. With everyone on his tail, Fernandez finally managed to flee to Brazil. He assumed a new identity as an economist with an advanced degree from the Metropolitan College Institute of London. "I couldn't get a doctor's degree in medicine because, you know, I was not a doctor," explains Fernandez. "An economist, who could know?" Samos, with his typical humor, provided Tony with a transcript including an "A" for off-shore banking.

Through early 1982, Fernandez liquidated his Sunshine State stock, leaving Ray in control. When the DEA caught up with him in Brazil, he actually seemed relieved. Back in the United States, he pled guilty to narcotics smuggling. Drawing a 23-year sentence, he turned state's evidence on his partners and entered the witness protection program.

□ 4 □

IN THE MEANTIME, the Sunshine State Bank appeared to be growing at a rapid clip. Its assets increased sixfold between 1978 and 1983, reaching a peak of nearly $120 million. But problems were building below the surface. An FDIC examiner commented, "Each of the six Corporation examinations conducted since the Corona family obtained control . . . have revealed an increasing magnitude of problems." By mid-1982, the FDIC started to take action, using a relatively mild Memorandum of Understanding. But the next time it looked, the problems had exploded. Bad loans had grown to five times the bank's capital, threatening to sink the whole institution. In August 1983, the FDIC rolled out its heavy gun, the emergency cease and desist order. "Bank management has been entirely uncooperative," complained the federal supervisor. With the state regulators maintaining a united front, the examination moved inexorably to its logical conclusion, the closing of the bank. The FDIC was so pessimistic about the condition of Sunshine State that it prepared to liquidate it and pay off the depositors.

But weird things began happening. When state and federal examiners started a joint visit in September, the FDIC group, a crack team of its most experienced men, had the strong feeling that their room at the bank was bugged. A state examiner accused the feds of conducting a "witch hunt." And in January 1984, the state suddenly broke ranks. To the consternation of the FDIC, the State comptroller's office negotiated a Memorandum of Understanding with the Coronas.

The FDIC insisted at a minimum that Rafael and his two eldest sons should be removed. "They are collectively responsible for the serious condition of the bank," said its examination report. But the state merely kicked Ray upstairs. The erratic young pugilist was removed from the loan committee and forced to resign as president, but he remained on the board of directors. State officials proclaimed their satisfaction with the way Ray's brothers were complying, but the feds were appalled. The Coronas had agreed to pump more money into the bank. When the FDIC learned that Ray had borrowed $6 million from two small institutions in Texas, its staff had a fit. The Dallas office called the Texas Savings and Loan Department to ask why the People's S&L of Llano had just wired $3 million to "a Mafia bank that was a five-graded bank [the worst]."

This surprising metaphor underlined an irony of Sunshine State. Even though it was founded with drug money, the reason for the Coronas' later indictment, its problems had little to do with drugs or unwashed currency. Although the "Mafia" charge was not substantiated, the bank attracted characters from an all-American tradition of shady dealing. One major borrower, a former stockbroker, had been disciplined by the National Association of Securities Dealers for securities violations. Another client, a real estate corporation with multistate dealings, had been sued by the attorney general of Arizona for a deceptive sales pitch. Sunshine State's largest individual borrower, a Philadelphia businessman named Leonard Pelullo had recently been involved in the failure of a bank in Denver, Colorado.

Yet state officials by now were firmly in the Coronas' corner. A delegation of the Coronas, their counsel and the two top bank supervisors from the state comptroller's office journeyed to the FDIC's Washington headquarters to get the Atlanta office off their backs. "It was a very heated conversation," testified Felix Adams, head of the Florida Banking Department. The midlevel FDIC man "did not want to hear us." Backed by Washington, the Atlanta office pressed ahead with its attempt to remove all three Coronas. On March 15, it served them with an Immediate Suspension Order, and the Coronas replied by going to court. News of the suit hit the papers. A run hit the bank. Over the next few days, anxious depositors pulled out $10 million and pestered clerks by asking when the bank would shut down. But the run subsided miraculously when the Coronas won in court, getting a restraining order blocking the FDIC. This was the first in a series of legal miracles for Sunshine State.

All of the FDIC's futile notices and orders were now bundled into an extended hearing before federal Administrative Law Judge Alan W. Heifetz. After six months of hearings and 14,000 pages of transcripts, documents, and legal arguments, Judge Heifetz found in favor of the Coronas. A central issue was whether the examiners had done a "hatchet job" in "classifying" the Sunshine State loans. An important part of a bank examination is to identify problem loans and divide them into three categories: substandard, doubtful, and loss. The bank then has to write them off on a sliding scale. Too many write-offs can mean the bank's demise.

"The judge went back and redid the classifications himself!" exclaimed an FDIC lawyer. Where the federal examiners classified $32 million in loans, nearly one-third of the bank's assets, Judge Heifetz saw problems with only $19 million worth. "Loan classification," said the judge, "is highly subjective." The page on the report that divided these loans into three columns, he remarked, has the nickname the "Ouija Board." But the FDIC board of directors was not impressed. Commenting stringently on the judge's ignorance of bank examinations, the FDIC Board rejected Heifetz's 100-page opinion and wrote a 325-page opinion of its own upholding the examiners. In 1986 the Coronas took the case to the United States

Court of Appeals, where a three-judge panel sided with the FDIC—
the first time that federal judges held that a bank examiner's judgment deserved "deference" from a court of law.

The administrative judge may have been launched on his own,
however, by one of the most peculiar points of the case, the attitude
of the state supervisors. "The curious aspect of distilling this cauld-
ron of charge and countercharge," he wrote, "is that at trial, while
one would expect that representatives of the State of Florida's Office
of the Comptroller would support the position of the FDIC, the
opposite was true."

This split was exploited to the fullest by Sunshine State's lawyer,
a large, sweaty, and brilliant former state attorney general named
Robert Shevin. Respected widely for his ability, if not his clients,
Shevin did more than anyone else to keep the Coronas in business.
But the state comptroller gave him plenty to work with.

The FDIC didn't reverse its own administrative law judge until
well into 1985, but by August it looked like the game was up. Ray
Corona and his father, Rafael, had long since been indicted and
removed from the bank. The state was ready to close Sunshine State
and appoint the FDIC as receiver. But the state comptroller's lawyers
chose an unusual procedure. Instead of closing the bank by fiat and
going to court later, the more common way of doing it, they applied
to Dade County Circuit Court first. Attorney Shevin had a few hours
to act. He managed to block the state comptroller in court and tie
up the FDIC by bringing a personal civil suit against Chairman Isaac
and most of the Atlanta office. They were engaged in a "conspiracy"
against the Coronas, he charged. Sunshine State had become "the
bank that wouldn't die."

The case had become intensely disillusioning for both federal
and state regulators. For the FDIC's regional examiners, the frustration was understandable. "They were so emotional about it that
their voices would crack," recalled FDIC Director Sprague. In addition, a number of the state comptroller's own staff began to wonder
what was going on. "We began to realize that something in the office
was wrong," said one of several who resigned or were purged during

the case. In their views, the Coronas survived because of a general breakdown in the state's financial regulation.

This breakdown came from a pervasive political weakness. The state government operates under one of those post-Reconstruction southern constitutions designed to make the governor as weak and pliable as possible. Only a portion of the government offices, such as budget, report directly to the governor. Major departments such as law enforcement and natural resources fall under control of a cabinet composed of the seven elected state officers. State government sometimes looks and acts like a South American junta.

This weakness came home to roost on the state's financial institutions. Florida is the only state in the nation that places every scrap of its financial regulation in the hands of elected (and intensely political) public officials. The supervisor for banks, thrifts, and securities brokers is the state comptroller, a tormented Harvard graduate named Gerald Lewis, under attack for years for spectacular lapses such as the Sunshine State Bank. Insurance, and a grab bag of related businesses such as Health Maintenance Organizations and "life care" retirement homes, are the province of the state treasurer/insurance commissioner, at the time a red-haired, self-proclaimed consumerist named Bill Gunter. (Gunter left his post in 1988 for the latest of several unsuccessful runs for the United States Senate.) If these two offices collaborate, as Gunter and Lewis did, they have a squeeze on the state's $130 billion financial services industry, and they can milk it constantly for campaign money.

The institution that makes the junta work, however, is the political law firm. Robert Shevin's Sparber, Shevin, Shapo & Heilbronner was one of several before it broke up in 1988. These firms play on personal friendships and employ former senior bureaucrats, but they also raise money. On a good night of fund raising, one of these lawyers can generate over $100,000 in campaign contributions, a lot of it from clients with business pending before the regulators. The final loop is the widespread notion that clients of these firms get preferential treatment.

No one wants to accuse a distinguished lawyer like Robert Shevin of unethical behavior. But his clients, and clients of other well-connected law firms, have had spectacular success with state government. At one point, the entire state cabinet joined to help Sunshine State Bank pull through. One of the bank's assets was a second mortgage on a potential development on Don Pedro Island, off Florida's west coast. When the bank needed cash, the cabinet voted to purchase the island with money from its environmental defense fund, even though the property was well below the cut-off point on the list of desired acquisitions.

With this kind of help from the state, Ray Corona may well have hoped to find some kind of leverage over the federal regulators. His dealings with William Isaac back in 1977 seemed to offer a pressure point. During the hearings with the administrative law judge, Corona made an issue of Isaac's participation.

□ 5 □

ON JANUARY 25, 1985, Ray Corona and Robert Shevin filed their first motion for the disqualification of William Isaac. The two were demanding that the FDIC chairman stay out of their case because of his "spiteful and malicious" conduct. This attitude, they claimed, "relates back to a *prior transaction* with the Coronas." (Their emphasis). Isaac refused to rise to their bait, and the FDIC board turned down the motion. The allegations, said the board, "were superficial, vague, and conclusory." Three weeks later, Corona and Shevin tried again, with more detail. "Whether vague or not," they wrote, "Mr. Isaac is, we are confident, well aware of the incidents referred to in the motion. We had hoped he would candidly assess those incidents and recognize that further specification would be unnecessary." Ray Corona added a sworn affidavit stating what he thought he held over the FDIC chairman.

The incident, said Corona, had came up in Isaac's attempts to sell Guillermo Hernandez-Cartaya's National Bank of South Florida, toward the end of 1977. Isaac was general counsel for the Louisville bank, and the two sets of would-be buyers met on the eighth floor of the First Kentucky Corporation.

In Corona's words:

> William M. Isaac informed your affiant, in the presence of others, including Gustavo Vollodo [sic], that in addition to a down payment of $500,000, an infusion of $500,000 capital into National Bank of South Florida, and an $800,000 non-recourse note, an additional cash payment of $200,000 would be required to be delivered to William M. Isaac at the closing of the transaction. Mr. Isaac explained that this sum had to be paid to Juan Evelio Pou, who had acquired the interest in Cartaya's stock of National Bank of South Florida, because Pou was not the real party in interest in the stock but, instead, was representing a Colombian "drug family" named "Arango", and if the sum were not paid by Pou to the Arango family as a partial recoupment of their investment, the Arango family would kill Pou.

Ray thought he was being shaken down for Isaac's own pocket, but other sources refute that. Isaac himself denies Corona's whole story, but there were certainly questioned about Pou and Villoldo. Two months earlier, the FBI had received a confidential report that the Pou group of bidders was actually financed "from an account owned by Sheila Arana [sic], wife of Julio Cesar Nasser-David, a friend of Cartaya's, who has accounts in the bank that Cartaya owns in Colombia." Regulators suspected at the time that Pou and Villoldo were acting as front men, although they thought the hidden party was Hernandez-Cartaya himself. Pou certainly showed an extreme case of nerves for several years after the collapsed deal. As mentioned before, he was arrested twice for trying to keep his loaded gun with him on airline flights.

It's not clear what Ray hoped to gain from this revelation, but it backfired badly. "Isaac was furious," reported Director Sprague. The FDIC board brushed aside the motion as curtly as before. Excluding the part that "amounts to mere rumor or opinion," it wrote, "The Corona affidavit documents nothing more than an unsuccessful business negotiation involving Chairman Isaac. . . . The facts of these negotiations do not reflect . . . the appearance of any impropriety."

For the Coronas, things went downhill rapidly. They were tried in early 1985, along with members of Tony Fernandez's operation, for participating in a "vertically integrated drug smuggling conspiracy." Their first trial ended in a hung jury, but the federal prosecutors tried again later that year. This time Ray and his father were found guilty. Ray received a 20-year sentence.

Incredibly, Sunshine State itself stayed open until the end of May 1986. At the end, one of the bank's largest and most troubled borrowers, the Miami-based Royale Group, Ltd., made a bold offer to take it over. The Royale Group, noted for its sputtering effort to renovate Art Deco hotels in Miami Beach, proposed a deal forgiving its loans at Sunshine in exchange for unspecified real estate in the casino strip of Atlantic City and control of the bank. The deal was a curiosity in light of Royale's banking track record. Its principal, the Philadelphia businessman, Leonard Pelullo, had been named in connection with the failure of Dominion Bank in Denver, Colorado. The FDIC had no trouble persuading a federal court to prohibit the deal and, finally, close the bank. The bank's capital had long since been exhausted by, among other things its legal fees, said to have reached $3 million.

□ 6 □

"WHAT GOES AROUND, COMES AROUND." It's a popular saying in both board rooms and jail cells, and it applies with some irony to William Isaac's career as bank regulator. One can read the facts of his case in a way that leaves his reputation unimpaired. But it strains credulity to argue that Isaac's background had absolutely no influence on his work. Isaac unquestionably dealt with some shady characters in rescuing the First Kentucky Corporation from its involvement with Guillermo Hernandez-Cartaya. Lawyers are prone to encounter strange types, and there is no convincing evidence that Isaac's conduct was anything less than above board. But these contacts left him open to a variety of pressures, both subtle and crude. The crude pressure came from Ray Corona, not the most credible person in the world. On the surface, Corona's charges against Isaac didn't make much sense. Why should Isaac bear a grudge against Corona or the Sunshine State Bank because of a business deal that collapsed through no fault of his own? The more plausible explanation is that Ray thought he could scare Isaac off his case by threatening to reveal the details. Isaac deserves credit for not backing down. As far as Sunshine State is concerned, the FDIC has nothing to be ashamed of (although the Florida state comptroller does).

The episode with Ray Corona and Hermandez-Cartaya's Hialeah bank dramatizes a new set of pressures on bank supervision. The quiet men in green eyeshades are now at the front in the war on drugs. Some offices, such as the Florida state regulators, are not willing to fight. Others still lack the means. Federal bank and thrift examiners, for instance, have lobbied for years to be covered under the statutes making it a felony to harass or obstruct some categories of federal officers. Not only are they still not protected, the federal thrift examiners have no procedure to follow if their personnel receive threats. Yet more than ever, examiners are encountering dangerous types who make Jake Butcher look like an all-American hero.

(A word in favor of the Butchers: Jesse Barr reported receiving several overtures to conduct a drug money operation through his banks. It looked like a natural to his acquaintances from the Eglin federal prison, "the drug business graduate school of the world," but he turned them down. "We were crooks," he said, "but we weren't that kind of crook.")

The more subtle pressures on Isaac came from the Butchers. Something clearly went wrong in supervising their banks. Isaac himself said, "The FDIC should have done a better job. We should have spotted it sooner." The question is, why the inaction? It grows more troubling when we consider how well the Butchers were known at the top of the FDIC. Isaac dealt with both brothers, although briefly. By his own account, his campaign for the FDIC appointment relied heavily on their circle of friends. He had doubts about them in late 1978, especially after reading a detailed series of articles in the *Memphis Commercial Appeal*. Isaac supported the Memphis regional office in its critical January 1979 examination. But the effort petered out.

Even more puzzling is the role of James Sexton, the Memphis asistant regional director who conducted that 1979 examination. Sexton wound up in the Washington office in charge of all bank examinations, first as deputy and then as director. Yet for three years he appeared to lose all interest in the Butchers. Isaac argued that he lost his own leverage when he reverted to the status of minority director on the accession of Irvine Sprague. Yet Sexton had line authority for the Butchers all through this period. Did Sexton get the message that too much attention to the Butchers could be unhealthy for his career? He denied it, but that was the impression left with his colleagues in the field. Finally, Irvine Sprague: as a former staff director of the congressional Democratic Policy Conference, Sprague had many friends on Capitol Hill who weren't bashful in giving him advice about the Butchers. Yet he said he never heard the concerns about the Tennessee bankers until mid-1982.

Sprague and others argue that from 1980 to 1982, the FDIC board was preoccupied with the interest rate squeeze on mutual savings banks, the parallel to the Bank Board's problem with the S&Ls. For scandals, it had the Penn Square nightmare and the bailout of Continental Illinois. "The Butchers were not at the top of our list," said Sprague. He admitted, in effect, that the FDIC couldn't walk and chew gum at the same time. If the headquarters staff lacked the means to track emerging problems, then it was poorly managed. This failure is particularly ironic in light of the FDIC's current ambition to shoulder not only its own caseload, but the entire weight of the failing savings and loan industry.

The early warnings failed in part because examiners seemed unwilling to look for trouble. The Butchers' fraud was not "well hidden," as some have argued. As far back as 1977, Regional Director Jackson wrote that their basic tactic of "reciprocal arrangements among the banks" could be "easily determine[d]" by "the most casual observer." The FDIC let this trail grow cold through a failure of will, not of insight. In congressional testimony, Isaac admitted that the man in charge of the 1981 examination of Jake's

UAB-Knoxville had let the bank's management talk him out of more than one-fourth of his loan classifications. But the grunts in the field yield to that kind of pressure when they know they won't get support from their superiors. Once more, the blame comes around to the top.

Plenty of FDIC file memos testifed to the Butchers' practice of displaying their political clout. Through 1980, FDIC examiners or regional administrators were well aware that Jake had a buddy in the White House. Even after Carter left office, C. H., Jr. could call his friend and beneficiary on the Senate Banking Committee, Senator James Sasser. Members of the Senate continued to second-guess the regulators right through the collapse of the Butcher empire. Senators Wendell Ford and Walter Huddleston of Kentucky, as well as Tennessee's Sasser, put their names on a July 25, 1983 letter to James Sexton, director of FDIC bank supervision, protesting the treatment of loan participations at one Butcher-related bank in Kentucky. This remarkable example of congressional micromanagement makes one wonder what else congressmen were up to.

The Butchers themselves had mastered the art of negative political influence. That is, they would counter criticism by yelling "vendetta." This tactic seemed especially effective with the Tennessee state regulators after Jake's failed campaigns for governor. Lamar Alexander, the Republican who beat him, explained that he called off state regulators in the 1982 joint examination to avoid any appearance of getting even. The picture is slightly more complicated, however. C. H. Butcher Jr. gave Alexander substantial financial help in his 1982 reelection campaign. Governor Alexander went out of his way to help C. H., Jr.'s attempt to merge and save his surviving banks.

One thing is missing from this picture: the means by which politics actually intruded on the regulators. We don't have the sworn testimony about meetings and phone calls, if any, that the House Ethics Committee assembled for the savings and loan debacle. In the case of the Butchers, politics may have asserted itself more as an atmosphere, a background miasma that dampened initiative and induced examiners to back down from their judgment calls.

Even a decade ago, this miasma took its toll. If the Butchers had been stopped in 1979, instead of in 1983, the FDIC could have saved itself at least $500 million, by its own estimate, and it could have spared Tennessee the economic disruption of a wave of bank failures. At the time, the Butchers' collapse ranked high on the list of federal regulatory failures. Now it pales in comparison to the S&L disaster, in which billion-dollar failures have become commonplace. But the Butchers were precursors. Intimidation of the supervisors, which in their case was indirect and elusive, later became crude and blatant. One would think the experience had taught Washington to take supervision seriously, but the lesson had to be learned over and over, each time at a greater cost.

PART THREE

Interlude:
The Ohio Bank Crisis

□□□

CHAPTER EIGHT

The Friends of Marvin Warner

□ 1 □

ON FRIDAY, MARCH 8, 1985, Home State Savings Bank of Cincinnati announced that it would not reopen the next day, or any day for the forseeable future. The thrift was in the middle of a roaring run. In three days, stolid Cincinnati depositors had pulled out $100 million. Home State was by far the largest member of the state's private insurance system, the Ohio Deposit Guaranty Fund; it was so large that it had managed to lose more than four times the amount the fund held in reserve for all 71 of its members. With much of the ODGF gone, the bank turned to the Federal Reserve for help. But the depositors were taking the money out the front door faster than the Fed could shovel it in the back.

With Home State closed, other privately insured thrifts in Ohio woke to lines of depositors waiting to rescue their savings in the blustery March dawn. It wasn't another 1842 bank riot. No one tried to break into Home State's lobby with crowbars and sledgehammers to force open an empty vault. No angry mobs of workers chased lawyers down Pearl Street. But, as with its nineteenth-century counterpart, the Home State closing shocked the country. As serious runs hit five more thrifts, the sleepless and politically embarrassed Governor Richard Celeste declared a bank holiday for all 71 privately insured S&Ls. Network television descended on southwest Ohio. The *New York Times* devoted a special section to the "Ohio Bank Crisis."

It was the largest bank holiday since 1933, and pundits wrung their hands about the "failure of the financial system."

There *was* systemic failure, but not the sort these wise men had in mind. Like the national savings and loan debacle three years later, the Home State crisis was caused by fraud, fraud that slipped past the supervisors under the cloak of political influence. The story of this fraud introduces a new cast of characters, and some who surprisingly aren't new at all. The main actor is the owner of Home State, a manipulative charmer named Marvin Warner.

Born in 1919 in Birmingham, Alabama, Warner grew up in the city's small, closely knit Jewish community, the origin of some of his most important business ties. After serving in the army in World War II, he saw the potential in the federal subsidies available to build low-cost housing for returning servicemen. He became a developer, relying on political contacts to speed his paperwork with the government. There is a story, unconfirmed but indicative, that he used his first bank loan to make a campaign contribution to the senator from Alabama, John Sparkman. Moving to Cincinnati, his main housing market, he gained a mixed reputation for his tough negotiations, at once both charming and squeezing. In the late 1960s, he abandoned housing for finance and plunged into big-time political fund raising. He backed Jimmy Carter early in 1976 and reaped his reward when his friend Bert Lance helped make him ambassador to Switzerland.

By this time the trim, perpetually tanned Warner was reaping other rewards. Worth tens of millions and divorced, he dated a series of glamorous, influential women, including Carter's White House secretary. Denied a pony in his youth, says the legend, he acquired two horse farms in Ohio and Kentucky, with 200 thoroughbreds. He bought pro football teams and once owned 10 percent of George Steinbrenner's New York Yankees.

From his Warnerton Farm just east of Cincinnati, Warner presided over a financial empire increasingly active in Florida. Home State became the cash cow backing raids and horse trades of banks and thrifts from Miami to Tampa. These Florida deals created the Ohio thrift crisis.

In almost all of Warner's buying, selling, and merging, he relied on the talents of his son-in-law, a bright, aggressive young attorney named Stephen W. Arky. Arky was born in St. Louis, Missouri, in 1943 and stayed there for his education, graduating from the law school at Washington University in 1967. Soon after, he moved to Washington, D.C., to join the enforcement division of the United States Securities and Exchange Commission. It's ironic in view of his later career that he used his SEC experience to write an article on "The Need for Regulation of [securities] Transfer Agents." While on the SEC staff, Arky transferred from D.C. to Miami, and in 1971, he left for private practice. His ambition and tenacity soon made him lead partner in his own law firm, and his client list began to terrorize Florida's banking establishment. There was Warner, of course, whose raids forced several banks to merge in self-defense, but there were others as well. A decade after leaving the SEC, Arky played a role in four of the biggest bank scandals of the time. He seemed arrogant, ruthless, and self-sufficient to the end, which came on July 22, 1985. As an Ohio legislative committee 2000 miles north prepared to take testimony on his involvement in the thrift crisis, he stepped into the bathroom of his home with a .38 handgun and killed himself.

In his suicide note, Arky singled out his "betrayal" by his former client and close buddy Ron Ewton, a founder of the failed E. S. M. Government Securities firm. This fatal friendship began upon Arky's arrival in Miami. Ewton, a "country slicker" from Tennessee was commanding officer of Arky's unit of the National Guard. "I liked Ronnie right away," Arky later told an interviewer. "He was the only guy to show up at meetings in a new Cadillac."

Ronnie Restine Ewton was born in Nashville, Tennessee in 1942. He went to small colleges in Tennessee and Kentucky and sold life insurance for a year and a half before starting his checkered career in government securities. He drifted from one scandal-ridden firm to another before winding up in Fort Lauderdale, Florida, a world capital of financial scandals. In early 1975, his employer was expelled from the National Association of Securities Dealers for a long list of offenses, and Ewton himself was censured. A regulator later, described Ewton and his colleagues as "suede-shoe types, slickers, high pressure salesmen." In 1975, Ewton and two other "Memphis bond bandits" named George Mead and Robert Seneca decided to start their own firm. With Arky's help, they incorporated E. S. M. Securities, Inc., taking the name from their initials. This dealership was regulated by the SEC; the partners later channeled most of their business into a companion firm called E. S. M. Government Securities, Inc., devoted to the wholly unregulated and highly volatile secondary market in federal agency bonds.

The financing of the federal government has this peculiarity, that after government bonds are issued by an exclusive club of some 35 "primary dealers," the bonds fall into the hands of riverboat gamblers. The United States Treasury insists on keeping the secondary market unregulated, to preserve its "efficiency." But this policy also creates a niche in which types like Ron Ewton have flourished. And after the ups and downs of working as salesmen for other firms, Ewton and his colleagues lived like gamblers on a roll. The company bought a Rockwell Commander airplane for close to $1 million but lost it to the Drug Enforcement Administration in a drug bust. (Three nonemployees had leased the plane and allegedly flown cocaine to Fargo, North Dakota.) Ewton joined racehorse syndicates and took up polo. He showered his first wife with jewelry, including a gold choker with three diamonds and two sapphires, a bangle with two horseheads flashing ruby eyes and a Piaget watch with 32 diamonds. Another founder, Robert Seneca, bought a 1953 Bentley and romanced his second wife in a shopping spree up and down the East Coast. In their protracted divorce, she testified that he also used cocaine virtually every day. (Seneca's lawyer, one of Arky's senior partners, retorted that the former Mrs. Seneca "had zero credibility.") Seneca left E. S. M. after filing for divorce in 1978, but his successors carried on the spending tradition. A later president kept two show dogs worth $80,000.

But the high living was a front. Almost from the start, E. S. M. had been losing its bets on the bond market. The firm's only profitable year was its first, with earnings of $737,000. Thereafter, the

The failure of the Bank of United States in New York City (11 December 1930) climaxed the first wave of depression-era bank runs. (UPI/Bettmann Newsphotos)

The 1980s witnessed more bank and S&L failures than any period since the Great Depression. Here, depositors line up to claim their savings at Molitor Savings & Loan in Cincinnati (March 1985) in the wake of the failure of Home State Savings Bank. (David Kohl)

William M. Isaac, chairman of the Federal Deposit Insurance Corporation, and Edwin J. Gray, chairman of the Federal Home Loan Bank Board, in 1983, as the two regulators were struggling unsuccessfully to prevent the abuse of the deposit insurance funds under their control. (AP/Wide World Photos)

Democratic congressional leader Tony Coelho and House Speaker Jim Wright. Both were forced to resign their seats in 1989 amid allegations of financial wrongdoing as the S&L crisis neared its climax. (UPI/Bettmann Newsphotos)

Right:
Florida State Comptroller Gerald Lewis, elected regulator of the state's scandal-ridden banking and securities industries. (Gerald Davis)

Below:
Rafael L. Corona and his son, Ray L. Corona, outside the Miami, Florida courthouse where they were convicted on charges involving drug-money control of their South Miami bank. (AP/ Wide World Photos)

Left:
Guillermo Hernandez-Cartaya, center of the 1977 financial scandal at his WFC Corporation. (*New York Times*)

Below:
Jake Butcher, his family's fraud-based banking empire in collapse, testifies in Anderson County Chancery Court in Tennessee. (21 June 1983). (AP/Wide World Photos)

Above:
Marvin Warner on trial on bank fraud charges stemming from the collapse of his Home State [Ohio] Savings Bank. (David Kohl)

Right:
Shepard Broad, founder of American Savings & Loan Association of Florida, whose split with Marvin Warner triggered the Ohio bank crisis. (*The Miami Herald*)

Above left:
Durward Curlee, lobbyist for the Texas Savings & Loan League and spokesman for the thrift "high flyers." (*Washington Post* Staff Photo)

Above right:
Herman K. Beebe (r.), behind-the-scenes influence in over 100 Southwest banks and thrifts, with Edwin J. Edwards, former governor of Louisiana. (Jack Barham/*Shreveport Journal*)

Left:
Donald Ray Dixon, whose Vernon Savings and Loan in North Dallas had losses of $1.3 billion when closed by FSLIC. (*Dallas Times Herald*)

Condominium town houses in Mesquite financed by Empire Savings & Loan, being bulldozed because of their shoddy construction. (James M. Thresher/ *The Washington Post*)

FSLIC officers prepare to auction off assets seized from failed thrifts in the wake of the Texas banking debacle. (Dan Ford Connolly/Picture Group)

losses built up rapidly. By 1981, the accumulated deficit exceeded $135 million. E. S. M. kept going by pure and simple fraud.

The mechanics of the fraud sounded complex because of arcane terminology and obfuscatory bookkeeping. But it boiled down to a case of eating your cake and selling it too. The E. S. M. fraud was built on the "repurchase agreement," also called a "repo," which was a fancy form of short-term loan. A salesman on the E. S. M. phone bank would call a small town money manager with a "no-risk" scheme to make a quick profit. The manager could buy a batch of government securities with an agreement that E. S. M. would repurchase them a few days later at a higher price. In essence, the money manager was making a loan to E. S. M., taking the securities as collateral, and collecting interest through the higher price when he sold the securities back.

This kind of loan is called a "reverse repo," mainly to confuse the public. Banks, pension funds, and other large pools of money use this kind of loan frequently. The hitch lies in the collateral. Prudent managers insist on getting the securities in their hand before they part with their money. But this prudence is highly inconvenient. "Sophisticated" investors will take the word of a transfer agent that the securities are credited to their account. For a similar arrangement, imagine that a stranger accosts you on the street and asks to borrow $100 against a savings bond, which he offers to leave in his uncle's desk.

Of course, E. S. M. didn't rely on strangers for its loans. Thanks to Marvin Warner, it could count on a constant series of hundred million dollar deals with the banks and thrifts he influenced. With this kind of backing, E. S. M. could shop the same batch of bonds to several different lenders. As long as no one asked to see the collateral, the money rolled in. (Some lenders did ask to see their bonds, or at least to verify their existence. When the treasurer for the City of Fort Worth, Texas, wrote directly to E. S. M.'s main clearing agent, the Bradford Trust Company of New York City, he received what could best be described as a runaround. Another clearing agent for E. S. M.'s deals was owned jointly by Home State Savings Bank and E. S. M.) By the time E. S. M. collapsed in March

1985, it was more than $400 million in the hole. It had covered $100 million of its losses by phantom repo deals (that is, unsecured loans) with naive city treasurers from Pompano Beach, Florida to Clallam County, Washington. Another $200 million came from Marvin Warner's thrifts. The news of the collapse of E. S. M., at a possible $150 million loss to Warner's Home State Savings Bank, triggered the Cincinnati runs and the Ohio Bank Crisis.

□ 2 □

THAT E. S. M. HAD SURVIVED for nearly ten years meant once again that the regulators had failed, but not for lack of trying. The outfit had aroused suspicions from the beginning. When the E. S. M. scandal broke in 1985, the Office of the Comptroller of the Currency released documents to show that it had been on the case as early as 1977. Astonished veterans of the WFC investigation learned that Ewton and his crew had popped up in a shady deal with the National Bank of South Florida (NBSF), the Hialeah bank that had so vexed William Isaac. The OCC's regional office, led by Lou Frank, forced E. S. M. to unwind the transaction and then put further restrictions on Ewton and Seneca. The OCC acted on a complaint from the parent of the NBSF, the notorious WFC Corporation. In a supreme irony, the first man to blow the whistle on E. S. M. was none other than Guillermo Hernandez-Cartaya.

The E. S. M. files from this period provide a field day for conspiracy buffs. A note of November 22, 1976 from Hernandez-Cartaya to Ronnie Ewton thanks him for "your kind offer of assistance" in buying or brokering the sale of Cartaya's Jefferson Savings and Loan Association in South Texas. (Hernandez-Cartaya had recently purchased the thrift from Lloyd Bentsen, Sr., father of the senator and 1988 Democratic vice-presidential candidate.) There's an employment contract between Ewton and Seneca and a Miami banker named Donald E. Beazley, who had just put in a brief stint with Hernandez-Cartaya's operation. Beazley ended his association with Ewton and Marvin Warner in 1979 to become president of Australia's Nugan Hand Bank, a cause célèbre on three continents. The collapse of the bank after the suicide of a founder fueled interminable speculation that it was involved with the CIA, tax evasion, drug money laundering, or all of the above. The E. S. M. files contained a May 31, 1977 mailgram from Robert Seneca to Michael J. Hand (one half of Nugan Hand) in Sydney, expressing "a definite interest" in "your proposal involving international money markets and future joint ventures involving offshore companies."

These lurid connections aroused curiosity about Ewton's involvement with Hernandez-Cartaya. Records of the aborted NBSF deal in the box-lined Fort Lauderdale office of E. S. M.'s receiver, suggested a lead, the name of the salesman, and his home address. A check of the phone book showed he was still there, and a call determined that he was willing, indeed eager, to talk. Dan Fromhoff, the saleman, worked in a small investment and money trading firm, and I drove to meet him at his office, tucked in a modern low-rise behind an overgrown North Miami intersection. Large and affable, Fromhoff had been waiting for years to do an interview about the early days of E. S. M. I asked about the connection with Cartaya, and he gave an embarrassed laugh.

"That was my fault," he said. "I was in Texas. My wife has relatives in the Rio Grande valley. On the plane coming back, I met Hernandez's father." The father talked proudly about his son, the international banker; Fromhoff saw the chance to land a large account, and E. S. M. met WFC. "Ronnie and Hernandez-Cartaya seemed to get along very well," Fromhoff said.

The explanation for this strange connection may be an anticlimax, a chance meeting on an airplane, but the result was big trouble. Fromhoff began trading for the NBSF in early December 1976. The OCC's Lou Frank described the deals in a dyspeptic internal memo as "a clear case of unsafe and unsound bond transactions." Fromhoff made money for the bank at first, with what Frank called a "sucker transaction." He reported a quick profit to the NBSF president who, said Frank, "must at this point have been ecstatic about the bank's good fortune." But to protect its short-term gain, NBSF found itself saddled with the several million dollars worth of bonds it was trading, and it was forced into a repo (a loan) from E. S. M. to cover the cost. Harrumphed Frank, "Only a very inexperienced and unlearned banker coerced by an unscrupulous and unethical bond broker would try to trade such issues."

But Hernandez-Cartaya would not be outfoxed by anyone. In several stiff letters to E. S. M., he demanded a refund and said pointedly that he had learned from the Florida Division of Securities that at the time of the trades E. S. M. was not properly licensed. By the end of February under pressure from the OCC, E. S. M. paid back nearly $90,000 in losses. The deal, however, had already attracted the attention of the SEC. In April, a veteran SEC investigator visited E. S. M. in Fort Lauderdale to check the books of E. S. M. Securities, the Arky-incorporated part of the group that still dealt in the regulated stock market. The visit launched years of lawyering that ended in a rare defeat for the SEC.

The SEC was already investigating another Fort Lauderdale bond trader, the firm where Ewton and Seneca had previously worked. Lou Frank's "suede shoe" memo apparently convinced the Atlanta regional office that something more was afoot. By May, Atlanta was ready to ask Washington for a formal Order of Investigation. "The common thread," Atlanta explained, "is the fact that dealers in United States government securities have a relatively large and aggressive sales force that prey on relatively small financial institutions. . . . As with every other bubble, the eldorado portrayed by the salesmen burst when interest rates declined and clients were obligated on losses."

The investigative order was approved, giving the regional office subpoena power, but its investigators decided to rely on Ewton's cooperation when they returned to E. S. M. Ewton and Seneca later claimed that the two SEC agents showed up asking to be educated about government securities trading, and that they happily answered the agents' questions until the conversation inexplicably kept turning to the trades with the National Bank of South Florida.

Ewton ended his cooperation in mid-November, and the SEC's men produced their subpoena. At this point, Stephen Arky, Ewton's friend and lawyer, jumped into the case with both feet. The Arky,

Freed firm went to court to quash the subpoena, claiming that the SEC had used "fraud, trickery, or deceit" in its visits to E. S. M. The case grew into a four-year battle. Arky's firm used every trick in its substantial arsenal, including a personal lawsuit against the lead SEC agent.

In the maneuvering, the SEC demanded to see the trades for three companies controlled by Arky's father-in-law, Marvin Warner. One of the companies was the Home State Savings Bank. The *American Lawyer* magazine later raised the question whether Arky had a conflict of interest in blocking an SEC inquiry presumably meant to protect customers such as Warner, whom Arky also represented. One of Arky's associates replied that Home State must have given "implicit" consent to the dual representation. Indeed, there is no record that Warner complained about Arky's "ferocious defense" of E. S. M., which went to the United States Fifth Circuit Court of Appeals. In May 1981, the Fifth Circuit ordered the lower court to consider Arky's objections to the four-year-old subpoena. The SEC dropped the case in disgust. The original complaint, it said, had gone "stale." By the end of the year, E. S. M. had accumulated losses of $135 million.

□ 3 □

SHORTLY AFTER THE E. S. M. CASE BEGAN, Ewton and Seneca backed into another SEC problem. Around the end of 1976, the two partners began actively shopping for a bank to call their own. They seemed to have a lot of cash to spend. One veteran Miami banker was trying to unload a troubled branch in Broward County when Ewton and Seneca offered him twice its book value. He became so suspicious that he turned them down. Arky came up with another prospect, a chain of small banks in Miami, weakened by one of the town's periodic real estate development scandals. Warner had looked at them briefly and then passed.

Ewton and Seneca picked up the chain, then called American Bancshares, Incorporated (ABI). Their nerve aroused Warner's interest, and he asked Arky to bring them together. "I sure would like to meet the turkey who would buy a pig in a poke like that," he said. "They must have a hell of a lot more money than I got." Warner said he met Ewton and Seneca for the first time on February 15, 1977, a fateful date for them all. As the four lunched at Bernard's Restaurant at Miami Beach, Warner must have concluded that Ewton and Seneca were his kind of guys. He started doing business with E. S. M., and he started lending the partners money.

Ewton and Seneca said they bought the bank with "working capital" from E. S. M. Whatever the source of the cash, they apparently had to pay it back quickly, and they eagerly accepted Warner's offer to refinance them with a $3 million mortgage from Home State. Warner didn't let their budding friendship disturb his practice of extracting every bit of advantage from a deal. With the loan, he demanded and got, an option to buy 50 percent of ABI's stock. The bank proved to be a money pit, and within months Ewton needed $3 million more. This time Warner insisted that Ewton sell him Class A preferred stock, with a warrant to buy more. Within a year, the bank fell into Warner's outstretched hand.

Warner claimed that he wasn't interested in ABI when Ewton took it over. With his long-time partner, Hugh Culverhouse, Sr., a prominent Jacksonville attorney, he was trying to buy a big bank holding company, such as Flagship, Century, or Florida National Bank. Soon after the February 1977 lunch, he packed up for his stint as ambassador to Switzerland. But the SEC saw it differently. After Warner took over ABI (the larger prizes having been elusive), SEC agents asked whether he had used Ewton as a stalking horse.

In November 1978, the SEC issued a Private Order of Investigation involving ABI, Ewton, Seneca, Warner, and Warner's bank holding company, ComBanks Corporation. When the SEC subpoenaed Ambassador Warner two months later, he furiously pulled strings. In late January 1979, Arky called William Nortman, the SEC's Miami regional administrator, to say that it would be damaging to Ambassador Warner's official position to have his name "on that ticket." According to an internal SEC memo, Arky went even higher. He called Stanley Sporkin—his old boss, the supposedly tough head of the SEC's Enforcement Division—and asked to arrange a meeting on February 8 between Sporkin and Warner. There is no publicly available record of the meeting, if indeed it took place. But after sputtering on for nearly a year, the SEC investigation quietly disappeared.

The United States Comptroller of the Currency had little more effect on Ewton and Seneca than did the SEC. After chasing them out of Hernandez-Cartaya's Hialeah bank, the OCC was not pleased to learn they had just bought a chain of banks it regulated. It responded by going to the boards of directors of each of ABI's six subsidiaries and obtaining a voluntary agreement prohibiting the banks from making any loans or deals with E. S. M. or its principals. Ewton dealt with the restrictions just as Jake Butcher had in an earlier case; he switched the ABI banks to state charters. By late October 1978, Beazley and Arky told the ABI board that the Florida Banking Division looked favorably on the conversion, in spite of gnashing of teeth in the OCC's Atlanta office. Beazley said the banking division wouldn't require the agreements imposed by the OCC. The following March, the voluntary restrictions were rescinded by the ABI board.

Warner always insisted that he had nothing to do with Ewton and Seneca's bid for ABI. "I declined for bona fide business reasons to purchase ABI before E. S. M's principals bought it," he wrote the *Wall Street Journal* after the Home State collapse. "They improved ABI, and I then decided to buy ABI." When he took over after his 1979 return from Switzerland, his management was a combination of interference on some nickle-and-dime decisions and complete aloofness on others. Several key figures on his always quarreling staff decided to bail out when he resumed full-time control. Others took the rap when things went wrong.

So Warner escaped personal embarrassment in late February 1981, when a caravan of federal agents pulled up outside the ABI branch in North Miami, now renamed the Great American Bank, and raided its records in a money laundering investigation. The raid produced the indictment of the bank in December 1982 on charges of failing to report more than $34 million in large cash deposits by a Colombian drug organization. The bank and three of its employees pleaded guilty, and, in the first judgment of its kind, Great American was fined $375,000. But the United States Attorney's office could never make a case against Warner or the senior staff.

One investigator recounted that subpoenas had been drawn up for Arky, who then went to United States Attorney Stanley Marcus and persuaded him "that the investigation shouldn't take that direction." Two days before the indictment of Great American, the Florida state comptroller approved the merger of its holding company with Barnett Banks, the state's second largest chain. The director of the State Banking Division acknowledged that he knew about the impending indictment.

Arky, Ewton, and all of Warner's interests had good reason to expect favorable treatment from Florida State Comptroller Gerald Lewis. The elected official in charge of every facet of their regulation, from securities dealing to thrifts to banks, Lewis was also Warner's second cousin. Born in Birmingham in 1936, he grew up in the shadow of the older and more glamorous Warner. The mothers of the two were close friends. There's a story that in Lewis's 1978 reelection campaign, he complained about the niggardly support that Warner was providing. His mother overheard him and got on the phone to Warner, shaking loose thousands in campaign contributions. Arky got along even better with the Harvard-educated Lewis, calling him "Uncle Gerry."

After the collapse of E. S. M., Lewis claimed that he heard nothing about its problems until mid-1984. Yet the OCC had warned the state regulators almost as soon as Frank had finished his "suede shoe" memo. A former member of Lewis's staff remembered sitting on the couch in the comptroller's office in 1977 when the memo arrived. "He lit up a cigar and read it intently," said this witness. Lewis handed the memo to another staffer for investigation, and nothing more was heard about it.

Once the regulators were neutralized, Warner's Home State and Ewton's E. S. M. were free to develop what the E. S. M. bankruptcy trustee later called their "symbiotic relationship." In early 1977, Warner was looking for a new investment agent. He later told the

SEC that he had just been badly stung by his previous broker, a New York outfit called Argent Investors Management Corporation. The FDIC had its own suspicions about Argent. Its examiner found that the broker had generated nearly $75 million in purchases and sales for Warner's ComBanks in less than four months, producing a gain of only $156,000, which was $100,000 less than its management fee. A similar arrangement with a bank in Georgia, said an FDIC memo in mid-1977, had "disastrous effects," with more than a $250,000 in losses. The bank, it appears, was Bert Lance's own National Bank of Georgia, which hired Argent on the recommendation of ComBanks. In a comment similar to later charges about E. S. M., FDIC Regional Counsel Stephen B. Woodrough concluded, "there appears to be a very real threat that Mr. Warner may be 'siphoning' funds from banks within the holding company."

(The FDIC based this suspicion, however, on the premise that Warner indirectly owned Argent, which its officials, now based in Stamford, Connecticut, deny. A filing in another case states that at the time Warner owned 20 percent of its common stock and 100 percent of its preferred stock. It doesn't appear that either federal or state officials took further action.)

The ties between E. S. M. and Home State didn't really flourish until 1980, when the Cincinnati thrift encountered another milestone. On December 15, 1980, Home State copped a plea on a two-count federal fraud indictment. The scheme involved "standby loan commitments" that Home State sold to developers at high fees to enable them to get long-term financing elsewhere at good rates. The commitments were hedged with so many self-contradictory conditions that, as one banker told an unfortunate purchaser, "it was not worth the paper upon which it was printed." Home State was required to refund nearly $800,000 in fees. One of the victims, curiously, was a Tennessee corporation involved with the Butchers.

The federal prosecutors ended the one-and-a-half year investigation in their usual deep frustration. Then United States Attorney James Cissell wanted to bring the case under the new federal Racketeer Influenced and Corrupt Organizations law (RICO), but he was overruled by superiors in the Justice Department. "I was absolutely furious," he told the Associated Press. (He added later that he considered it a policy dispute over the RICO statute, not a cover-up.) Nonetheless, Warner kept his name off one more ticket. Home State was allowed to plead no contest to the fraud charges; none of its officers were indicted.

The prosecutors worked under the fear that their case could set off a run at the thrift, and that a RICO judgment could bankrupt the private fund that provided its deposit insurance. The first newspaper stories about the investigation led off with a profuse assurance of Home State's safety from an Ohio Commerce Department official. The spokesman was Clark Wideman, superintendent of the Division of Building and Loan Associations, who had drafted some of those self-contradictory clauses in the "worthless" standby commitments.

There was no run, but Home State had a problem. Without the standby fees, the thrift would lose money. The losses increased in 1980, as several large real estate loans went bad and the thrift fell into the interest rate squeeze that hurt the whole industry. E. S. M. stepped in to fill the gap. The deals with Home State grew rapidly, and the thrift relied on its short-term trading profits to stay in the black. In 1981, day-trade profits of $3.3 million covered an operating loss of $2.5 million.

In return, Home State kept E. S. M. going by providing it with the government bonds to support its other deals. When Home State borrowed from E. S. M. in a "repo," it provided bonds worth more than twice the amount of the loan as collateral. In one deal, it provided nearly six times the necessary collateral.

E. S. M. hid the growing deficit with phony books and bribed its outside auditor to look the other way. The auditor, José Gomez of the firm of Alexander Grant, pleaded guilty to the fraud. This nearly unprecedented incident of bribery later gave Warner and other investors an excuse for claiming ignorance of the fraud. Each company was able to cover the weakness of the other, for the short term. In the long run, said Miami lawyer Thomas Tew, E. S. M.'s bankruptcy trustee, it looked like "two rocks that were tied together with the hope that they then could float."

But the rocks did float. Warner and Ewton "were umbilically tied together," as Ewton put it in his later voluble testimony, in "somewhat of a self-preservation mode." After the collapse, Ewton spilled his guts in debriefing sessions that resembled scenes from a John Le Carre spy novel. The SEC and the E. S. M. trustees interrogated him on alternate days, as investigators from a range of agencies took handwritten notes on yellow legal pads so that, as "work product," the record couldn't be subpoenaed by defense counsel. Ewton recounted a relationship that was often strained and filled with noise. He testified that, on September 6, 1983, Warner summoned Novick and Ewton to Cincinnati when one of their deals stood to lose Home State $30 million. Said Ewton, Warner began screaming in his office about his own $5.7 million in losses. Ewton agreed to reimburse him. As they drove back to the airport, said Ewton, Warner launched into another tirade. Ewton cracked.

"Damn it," he yelled in Warner's face, "listen to me. Coming up here on the plane this morning I found out we had taken a $40-odd million loss, which happens to be three times our net worth. Now I'm here to tell you something. I don't want to hear about your problem anymore."

The scene recurred in a meeting at Manhattan's Waldorf-Astoria Hotel in early 1984. Warner demanded a break in interest rates to put Home State back in the black. "Well, Ron, you've got to do this," Warner said. "You got us into this and you've got to do that."

"Marvin, we can't do this," Ewton pleaded. "We've already taken more losses than we can. Marvin, Hell's bells, we're bleeding out both ears as it is."

Himself no model of austerity, Ewton had to marvel at Warner's dominant passion. "Marvin is a money-making machine," he testified. "And I'm not saying this to his detriment at all.

"He thinks about it 24 hours a day, seven days a week. He plots and plans, not that that's bad. And his focus is in that direction. Anything that is moving him in that direction is his buddy for life. The minute you don't move in that direction, you are in some deep trouble."

□ 4 □

THIS WAS THE MIRACLE OF THE FLOATING ROCKS, of the umbilical tie
between Home State and E. S. M. In the end, they were severed,
not by the regulators, but by boardroom intrigue and a clash of strong
personalities. This remarkable story begins with yet another veteran
of Hernandez-Cartaya's outfit. Somehow Stephen Arky had become
lawyer and friend of a Venezuelan Horatio Alger named Juan Vicente
Perez Sandoval. Born in a poor section of Caracas in 1944, Perez
started his career in a Pepsi bottling plant owned by a powerful
Cuban émigré family named Cisneros. Detractors say his first job
was driving a truck. But he was sleek and handsome in a slightly
goofy way (his picture vaguely resembles the late comedian Andy
Kaufman), and he rose rapidly, especially after he married the sister
of Oswaldo Cisneros.

In addition to the bottling plant, Oswaldo's branch of the Cisneros family owned real estate, financial companies, and a chunk
of the Venezuelan subsidiary of General Electric. In 1975, Oswaldo
and Vicente became partners of Hernandez-Cartaya. They sat on
the board of Cartaya's Panamanian bank, along with officers of the
Mercantile Bank of St. Louis and the First National Bank of Louisville. Perez became the WFC Corporation's agent in Venezuela.
During the WFC debacle, Perez and Cisneros escaped scrutiny and
were happy to play down the connection. Around 1979, Perez became a player in Florida's frenetic world of banking. As president
of a Cisneros-owned finance company called Sociedad Financiera
Credival, he controlled enough capital to think seriously about buying a major Florida banking chain.

Perez Sandoval became formidable when he somehow linked
up with Arky. (One connection might have been Arky's counsel
Alfredo Duran, son-in-law of a former Cuban president and the first
Hispanic to be named head of the Florida Democratic Party.) Arky
and Perez took a run at Flagship Banks in 1982, forcing it to take
refuge in a merger with another large chain. Together they invested
in a United States Football League franchise, the Tampa Bay Bandits.

But the venture that started the trouble was their attempt to take over the Freedom Savings and Loan of Tampa.

Freedom, considered one of the worst thrifts in Florida, never ceased to fascinate Warner's alumni. Arky put together a syndicate to buy Freedom, much to the relief of its owners. Perez Sandoval and Ronnie Ewton were investors. Some of Arky's friends speculated that he may have been trying to impress his father-in-law. But the move backfired. "Warner was very upset with Arky," said a mutual friend, "very upset." He had his own designs on Freedom. In a celebrated recent maneuver, he had tried to sell his holding company, ComBanks, to Freedom. When shareholders of the thrift refused to approve the purchase, he ordered Home State to buy enough of its shares to tip the vote in his favor. Home State now owned 7.5 percent of Freedom, and Warner was afraid that Arky's bid was hurting its market value.

Warner counterpunched in March 1984 with a suit charging that Perez Sandoval lacked the moral character to own a thrift. Warner was a better prophet than he knew. Perez had a big personal problem. His affections had shifted from his wife, Milagros, to her niece, a coed in Miami. Oswaldo Cisneros was not graceful about Perez Sandoval's ensuing divorce and remarriage and his own conversion from brother-in-law to father-in-law. He severed their business ties, and bad things began to happen. Without Cisneros as a counterweight, Perez ran his Venezuelan banks into the ground. His holdings included the Banco de Comercio, one of Venezuela's largest. Government investigators later charged that Perez Sandoval had systematically looted the Banco de Comercio to finance his bank buying sprees in Florida. In mid-1985, the government bailed out the bank at a one billion Bolivar charge to the country's new Deposit Guaranty Fund. A Venezuelan court charged Perez Sandoval with misappropriating $70 million and declared him a fugitive. (He remains a fugitive to this day.)

In 1984, however, Perez Sandoval was still holding things together. Stymied by Warner's resistance, he and Arky negotiated a deal to sell him their shares in Freedom. By July, Warner and Perez, both relying on Arky as their lawyer, worked out a deal in which

Freedom would be absorbed by the American Savings and Loan Association of Miami (ASLA). In return for his Freedom stock, Perez would become a large shareholder in American.

The deal threatened to upset a delicate balance at the $3.7 billion ASLA. The thrift had been founded in 1950 by Shepard Broad, a successful lawyer who had immigrated from Minsk in Russia shortly after the Revolution. ASLA suffered badly in the interest rate squeeze of 1982 and had welcomed an offer from Warner to invest $10 million. To avoid losing control, Broad and his son Morris had worked out a "voting trust" with Warner that gave each party six seats on the 12-person board of directors. They also included a buy-sell agreement in case either side became disgruntled. Warner could offer to buy out Broad, or vice versa, but whoever invoked the agreement had to give the other the choice of buying or selling.

By March 1984, Warner had taken control of ASLA and started making changes. He brought in his own managers. He branched into unconventional investments, such as a New York brokerage house and a development corporation, using the broadened powers of Florida's new savings and loan code. He put Ronnie Ewton on the board of directors and started doing big business with E. S. M. This development bothered Shep Broad, a feisty octogenarian with a Mel Brooks accent.

The last straw was Warner's free-wheeling deal with Freedom Savings and Loan. Warner took the occasion of the purchase talks to unload the Freedom shares that he had saddled on Home State in his earlier coup. In mid-June he called ASLA President William Cooper to meet him at the airport. Warner showed him an agreement to buy Home State's holdings and told him to sign it. The executive committee of the board had approved it, Warner told Cooper, but he couldn't sign it himself because of insider problems. This was big news to Shep Broad and his half of the directors. Also on his own say-so, Warner committed the thrift to paying Perez Sandoval $5 million for his stock option. Again he acted without going to the board of directors. Arky helped close the deal, acting both for Warner and for Perez, a dual role that later caused ASLA to sue his estate for conflict of interest. In the ultimate insult, the deal promised Perez two seats on the board. Control of American would have tipped firmly to Warner.

The deal hit the fan at the next board meeting, on the morning of July 31. Shep Broad was travelling in Europe, but he made his presence felt with a detailed memo that the directors debated the day before in an informal "workshop." The preparation made the board meeting even more tumultuous. Questions and objections came from all sides. Arky showed up with Warner and did his share of talking, even though other directors noted that he hadn't been formally invited. The board minutes called it a "frank and free discussion," a term that in the diplomatic world means a shouting match.

Passions hadn't cooled by the September 10 meeting. Cooper, the ASLA president, was called on the carpet to explain how he came to sign the Home State document. Shep Broad called it "a disaster." In short order, the board voted to "repudiate and reject" Warner's deals with both Home State and Perez Sandoval. But if Shep Broad was Warner's match in shrewdness, Warner was nobody's slouch in stubbornness. Complaining about the "stalemate," he invoked the buy-sell agreement. Once again, Broad matched his move. The old man declared that he would be the purchaser, not Warner. Weeks of acrimonious niggling and shuffling followed. "Please stop all this foolishness," Shep admonished Warner at the end. "Let's act like gentlemen should." As 1985 began, Broad had taken back the thrift he had founded.

As the conflict with Warner was building, Shep Broad had another worry. Ronnie Ewton had committed American to a huge and baffling arrangement involving $1 billion of Treasury bills. As far as Broad's lawyers could figure out, it amounted to a $110 million unsecured loan to E. S. M. The deal originated on May 16, after a meeting of the board's executive committee had disbanded. Warner called Shepard and his son Morris to his private office to explain E. S. M.'s written proposal for the $1 billion "leveraged arbitrage" deal. Warner claimed it was a "risk-free" way to earn $5.6 million.

Shep had qualms and asked the chief financial officer to see what other brokers offered on a similar deal. But no other brokers would handle that kind of "arbitrage." The financial officer, Robert Luther, went ahead with $500 million of the purchase. At a management committee meeting a week later, Luther told ASLA President Cooper that the order had been approved by the board's executive committee. Cooper replied, that he was at that meeting and didn't remember that. Luther said, actually, that it happened at an executive session following the regular meeting. Shep Broad was away in Canada at the next executive committee meeting, so the remaining members, Warner, Ewton, and Morris Broad, voted formal approval in language tucked into a broader resolution on securities transactions. To finance the deal, American Savings and Loan handed E. S. M. $110 million of United States Treasury notes. The bankruptcy trustee later concluded that the notes, and the collateral they provided for the Treasury bill purchases, helped keep E. S. M. afloat, "despite its staggering losses."

Like a huckster with a live one, Ewton tried to keep his streak going. He wrote Warner, offering to help correct American's "under-leveraged/over-capitalized structure" with another billion dollars in deals, including brokered CDs and an offering on the unregulated Euro-note market. But Shep Broad had had enough. Back on the scene, he pushed for documentation, written loan agreements, close tabs on American's notes, the details that would disrupt Ewton's game. He commissioned lawyers' studies and accountants' reports. As summer turned to fall, and the Perez Sandoval dispute came to a head, he demanded the "unwinding" of the arbitrage deal. Ewton managed to scrape together $45 million, part of which Broad apparently used to finance his buyout of Warner.

The unwinding of the arbitrage meant the unwinding of E. S. M. The refund to Broad destroyed the cash flow that covered the firm's fundamental bankruptcy. In November, E. S. M. President Alan Novick died at his desk of a massive heart attack. Among their other crimes, the survivors at E. S. M. tried to straighten out affairs by forging his will. (It left all his estate to his wife, who, according to a still unexplained rumor, possessed a mysterious tape recording he had made.) By January, the game was up. A week after making a $300,000 downpayment on a $1.3 million yacht, Ewton resigned from the company. Only the "M" of the outfit, the workhorse sales-man George Mead, was left to carry on. At 6:00 P.M. on Monday, March 4, in a special session of the United States District Court, E. S. M. went into receivership. American Savings and Loan had lost $55 million. Home State Savings Bank had lost $150 million. Both rocks had finally sunk.

CHAPTER NINE

□□□

The Time Bomb Explodes

□ 1 □

SYLVESTER HENTSCHEL WAS NOT SURPRISED when E. S. M. went bust and Home State Savings Bank closed its doors. As senior examiner for Ohio's Division of Savings and Loan Associations, he had been predicting the disaster for two and a half years. What shocked Hentschel, a quiet bear of a man, was that no one higher up would listen to him.

"You may be losing much precious time if you intend to wait until after the report is typed," Henschel had written in sending a "pencil draft" of his October 1982 examination of Home State directly to Clark Wideman, then the savings and loan superintendent. In a "Dear Clark" memo handwritten on legal pad, Hentschel strongly urged a cease and desist order to ban new repo deals with E. S. M. "It is important," Hentschel wrote, "that the restriction be placed on the association immediately to protect its savings depositors and the Ohio Deposit Guarantee Fund and its member institutions." The memo was dated October 8, 1982.

But Wideman never replied. When the final version of Hentschel's examination was typed, someone deleted his recommendation, repeated three times, for an official cease and desist order. But four terms of Republican Governor James Rhodes were drawing to a close. Hentschel, an experienced bureaucrat, decided to try his luck with the new administration of Democratic Governor-elect Richard F. Celeste. He delayed his formal review of the final report until Celeste's inauguration on January 30, 1983. Then he wrote Chief Examiner Kurt A. Kreinbring that the new superintendent "should be alerted to the veritable time bomb ticking away."

Shortly afterward, Hentschel called Kreinbring to find out what was happening. Kreinbring had supported Hentschel earlier. "I have discussed this matter at length with Kurt, and he is as concerned as I," Hentschel had written in his "Dear Clark" memo. This time, however, the chief examiner was embarrassed and evasive. "He said he did not care to discuss it with me," Hentschel recalled.

Hentschel put his concern right on the front page of his examination report. "Securities with a book value of $208.2 million are assigned to a securities dealer in Florida under repurchase agreements," he wrote. "The association has borrowed $83.8 million on those securities. . . . The association is therefore vulnerable to a potential loss of about $125 million, should the dealer be unable for any reason to redeliver the securities upon expiration of the repurchase agreements. The association's net worth is less than $12 million." A potential loss this big, he added, was almost twice the assets of the Ohio Deposit Guarantee Fund. Another examiner a year later gave the same warning, with bigger numbers. Paul Albin wrote that Home State had borrowed $615 million from E. S. M. and given it $773 million in bonds as collateral, a potential loss of $158 million. Even more urgent, Home State's net worth had been eaten up by bad loans. It was clearly a thrift in trouble.

The examiners may not have realized, however, that their boss, Chief Examiner Kreinbring, was as worried and frustrated as they were. For various reasons, the politically appointed thrift supervisors were not responding to the department's professionals. Under Governor Rhodes, Superintendent Wideman kept close ties to Home State, far too close, it turned out. He admitted helping Home State draft its standby loan commitments, later labelled fraudulent in federal court. After leaving office with Governor Rhodes, Wideman set up his own legal and bank consulting practice; within a month he had signed up Home State as one of his first clients. He said later that, until state officials cleared him to help with the thrift crisis, he handled only matters he hadn't dealt with in office. This, to his mind, complied with a state "revolving door" law that banned ex-regulators for one year from working for companies they had regulated. Wideman did handle Home State's applications for new branches, ten in all, in the year before its collapse.

Wideman argued that he was inhibited in disciplining Home State by the fear of starting a run. At the time, he says, Ohio law required a public hearing before the state could enforce a cease and desist order. (There is no such requirement in federal law.) One wonders, though, how a state regulator with that attitude could ever enforce anything.

Wideman's alternative, he said, was to threaten such an order in a conversation with Home State President Burton Bongard. He said he sent word of the problem through the chain of command to Governor Rhodes, who had appointed Warner to an honorific state board. Rhodes said "go ahead," to the threat. Bongard replied with a promise to start unwinding the E. S. M. commitment when the repo contracts expired in June 1983. This promise came in late January 1983, just before the change in administration and Wideman's contract with Home State.

Wideman's successor, Lawrence Huddleston, was a different problem. Younger and much more naive, he came to the job with a background in consumer law but none in bank regulation. As one of the governor's new wave of "Celestials," he had a fatal predisposition toward discounting the warnings of his own staff, thinking of himself as the moderator of their bureaucratic extremism. He was also easily conned by Home State. The June deadline came and went, and Home State's repos ballooned. In the September 1983 examination, State Examiner Albin found that Home State had tripled the collateral in E. S. M.'s hands, and that its exposure had increased by $25 million. Huddleston reacted in October by calling a large meeting. Along with officials of the Ohio Deposit Guarantee Fund (ODGF), he asked Home State officers to meet with him at its Cincinnati office. Two principals of Home State flew up from

Fort Lauderdale. After Huddleston agreed that the urgency justified a technical violation of the state's "revolving door" law, former Superintendent Wideman also attended and was later indicted for it. (He was found not guilty in a municipal court trial.)

The folks from Home State and E. S. M. defended themselves vociferously. The regulators were overwhelmed and settled for yet another written promise from Home State to unwind the repos. The fascinating feature of the meeting, however, was the absence of the Home State directors. A special investigating committee of the Ohio legislature later noted that it "received conflicting testimony" about the board's awareness of Home State's condition. Home State Director Nelson Schwab, Jr., a Cincinnati attorney and long-time associate of Warner, testified, "At no time was the board asked to nor did it meet with the Superintendent of Building and Loans or with ODGF or with Arthur Andersen or with E. S. M or with any representatives of the above to discuss E. S. M or Home State's government securities repo program."

Schwab hired a lawyer to demand a retraction from the *Wall Street Journal* when it characterized the October 1983 session as a meeting with the Home State board. Yet State Examiner Hentschel had been trying to bring his report to the attention of the board at least since his "time bomb" memo of January 25, 1983. He wrote Kreinbring, "In view of former Superintendent Wideman's perfunctory letter transmitting this report to the association, I would appreciate receiving a copy of the board of director's response when it is received." In February 1983 the ODGF wrote the board of directors demanding that it reduce the collateral it was leaving with E. S. M. Five of the seven directors (excluding Schwab) responded by signing a resolution of compliance. Superintendent Huddleston wrote the board members in late December 1983, requesting a meeting at his office about the "extremely large" repos. Home State's lawyer, former Superintendent Wideman, produced the management instead.

One can understand why a Home State director would try to plead ignorance, but that hardly excuses the conduct of Schwab and the others. The director of a company takes personal responsibility for its safety and soundness. Weak or compliant boards of directors, as Comptroller of the Currency Robert Clarke has observed, constitute one of the most common elements in bank failures. By their own account, the directors of Home State, like the directors of all the Butcher banks before them, and the Texas savings and loans afterward, did a very poor job.

□ 2 □

AFTER THE INEFFECTUAL OCTOBER MEETING, Chief Examiner Kreinbring gave up on Superintendent Huddleston. "I was at my wit's end," he told the legislative committee. He decided to leapfrog his boss and approach Warren Tyler, head of the state commerce department. By Kreinbring's account, Tyler said he would talk to Marvin Warner at a social function they were both scheduled to attend. Afterward, Kreinbring asked Tyler what had happened. Testified the chief examiner, "he said Warner took him by the elbow out of the room and said, 'You've got to be very careful you don't say that around a crowd of people.' " (Tyler confirmed the meeting, except for the detail about being ushered from the room.)

Meanwhile, the regulators flailed more and more wildly at Home State. Through 1984, Huddleston's office addressed several more letters to the Home State board. The ODGF ordered Home State to unwind its deals and asked outside accountants to figure out what was going on. Even the SEC got back into the act, refusing to let Home State float a $30 million issue of debentures (that is, to borrow $30 million from the public) until it disclosed how it would be affected if E. S. M. went bankrupt. Home State cancelled the public issue instead.

Some of these blows began to bother Warner. In September 1984, Ewton testified, the Home State owner complained about the state regulators. "Ron, I'm going to have to do something about these guys; they are all over us," said Warner. "I may have to go over their heads."

By this point a feud had erupted between Tyler and Huddleston, further paralyzing the regulators. Tyler had made his reputation as an economizer, and he was blocking Huddleston's request for more staff. Huddleston was asking for, among other things, a securities analyst, who would have been useful in the Home State case. (His examiners, however, already understood Home State very well.) It took Huddleston six months of pestering Tyler to get him to interview a candidate for an open slot as examiner.

Huddleston put his staffing request squarely in the context of the developing national savings and loan crisis. More people were needed, he wrote Tyler, to cope with the expanded investment powers a new Ohio law had granted the thrifts. Some S&L managers were beginning to take wild risks: "There are so many who are so bad, we must substantially enhance our ability to control the bad." The Empire Savings and Loan failure in Texas had drawn the fire of Congress and shaken the regulatory world. One memo even fantasized about a hostile congressional investigation. Huddleston wrote: ("Mr. Huddleston, suppose you tell the committee why, when everyone around you was beefing up their staffs substantially, and you even knew how critical the condition of your industry, you didn't do anything . . .")

In October, Huddleston tried a leapfrog of his own. Although the thrift supervisor was part of the commerce department, a recent change in the law had made both officials direct appointees of the governor. Arguing that his department should be autonomous, Huddleston asked the state attorney general to give a written legal opinion. The attorney general kicked the issue over to the governor's office. On October 15, Huddleston asked for a meeting with Governor Celeste. Failing that, he asked for two hours with Celeste's Chief of Staff Joe Sommer, accompanied by his chief counsel and chief examiner. But Sommer agreed with the commerce secretary. When Huddleston came to talk about regulation, he received a tongue lashing about insubordination. Shortly after the meeting, Huddleston resigned. Before leaving, he wrote a memo listing his accomplishments. The seventh item was arranging "a special table at 1984 Democratic Victory Gala in Washington, D.C." The guests included House Speaker Tip O'Neill; a former staffer to Senator John Glenn named James Grogan, now at Lincoln Savings and Loan in California; and Ambassador and Mrs. Marvin Warner.

The first warnings of an impending thrift crisis began as Huddleston prepared to leave in January 1985. The Nebraska state guaranty fund had failed, and a segment on "60 Minutes" inspired "moderate outflows" at some Ohio thrifts. A "Celestial" to the last, Huddleston drafted his last memo to the governor, warning him against taking any hand in the affairs of the financial regulators. "There is no public upside to your involvement," he wrote, "and the potential downside is monstrous." Huddleston's post remained vacant until the March run on Home State.

It's not clear if Tyler pursued the Home State matter beyond his strange decision to chat about it with Warner. Early in the game, on March 8, 1983, he asked Huddleston to summarize his concern about Home State and "indicate how you plan to proceed." The purpose of this memo, explained Tyler, "is to advise the Governor early of the situation." But the follow-up, if any, has disappeared. Tyler steadfastly claimed that he never notified Governor Celeste. Shortly before the March run, Celeste transferred him from commerce to the Environmental Protection Agency, ostensibly to deal with its management problems. Said Celeste's press officer, "The governor is very high on Mr. Tyler."

Although tarnished, Celeste was not lethally wounded by the Home State crisis because no one could show that he directly intervened to help Warner. Up to the end, however, Warner could put calls through to the Governor's Mansion, and he had the ear of the governor's staff. One candidate for S&L superintendent reports that the governor's aides recommended he talk to Warner for a fix on the Celestial position on regulation. Warner's close ties to Celeste were common knowledge. At the end of the Carter years, Warner lowered his political sights to the state of Ohio. He cultivated warm relations with the Speaker of the Ohio House, Vernal Riffe. (Warner's third wife was Riffe's former legislative aide.) And he made a crucial intervention in the 1982 governor's race.

□ 3 □

IN THE SPRING OF 1982, Richard Celeste was lagging in the three-man Democratic primary for governor. In May, Warner called a number of heavy political contributors to a meeting in his nineteenth-century home. They raised or pledged about $100,000, according to some accounts. The cash saved Celeste's campaign and eventually helped put him in the governor's chair. The contribution reports don't specify just who attended Warner's gathering, but they do show that Celeste drew on an intricate multistate web of Warner's associates. During mid-May, Warner gave $23,000 (and a final total of $36,000). From E. S. M., Ronnie Ewton gave $10,000 and Alan Novick gave $5,000. Bernard Rapoport, a Waco, Texas insurance man and one of Warner's directors at Miami's American Savings and Loan, gave $25,000. Aaron Aranov of Montgomery, Alabama, an old friend of Warner and principal in the Kinder-Care day care chain, gave $10,000. Jake Butcher gave $5,000. Perhaps more surprisingly, $15,000 came from Carl Icahn, the corporate raider. Warner invested in some of Icahn's syndicates, and Home State helped finance his takeover bids.

Celeste drew on Warner's web once more in 1983, in his hardball campaign against two tax revolt initiatives. This time, he received $10,000 from partners in Bear, Stearns & Co., the New York brokers who underwrote some of Warner's business raids (and also backed Juan Vicente Perez Sandoval in his bid for the Flagship Bank). After his election, Celeste named Warner the chairman of the highly political Ohio Building Authority, in charge of constructing state buildings. It promptly switched to Bear, Stearns as lead underwriter.

This political background colored much of the way the Home State crisis was handled. Celeste said that his first hint of trouble came from Warner. On the morning of Wednesday, March 6, two days after E. S. M. collapsed, Warner called Celeste at the Governor's Mansion. The Home State owner wanted to tell the chief executive of Ohio that a *Cincinnati Enquirer* story about E. S. M. was about to devastate his thrift. The public might wonder about Warner's ability to reach the governor at home, and Celeste thought it was a matter for the savings and loan division, but he listened intently. "It was clear to me, just from the tone of his voice, that it was a matter of real concern, and I didn't take it as a casual conversation," Celeste told *Columbus Monthly* magazine.

Meanwhile, the interim head of the S&L division was meeting with the new commerce department secretary, Ken Cox; the head of the Ohio Savings and Loan League, the industry group; and Ray Sawyer, the governor's new chief of staff. Sawyer, as tall, beefy, and arrogant as the governor himself, became one of the most important players in the crisis. In principle, the problem should have been handled by the state-regulated but privately run Ohio Deposit Guarantee Fund. But regulatory neglect had let things get too far out of hand. Not only were the losses at Home State more than twice the resources of the ODGF, but Home State itself was too big to fit comfortably into an insurance scheme that had originated with neighborhood thrifts oriented toward southwest Ohio's immigrant German communities. Sheer weight had given Home State far too much say in running the ODGF, and now it was taking the entire fund down with it.

By Friday, March 8, the run on Home State had drained $150 million in deposits and virtually exhausted the ODGF. The state government reached its first crossroad. Instead of pouring more money into the fund, the state let it sink with Home State. Over the weekend, Celeste decided to back a new insurance fund for the other ODGF members. According to one sharp critic of his policy, Professor Edward Kane, this decision broadened the crisis. A long-time student of deposit insurance funds and professor of banking at Ohio State University in Columbus, Kane had a ringside seat for the Bank Holiday. The decision to abandon the ODGF, he argued, wiped out the capital that the 70 other ODGF members had contributed to the fund and still carried on their books as an asset; this blow pushed a few into insolvency. Second, it undermined public faith in the guaranty. Even though the fund was basically a private insurance pool, said Kane, the public assumed that in a pinch, the state would bail it out. Suddenly this assumption was out the window.

As Celeste struggled to find a buyer for Home State and the legislature voted a woefully inadequate $50 million for the alternate guarantee fund, depositors lined up outside six more ODGF member institutions. Professor Kane said these were "rational" runs. The thrifts were the weakest in the system. Depositors had learned how poorly they were regulated, and they had good reason to think that the state would bungle the crisis. As lines lengthened and hardware stores in Cincinnati ran out of home safes, one completely uninsured thrift well known for its conservative lending stayed open with no trouble at all.

The new runs changed the politics of the crisis. In the first week, the Republican-controlled Senate seemed glad to discomfit the widely disliked Celeste, especially as his connection with Warner became known. But now deposits were bleeding from thrifts owned by Republican interests. Influential GOP state senators from Cincinnati pestered Celeste for help. Celeste's aide Sawyer later claimed that the Republican senators were the crucial voice in the decision about to be made.

On the evening of Thursday, March 14, Celeste polled close advisers. Whether or not he knew it at the time, two of them were deeply indebted to Warner. Jack Kessler, an insurance man and developer from Columbus who sat on the board of the Federal Reserve Bank of Cleveland, had just received a multi-million dollar loan from Home State. Gerald Austin, Celeste's 1982 campaign manager and, later, the manager of Jesse Jackson's 1988 presidential campaign, was still drawing a salary as the thrift's state lobbyist. The crew munched on barbecued spareribs and Girl Scout cookies in the Capitol and watched footage of the runs on the television news. By 5:00 A.M., Celeste had rejected traditional strategies of coping with the runs and decided to declare a Bank Holiday. "Close them all," he said.

The Bank Holiday was probably illegal, but since it served bipartisan interests, no one in the state government was willing to challenge it. Instead, as in Franklin Roosevelt's original, the legislature quickly passed a bill putting it on firmer footing. It's even more likely that the "holiday" was unnecessary. Cynics have called it a cover-up to divert attention from the fraudulent collapse of Home State. At the least, the policy revealed the inability of Celeste and his regulators to distinguish between the healthy thrifts and the failing ones. At least 50 of the ODGF members were in reasonably good shape as they proved by their ability to qualify for FSLIC insurance and reopen. One thrift threatened to sue to prevent its closing. It changed its mind, however, when state officials reminded its president of the pressures that regulators could bring to bear, pressures not used on Home State.

The Bank Holiday may also have been meant to set the stage for a federal bailout. During the crisis, Celeste talked constantly with Federal Reserve Chairman Paul Volcker. ("These things are always worse than they seem at first," Volcker told him helpfully.) Although Sawyer later complained about the Fed's attitude, Volcker took steps to provide loans for the healthy ODGF thrifts. Sawyer and Celeste saved their most vociferous complaints, however, for the Federal Home Loan Bank Board. The state strategy, supposedly modelled on a 1976 crisis among self-insured Mississippi thrifts, was to allow ODGF thrifts to reopen after they qualified for FSLIC insurance. At first, charged Sawyer, Bank Board Chairman Ed Gray was not eager to pick up the pieces. Even after his posture shifted to effusive cooperation, the FSLIC insurance applications proved time-consuming.

□ 4 □

THE STRATEGY OF THE BANK HOLIDAY in large part was to make the Home State failure look like a failure of the entire financial system, an argument that diverted attention from the personal failures of Celeste and his staff. This argument received a superficial confirmation on March 18, the Monday after the closings, when the dollar plunged on the world currency market and the price of gold increased by $30 an ounce. This seemed like a disproportionate reaction to a crisis in Ohio, but Professor Kane explained it in terms that did matter globally, the impending crisis in the deposit insurance of the federal government. By this time FSLIC was already insolvent, an important reason for Bank Board Chairman Gray's reluctance to insure another batch of failing thrifts. The public was already hearing predictions of its demise, in part in the writings of Professor Kane. The value of the guarantees, argued Kane, no longer came from the money in the funds, but from the belief that incumbent politicians would inevitably bail them out. Hence the global shock when Celeste and the Ohio legislature didn't automatically do so.

The markets may have been surprised, but the political posturing in Ohio foreshadowed how Congress would react when the national FSLIC crisis emerged a year later. In analyzing the Bank Holiday, Professor Kane drew a number of cynical conclusions that proved just as true for a federal debacle whose stakes were one thousand times larger.

Kane saw the Ohio crisis as the product of a series of cover-ups by the thrifts, the regulators, and the politicians. As long as the thrift owner played with other people's money, especially insured money, the natural incentive was to keep on gambling. The further he fell behind, the greater his motive to take the big risk. You didn't have to be a crook to give into this pressure, but it helped. And while you were betting the bank, of course you told depositors and regulators that all was well. The regulators, said Kane, had more to gain by going along with the game than by closing it down. Their greatest reward, he argued, came in trying to make a "clean getaway."

What Kane said in his academic prose amounts bluntly to this: the salary of a bank or thrift supervisor isn't enough to make the job worthwhile. The greedy ones count on making up the difference when they leave the government. In the meantime, they don't want to do anything to hurt their chances for a good job in the private sector. Like many purely economic arguments, this one does serious injustice to the many people who display outstanding honesty, integrity, and courage, the unquantifiable virtues, but there are plenty of examples to bear it out.

There is less need to make this caveat when it comes to the politicians. Their game was to defer the crisis until it could be blamed on somebody else. In the meantime, in Kane's words, "managers and stockholders of insolvent firms may be willing to pay a high price in political contributions for authorities to overlook their insolvent condition."

The cover-up was possible on all sides because the government controlled the information. Bank and thrift records were protected from public view by long habits of confidentiality, enforced by bank secrecy legislation. The only check came from state examinations, and examiners themselves were sworn to secrecy. The examiners sometimes seemed to have more to fear from the banking law than did crooked bankers. Publication of the examiners' ratings, said Kane, would have helped discipline the troubled thrifts before their failure. But with deposit insurance in place, neither clients nor competitors worried about the lack of information.

These restrictions suited politicians as well, because they shielded them from criticism for a poor job. If a crisis broke, they had "deniability." (One of Huddleston's memos listed among the duties of the thrift supervisor, "to protect the governor.") Kane marveled that the "watchdog" press was so willing to accept "official misrepresentations" of the condition of the deposit insurance funds, in view of the "straightforwardness of incentives for officials to lie."

Kane's analysis applied equally well to the Maryland thrift crisis, a close parallel to Ohio. On May 14, 1985, Governor Hughes declared a state of public crisis for Maryland's privately insured thrifts. The Maryland Savings-Share Insurance Corporation (MSSIC) was about to be wiped out by runs on a handful of its 120 members. It was a large handful, however, including its second- and fourth-largest members. Once again a few thrifts had been looted by several masters of financial fraud while the regulators watched in paralysis. The owner of one of these thrifts had been accused of diverting funds for his own use in 1978. Examinations of his thrift, Old Court, showed numerous violations in 1983 and 1984. After six months of dithering, the MSSIC board had not taken firm disciplinary action by the time the crisis erupted. The trigger of the crisis was the failure of yet another government securities dealer, Bevill, Bresler & Schulman of New Jersey. (Six of these securities firms went belly up during this period; Ron Ewton had worked for three of them, including Bevill Bresler.)

One new twist came from MSSIC's lawyers, the ancient and powerful Baltimore establishment firm Venable, Baetje and Howard. A senior partner of Venable served the MSSIC as general counsel while taking a retainer from one of the fund's most predatory thrift owners. The Venable partner persuaded MSSIC that its guarantee extended to every single account in a thrift, rather than simply to the depositor. He also discouraged the fund from disciplining his other client. The Venable firm ultimately paid the state $27 million in a legal malpractice settlement, the second largest on record.

Both Ohio and Maryland discovered that it is easier to start a Bank Holiday than to end one, something Roosevelt's Treasury Department could have told them. It took nearly a year for the last of the closed ODGF thrifts to reopen. Limits on withdrawals from some MSSIC institutions lasted for more than two years. Nearly all of the main participants in Ohio received some legal punishment, thanks mainly to the hard work of its Special Prosecutor, Cincinnati Attorney Lawrence Kane. E. S. M.'s Ewton received a nine-year sentence in an Ohio fraud trial, to be followed by a 15-year federal term. Home State President Burton Bongard was sentenced to ten years. Warner was convicted in Ohio state court and given a three-and-a-half year term (now on appeal), even though a federal jury in Michigan found him innocent on federal charges. The Michigan jury foreman called him a victim of fraud rather than its perpetrator.

At the time, these examples seemed like powerful deterrents. I thought that the scandal of Home State would discourage political interference in regulation for years to come. I was younger then. As Edward Kane described it, the perverse incentives of deposit insurance were too powerful, both for crooked thrift owners and for politicians. Completely oblivious to the proven potential for damage, elected officials became more heavy-handed than ever in their bullying of the regulators when the regulators refused to play their game. In the earlier incidents, the influence of the Butchers and Ambassador Warner had been subtle, circumstantial, and hard to pin down. From 1986 on, as the costs multiplied a hundredfold, the political interventions became blatant and well documented, and no one seemed to feel ashamed.

CHAPTER TEN

□□□

The Seamless Web (I)

□ 1 □

IT MAY SEEM PECULIAR THAT so many people in this story knew each other. Of course, the world is filled with hidden structures; networking, the sociologists say, comes naturally to human beings. Nothing is illegal or even sinister about people who know each other through their sports or their politics and do business together. But citizens should be concerned when business ventures linked by political connections start to cost them money.

Even before the $300 billion debacle in the savings and loan industry, much of which will come directly from the taxpayer's pocket, bills were coming due. Ohioans had to pay more than $120 million for the collapse of Home State. The billion dollars it cost the FDIC to clean up the Butchers' empire came first from the banking industry, which passed the additional charge to its customers. Further down the road this debacle, and others like it, may drain FDIC reserves to the point that it too could become a public charge. By this measure alone, the regulators failed in a big way.

There was also a more subtle and more dangerous cost: the growing conviction that the regulators could be called off. In the spreading demoralization, respectable bankers were tempted to cross the line, and the crooks flocked to the industry. Did political ties help spread this corruption? Before we can answer that question, we first have to determine just what the political connections were.

A web does bind the characters we have encountered. Sometimes the strands connect only a few, but then someone at one end will connect with another group until the pattern becomes a closed loop. At other times, the bonds are strong, broad, and openly acknowledged. A host of minor relationships complete the loops, until the picture resembles the undistrubed product of a busy spider. A number of these webs, across the country, often share more than a few stray strands. The most troubled Texas and California thrifts have spun a sinister mesh of their own. Another trails across a number of smaller thrifts and banks in New York and New Jersey. But the trail we've followed from Florida through Tennessee and Kentucky to Ohio has its own coherent center. The main players, and a substantial supporting cast, all came together in Jimmy Carter's 1976 presidential campaign.

□ 2 □

THE CUBAN CONNECTION

AS THE WFC COLLAPSED AROUND HIM, Guillermo Hernandez-Cartaya gave an interview to one of Miami's Spanish-language papers claiming that he had made a large political contribution to Jimmy Carter. He personally doesn't appear in the Federal Election Commission's list of large contributors to Carter's main committee, but two of his associates do. Enrique ("Kaki") Argomaniz, the middle-aged playboy who first led Metro-Dade detectives from the dumpster to the WFC office, shows up as an "in-kind" donor of $1,000. A New York insurance executive named Reginald J. Denton is listed for $750. Denton, a native of north Georgia, was a close friend of Hernandez-Cartaya, dating from Guillermo's stay in Atlanta. As chairman of the Foreign Credit Insurance Association, a government-sponsored trade group to insure the billings on exports, Denton helped float the WFC by directing large deposits to it. A strong supporter of Carter, he was forced to resign from the FCIA shortly after organizing an expensive campaign bash at the chrome and glass "Windows on the World" restaurant at the top of the World Trade Center. But a recent FCIA official hinted that his campaign work wasn't the reason he left. The FBI heard from an informant that Denton later went to work for Bert Lance at Carter's Office of Management and Budget, but the report can't be verified. OMB says that personal records from Bert Lance's stay were lost when the agency switched to a new computer system.

Denton maintained a murky connection with the WFC. The weekend before Hernandez-Cartaya closed on his purchase of the Hialeah bank (later the National Bank of South Florida), Denton flew with him on a Saturday jaunt to Panama. Hernandez delivered $3 million to pay for the bank the next Monday. During the next year, the NBSF carried a $500,000 loan to Denton that a bank officer called an "evergreen," meaning unpaid. An OCC examiner found it "questionable." The WFC also carried Denton on its payroll, at $5,000 a month.

Hernandez-Cartaya employed a fascinating conduit for his payments to Denton. He frequently sent a short, heavy-set bodyguard named Salvador Aldereguia on a plane ride north to meet the Georgian. Aldereguia, a former veterinarian nicknamed "Gallego," the rooster, was an engaging clown whose antics constantly amused Guillermo. On one plane ride, Gallego passed himself off to a seatmate as Hernandez-Cartaya. The fellow traveller happened to be a banker; in their ensuing conversation, he was baffled by Gallego's utter ignorance of finance. WFC officers were dismayed by the incident, since they thought it hurt their reputation, but Hernandez-Cartaya laughed. Gallego, the Rooster, was also known in Miami's Little Havana as an agent of Cuban intelligence. "He doesn't deny it," said one well-informed Spanish-language radio journalist. A Cuban government defector, a former Finance Ministry adviser named José Luis Llovio-Menendez, reported seeing Gallego in Havana, in the corridor of the Ministry of the Interior. Llovio-Menendez said that the Rooster was known in Havana as "Samuel" (pronounced sam-WELL).

I first encountered Llovio-Menendez, now a good friend, through a fellow journalist specializing in Latin America. In their first interview, I suggested that my journalist friend ask about "Samuel." Jose Luis responded to the question by saying, "I thought we weren't going to talk about security." Llovio-Menendez has since written a highly recommended book, *Insider, My Hidden Life as a Revolutionary in Cuba.* When it appeared, he was roundly attacked by the Cuban-American National Foundation, a once-respected lobbying group that had fallen into the hands of a Miami clique that included former friends and business associates of Hernandez-Cartaya. (The president of the foundation, Jorge Mas Canosa, wrote a letter pleading for a light sentence for one of Hernandez-Cartaya's codefendents in the tax evasion trial.)

Aldereguia was astonishingly successful at disarming adversaries through his affability and his concentration on social work (that is, helping Miami refugees get their relatives out of Cuba). A mutual acquaintance, a fierce anti-Communist who said he once infiltrated Cuba to try to assassinate Castro, maintained a friendship with Aldereguia "because he never did anything to hurt anybody." He added, "I saved his life several times." Aldereguia, a naturalized United States citizen, now lives in Miami in self-proclaimed retirement. He declined a request for an interview, saying he wanted to live in peace.

Samuel became a cause célèbre on March 3, 1978, when the FBI arrested Aldereguia at Miami International Airport as he was about to board an Air Jamaica flight for Kingston, Jamaica. According to the *Miami Herald,* a search of his briefcase yielded a letter from a Cuban secret police agent addressed to " 'Samuel', a Cuban spy working in Miami," ordering him to come home. Denying that he was "Samuel," Aldereguia was charged with forging the passport that Hernandez-Cartaya used to flee Ajman. "It was a charge we came up with literally on a Friday afternoon," said then assistant United States Attorney R. Jerome Sanford. "We heard that Aldereguia was about to leave for Cuba, and we wanted to stop him." The prosecution case, "against two Cubans in Miami at the peak of the energy crisis," was almost hopeless, and both were acquitted.

But Gallego's briefcase contained other fascinating leads. In addition to Denton's phone number, the Rooster was carrying three business cards from the law firm of Levey, Levenstein and Cowan. Leonard L. Levenstein, a name partner, was one of the first large contributors to the political career of State Comptroller Gerald Lewis. Levenstein was also the first lawyer that the pistol-packing banker Juan Evelio Pou called after one of his arrests for trying to take a loaded weapon aboard an airliner. (Pou, you'll remember, bought the NBSF from Hernandez-Cartaya.) In 1983, Levenstein was charged with transporting cash from a client's drug-smuggling conspiracy to the Bahamas for laundering. Levenstein pleaded guilty. Comptroller Lewis was criticized for his delay in suspending Levenstein from his post as director of a Dade County bank.

It might raise eyebrows that a suspected Cuban spy had these names on his Rolodex: one, a political intimate of the Florida state comptroller and the other, a head of a quasi-governmental agency with ties to the White House. But that's not the end of the story. Says Llovio-Menendez of his former government, "1977 and 1978 were the years of our greatest penetration in the United States." The Carter administration opened a direct line to Castro, using yet another friend of Hernandez-Cartaya.

For more than ten years, the red-haired, bespectacled banker Dr. Bernardo Benes was one of the most controversial men in Miami. Born in Cuba in 1934 and educated at the University of Havana when it was a hotbed of revolutionaries, he came to the United States in 1960. In 1976, he became vice chairman of the board of Continental National Bank of Miami, the city's first Cuban-owned bank. A year later, while on vacation in Panama, he met an old university friend, then a high official in the Cuban government. This friend invited him to Cuba. Clearing the trip with the CIA and the United States State Department, Benes went, the first of 75 such visits, which included meetings with Fidel Castro himself. As planned, Castro opened direct contact with United States Cuban exiles. Benes helped free hundreds of political prisoners and opened Cuba to visits from the exile community. Although widely condemned in Miami, he may have done more inadvertent damage to Cuban communism than any of the anti-Castro activists. Exposure to the American exiles and their high standard of living unleashed a wave of discontent in Cuba that culminated in the Mariel exodus.

Benes moved in Carter's highest circles. "Cyrus Vance was my rabbi," he said. In 1979, his contact with Ricardo de la Espriella, vice president of Panama, president of its national bank, and also a close friend, led to the exile of the Shah of Iran to Panama's Contadora Island, a bit of shuffling that Carter's advisers thought would help resolve the Teheran embassy hostage crisis. (De la Espriella was also a close friend of Hernandez-Cartaya.) Politically, Benes was part of a circle of early Carter supporters known in 1976 as the "Eighth Street Latin Cabinet."

As usual, there was a dark side. In 1979, the Senate Banking Committee investigated money laundering in south Florida. Benes and his Continental National Bank were prominently mentioned. Benes drew further fire when he told NBC News, "It's not really up to bankers" to police drug money. (Although the United States Treasury did target the Continental National Bank, neither the bank nor Benes were ever charged with a crime.) In the contacts with Cuba, reported the *Wall Street Journal,* Benes was meeting with Colonel Antonio de la Guardia, in charge of an Interior Ministry unit running a network of front companies designed to break the United States blockade. Castro ordered Colonel de la Guardia's execution in the summer of 1989 after obtaining a confession that his network also helped the Medellin Cartel smuggle cocaine to the United States.

Benes has a close friend in the superbly connected Miami lawyer Alfredo Duran, who in 1975 had become the first Cuban, or Hispanic, to head a state Democratic party. Duran had also married the daughter of Cuba's last elected president, the notoriously corrupt Carlos Prio Socarras. At one meeting in Havana, said Benes, "Fidel put his arm around me and asked, 'Why didn't you bring Alfredo?' " As state chairman, Duran helped organize the 1975 state convention straw poll that was Carter's first campaign breakthrough. Duran was another member of the Calle Ocho (Eighth Street) Cabinet, named after the thoroughfare of small shops, cafes and exile offices that cuts through Miami's Little Havana, but his real strength lay downtown. He was counsel to Stephen Arky's law firm. He sat on the board of Marvin Warner's American Bancshares, Inc., later Great American Banks. He maintained trust accounts in the Coronas' Sunshine State Bank, and he acted as lawyer and trustee for the fugitive Venezuelan Juan Vicente Perez Sandoval. An informant's report from the files of the old Bureau of Narcotics and Dangerous Drugs, predecessor of the Drug Enforcement Administration, shows how ancient and intricate the ties can be that bind these networks. When Duran, a veteran of the Bay of Pigs, married the daughter of Carlos Prio in the early 1970s, another Brigada 2506 veteran, the drug dealer José Alvero-Cruz, shared a table at the wedding reception with the former state senator who was a target of the Blue Ridge Farms Dairy dumpster investigation.

□ 3 □

THE TALLAHASSEE JUNTA

HERNANDEZ-CARTAYA CULTIVATED FRIENDSHIPS among Anglo politicians as well. From 1976 to 1978, his story intersected broadly with that of the clique that was consolidating its hold on the state's financial regulation. William Dawson Gunter, a red-haired, round-faced Baptist from north Florida, was elected insurance commissioner and treasurer in 1976. One of the WFC officers said the company donated $21,000 to Gunter's campaign and gave him the use of the corporate jet. Large, curly-headed Robert Shevin from Miami was winding up two terms as state attorney general. Hernandez-Cartaya and associates contributed to Shevin's campaign, and the two became friends. In March 1978, when Cartaya was in deep trouble and Shevin was the front-runner for the Democratic nomination for governor, a Coral Gables detective reported the following incident.

Responding to Hernandez-Cartaya's complaints of death threats, the officer found the house a virtual armed camp, surrounded by six to eight bodyguards. He started to warn Cartaya about the legal use of weapons, when the financier interrupted.

"When Bob was here for his birthday, he gave me the legal advice I need," Hernandez-Cartaya said. "I know about the law for the guns."

"Bob Shevin?" asked the detective.

Hernandez-Cartaya said yes.

The only member of the cabinet junta untouched by Hernandez-Cartaya was State Comptroller Gerald Lewis, at the time a "good-government" reformer. In 1974, the slicked-down, Harvard-educated Lewis had beaten an incumbent under investigation for, among other things, selling bank charters. The incumbent was later convicted on lesser charges. In 1978, Hernandez-Cartaya approached Lewis with a campaign contribution, but an alert staffer knew about his legal trouble and persuaded Lewis to turn him down.

When Shevin left office in 1979, he rejoined his Miami law firm and built a strong practice before the bank regulators. He displayed his magic in the Sunshine State case, but it was by no means the only miracle he worked. He and his partners also became important political contributors and fund raisers. His firm was only one of several that played that role, however. The most dramatic rise among the political lawyers was that of Richard Swann, a dark-haired Orlando native widely known as the alter ego of Insurance Commissioner Bill Gunter. After meeting Gunter in 1963 at the South Orlando Kiwanis Club, Swann raised money for Gunter's campaigns for the State Senate in 1966, the United States House in 1972 and the United States Senate in 1974. (Gunter lost only the run for U.S. Senate, a goal that eluded him four times.)

Swann's big break, however, came in 1974, when Rosalynn Carter enlisted him in her husband's presidential campaign. (Swann met Rosalynn through a Rollins College student who rented a room over his garage and introduced him to a close friend of hers from Calhoun, Georgia.) Swann became Carter's biggest fund raiser in Florida, where the Georgia governor's primary victory put him in the front of the race. Swann too moved to the front rank. "Before the Carter campaign, Swann was just another Florida lawyer," said one associate. Afterward he became a formidable power.

As the Swann and Haddock law firm grew rapidly, Swann bought an Orlando thrift and took control of a troubled insurance company. Swann received some help with the latter when Marvin Warner's ComBanks, headquartered in nearby Winter Park, called a loan to the company, forcing out its previous management. In 1980, under the provisions of Florida's Sunset Law, the state banking code expired. Swann was influential in adding language to the new code that greatly expanded the investment powers for thrifts. This provision helped him pull off an unusual "reverse merger" of his insurance company into his thrift to produce a conglomerate called the American Pioneer Corp. Although financially troubled, Swann's thrift has not been accused of fraudulent practices. Carter gave Swann a patronage appointment carrying ambassadorial rank, but the Orlando lawyer's focus remained firmly local. His political and economic power rested firmly on a network of Orlando-area businessmen and political contributors such as the developer Everette Huskey.

Over the years, the Swann and Haddock firm helped several controversial characters win insurance company charters, in circumstances that have sometimes drawn the attention of federal grand juries, although no charges have resulted. The most interesting case involved Guillermo Hernandez-Cartaya, who tried to rescue his fortunes in 1978 by incorporating an insurance company. Gunter turned him down only after news of the scandal hit the *New York Times*. During this effort, according to later congressional testimony, Hernandez-Cartaya hired Swann to help drum up endorsements.

□ 4 □

THE BUTCHERS IN FLORIDA

AS THE BUTCHER BROTHERS neared the end of their run in Tennessee, they turned to the Florida network for help. In June 1982, C. H. Butcher, Jr. targeted a thrift in posh Palm Beach, the Home Federal

Savings and Loan. His confederates accumulated stock throughout the summer. After courtroom maneuvers, the board of Home Federal decided to accept a bid from C. H. Along the way, the Butchers fended off a rival bid from none other than Shepard Broad, chairman of American Savings and Loan, who wanted to expand up the Florida coast. The ubiquitous Stephen Arky brought C. H., Jr. and Jake together with Shep Broad and his son Morris for a lunch at the oceanfront Sheraton Key Biscayne, but C. H., Jr. wanted the deal for himself. Even before making a tender offer, he controlled enough stock to place his own man in the thrift. Home Federal soon bought loans from the Knoxville banks, especially development loans to the Butchers' friends on the Florida Panhandle's "Redneck Riviera."

The Florida venture grew more urgent as fall progressed. By the end of November 1982, examiners swarmed over the Butchers' banking chain. The round robin loans were about to unwind. By the first week in January, C. H. had raised $25 million, mainly in loans to himself, to complete the purchase. Half a million of the proceeds eventually wound up in a trust account at the Arky Freed law firm, where it disappeared from view.

The Butchers brought in an old Florida hand to help close the deal. C. H., Jr. incorporated two shell outfits, City & County Acquisition Services and C&C Interstate Financial Corporation. He put Randy Attkisson on their board, the same Attkisson who had recently resigned as Kentucky banking commissioner and who, as the second man in First Louisville's international department, had previously helped William Isaac dispose of Hernandez-Cartaya's bank in Hialeah. The chairmen of the corporation was Emmett J. Foster, who ran ten of C. H., Jr.'s banks.

To the FDIC examiners poring over the Butchers' books, the Florida thrifts looked like a new dumping ground for bad loans. "I think S&Ls in Florida were the key," reads one examiner's handwritten notes. "If they could have acquired them they could have buried a lot of the shit." The FDIC passed the word to the Home Loan Bank Board, which scotched the acquisitions. The thrift regulators also ordered Home Federal to send back the loan participations the Butchers had dumped on it. Some $22 million in bad loans flowed back to Knoxville just before the FDIC tried to freeze the round robin. The Bank Board and the FSLIC thus pushed $22 million in losses back into the FDIC's corner, a move that severely strained relations between the two agencies.

The Butchers tried to neutralize this type of regulatory interference when they first moved into Florida, but their target was the state. Comptroller Lewis had just won a hard-fought primary, but his campaign fund was deep in debt, a technical violation of Florida law. The Butchers offered to help out, with an elaborate deal in which the Florida State Democratic party picked up enough of Lewis's campaign bills to balance his books, and Butcher front men gave at least $50,000 to the state committee.

After the collapse in Tennessee, some of the Butchers' circle took refuge with their friends in Florida. Both Jake Butcher and Emmett Foster, chairman of a string of C. H. Butcher's banks, moved their families to lush neighborhoods in Longview, just north of Orlando, that were developed by Everette Huskey, a prominent local builder who was part of Richard Swann's fund-raising network. Before his incarceration, Jake moved to the uppercrust Sweetwater Oaks Club, where polite security men in a wood-shingled guardhouse turn away all outside traffic not cleared with the residents. Like Marvin Warner, Foster declared himself a Florida homesteader, which under state law protected his home from seizure in the event of a personal bankruptcy. By 1986, he had apparently prospered sufficiently from a bank consulting service to move from one of Huskey's middle-class developments into the Sweetwater Oaks Club itself.

□ 5 □

WARNER IN SWITZERLAND

THE FLORIDA-TENNESSEE-OHIO NETWORK has a global extension, perhaps explainable by Marvin Warner's service as ambassador to Switzerland. By the time Warner returned to the United States, he had become friends and partners with a shadowy Geneva multimillionaire named Bruce Rappaport. The founder of an empire of banks and chartered oil tankers, Rappaport at one point was so secretive he wouldn't reveal the time or place of his birth. He apparently feared that his Arab clients would be offended to learn that he was born in 1922 of Russian Jewish immigrants to Haifa, in what was then the British Mandate of Palestine and now is Israel. Rappaport became a naturalized Swiss citizen in the 1950s and built a far-flung chandling company. (Chandlers supply ships with ropes, linen, and other supplies, including, in Rappaport's case, frozen food.) He expanded rapidly into managing and leasing vessels and set up the privately owned Inter Maritime Bank as his financing vehicle.

Rappaport's most famous coup came in 1977, when he sued the government of Indonesia for $1 billion and tried to attach its shipping fleet around the world. The president of Pertamina, the Indonesian oil company, had signed $1.3 billion in promissory notes in arranging oil tanker charters with Rappaport, his close friend and golfing partner. The Pertamina head, General Ibnu Sutowo, had also received a $2.5 million loan from Rappaport's Inter Maritime Bank. The Indonesian government eventually settled with a payment of $150 million and declared Rappaport an "enemy of the state."

More recently, Rappaport attracted attention in the controversy about former United States Attorney General Edwin Meese. Rappaport was pushing a project to build an oil pipeline from Iraq to Jordan's southern port of Aqaba, the headquarters of Lawrence of Arabia in World War I. Rappaport hired Meese's close friend Robert Wallach, later a defendant in the Wedtech bribery case, to lobby for National Security Council support. Although Meese made inquiries, neither he nor Rappaport were accused of wrongdoing for it.

It's unlikely that Warner could pass up a chance to work with a wheeler-dealer of Rappaport's proportions, and the two became partners in an off-shore outfit called Swiss American Holding Co. This Panamanian corporation owned two banks in the Caribbean island nation of Antigua, whose stringent bank secrecy law is said to have been drafted by Stephen Arky. In 1982, Home State pledged $1 million for its share of the capital. Warner and Rappaport apparently had big plans to turn Antigua into a new financial center, with a Club Med, Israeli-tutored agri-business and an oil refinery.

But plans were disrupted by the failure of Home State. In the aftermath of the bankruptcy, Warner's half of the Antigua bank fell into the hands of the State of Ohio. This happenstance could have opened a rare window into the world of offshore banking. (According to an auditor's report, a large number of the bank's depositors were so concerned about confidentiality that they had instructed the bank not to forward mail to them.) But Ohio's trustees showed a remarkable lack of curiosity. One lawyer explained that they wanted to preserve the bank's value, which lay mainly in its secrecy. Rappaport eventually bought out Warner's share.

The Rappaport connection fascinated the agencies trying to track the flow of Warner's money. An SEC court filing noted that Warner vacationed in the Caribbean in January 1985, just as Ewton was bailing out of E. S. M. In mid-March, days after the failure of Home State, Warner flew to England and Switzerland. He arrived in Geneva by train on the morning of Saturday, March 16, the day after Celeste declared the Ohio Bank Holiday. According to his office memos, Warner planned to spend the weekend with Rappaport discussing the affairs of their Swiss American National Bank.

In a current suit, the SEC has accused Warner of handling offshore money for others as well, and there is a solid rumor that one of the Antigua bank's accounts involved Jake Butcher. It appears that a loan to Butcher may have been channeled through the bank. Whatever the details, there is good testimony that Jake knew Rappaport. From his jail cell, Jesse Barr followed the Meese-Wallach-pipeline stories with great interest. "Yes, it is the same one," he wrote me about Rappaport, "and he has been to Jake's house for dinner. In fact, Jake went to Switzerland to see him before he went to jail. . . Like you say, Small World."

PART FOUR

The Education of Edwin Gray

CHAPTER ELEVEN

□□□

The Making of an Outcast

□ 1 □

IN EARLY JUNE 1983, five weeks into his term as chief regulator of the nation's thrifts, Ed Gray flew to Dallas for one of the most remarkable parties of his life. He was making an appearance at the annual convention of the Texas Savings and Loan League, at the behest of a fellow member of the Federal Home Loan Bank Board. He spent the cocktail hour in the bedroom of a luxurious hotel suite, listening to the Texas League lobbyist Durward Curlee recount his politicking over an open seat on Gray's Bank Board. Curlee, a short, garrulous character who delighted in telling unvarnished tales about the state's thrifts, claimed that his friends were pushing the state's previous savings and loan commissioner for the seat because they wanted to replace him with their friend Linton Bowman. The commissioner, Alvis Vandygriff, had resigned but failed to get the federal appointment. Bowman, the new commissioner, sat and listened with the rest. At the end, he mentioned something to Gray about several problems that would be coming up. The names didn't mean much to Gray, who was new to the territory, and he promptly forgot them.

It was time for dinner, and Spencer Blain, the president of the Texas League, loaded the party into his blue Rolls Royce for the short drive to the restaurant. The place was filled with guests from the convention, including the head of the regional Home Loan Bank. "Everybody who was anybody was there," remembers Gray.

After dinner the group returned to the hotel, formerly the Registry, where Blain was staying in the penthouse. Bowman, the state commissioner, and Curlee, the lobbyist, pulled out guitars and played honky-tonk favorites. Gray says his taste runs to classical music, but he was thoroughly charmed. "I'd had a drink or two," he explained. "It was ten or eleven at night." Gray had a weakness for luxury, and he regulated an industry that was more than willing to cater to it, but this was the peak of their bonhomie. The good-ol'-boy spirit evaporated rapidly as the Texas thrift operators and their confederates found out that they had misread their man.

The national thrift lobby had pushed Gray for Bank Board chairman, perhaps because they counted on him to be a pliable free-market Reaganite. They misunderstood both Gray and free-market economics. Gray made compromises as great as any forced on a federal regulator and with far more costly impact. But by the same token, he took a stronger stand on principle than anyone, including himself, had reason to expect. His reward was vilification from the industry, Congress, much of his own administration, and a good part of the press. He bore the full weight of the most overt and most successful attempt to politicize regulation that we have yet encountered. It could have been crushing if his vindication hadn't been so thorough and dramatic. In the end, Gray outlasted his enemies. His instinctive understanding of the needs of a free market proved sounder than the prevailing doctrine of deregulation, in whose name so many crimes were committed.

□ 2 □

ED GRAY'S FATHER, EDWIN ARCHER GRAY, came to California from Texas as a boy, settling in the south-central Imperial Valley. "He had something like an eighth grade education," said Gray. "They were poor. He had to work." The family moved through central California, up the great San Joaquin Valley, working in the fields that stretch north and south as far as the eye can see. Edwin Archer settled in Turlock, 90 miles south of Sacramento, where he helped maintain the water pumps, lifeline of agriculture in that semiarid climate. He became a salesman for a company that sold the pumps. Then he bought his own hardware and farm machinery business and moved to Modesto, the commercial center of the region 13 miles north. Edwin John Gray was born there in 1935, to a family that knew the value of hard work and free enterprise. They had deep populist roots reinforced by Baptist fundamentalism. Although Edwin John was later called a "quintessential Reaganite," he grew up a Democrat and did not change registration until shortly before going to work for Reagan. Gray stood out at Modesto High School as valedictorian and champion debater, and he entered the College of the Pacific in Stockton on a debating scholarship. With his deep, sonorous voice, he was a natural for radio, and he earned his way through college as a broadcaster, switching schools twice because of the demands of his jobs.

After graduation from California State University in Fresno in 1957 and a stint in the National Guard, Gray travelled through Europe, studying a semester at the University of Barcelona and working on the side for United Press International. In 1963, he got married, came home to California, and settled into a job in public relations with the Pacific Telephone and Telegraph Company in Sacramento.

The decisive change in Gray's life came in 1966 with the election of Ronald Reagan, the fading actor and free enterprise spokesman for General Electric, as governor of California. Reagan's staff went to the telephone company looking for volunteers to help with the inauguration. The company seconded Gray, still on its payroll, and he took to the job like a duck to water. He remembered scouring California's Spanish missions for the oldest Bible in the state, to be used in the swearing in. At the Carmel Mission, he found the Bible brought to California by the eighteenth-century missionary Fr. Junipero Serra, now a candidate for sainthood, and, as part of the inaugural buildup, he displayed it in the window of a Sacramento jewelry store. Reagan took the oath of office a few minutes after midnight on January 2, 1967, a time gossip mongers claimed was chosen by astrology.

The occasion was propitious for Gray. Remembering his work, Reagan's chief of staff called him that fall and asked him to join the governor in his press office. Gray said that he had been a Republican for only a year and hadn't even voted for Reagan in the primary. Perhaps with Reagan's own late conversion in mind, the governor's men told him not to worry. For the next six years, Gray became Reagan's spokesman, learning his mind as well as anyone. Each year, he renewed his leave of absence from the telephone company.

Gray first turned his attention to the thrift industry when a friend from the governor's cabinet left to head San Diego Federal Savings and offered him a job. Several years later, at the end of Reagan's last term, Gray took up the offer. He worked as senior vice president for public affairs for the next six years. In 1980, the Reagan people called again. Reagan had just won the New Hampshire primary and fired his campaign director. Would Gray come on board as press secretary? Gray hesitated to accept the cut in salary and took the fateful plunge only after Reagan himself asked for his help. I first met Ed Gray at this time, at the nondescript Reagan national headquarters near the Los Angeles International Airport. I was working for the *Wall Street Journal* editorial page and had been asked to harass Gray a bit about some state secret that had been leaked to the *Journal* and then picked up without attribution by the Reagan campaign. Gray, medium height, squarely built with a square jaw and an open, friendly smile, was extremely pleasant, explaining that they too had received the leaked document and that if they cited the *Journal* as a source, other papers wouldn't report it. As he fumbled in his briefcase for the document, without finding it, I thought that the real story might be the understaffing of the Reagan campaign. Gray was a nice guy, no doubt about it, but his bumbling, homespun style made him easy to underestimate.

The same was often said of Gray's boss, soon-to-be President Reagan, and looking back, one can see that both men had a great deal of overlooked substance. During and after the transition, Gray moved into the office of policy development during one of the greatest policy upheavals of the generation. But his family couldn't take the steamy climate in Washington, and he missed California. "I just decided I don't need this for the rest of my life," he said. "I'd used up literally all of my savings and borrowed on my house." So he moved back to his San Diego thrift. He became a leading voice in support of the impending Garn-St Germain Act, and the phone calls started. Nearly every day, Gray recalled, someone from the industry would telephone urging him to consider becoming chairman of the Federal Home Loan Bank Board. "You know the President," they would say. "You know the industry."

In January 1983, the call came from the White House, and Gray said yes again. His confirmation, he said, was as smooth as could be, "like a knife cutting through soft butter," except for one extraneous and portentous complication. Under pressure from the Texas thrifts, the Bank Board was considering relocating its southwest regional Home Loan Bank from Little Rock, Arkansas to Dallas. In a last-ditch protest, the two senators from Arkansas tried to hold up Gray's nomination. But the Bank Board had made up its mind, and Gray later voted for the move as well. He was sworn in as a member of the Board on March 24, 1983 and became its chairman on May 1.

The honeymoon lasted into the summer, two months after that evening in Dallas with the Texas Savings and Loan League. Gray dates the beginning of his awakening to August 1983, at a monthly briefing by his Office of Examinations and Supervision. "They said we had a real problem," Gray recalled. "The spread cases were turning into bad asset cases." And the bad asset cases were five to six times as bad. Up to that point, the policy of the board, and Congress, had been to relieve the pressure on thrifts from their negative "spreads," their inability to earn more on their loans than they paid out in deposits. Garn-St Germain, and the Bank Board's regulations, had given the thrifts new investment and lending powers in an effort to boost their earnings. But now these new investments were going bad. Some owners had turned truly reckless because none of their own money was at stake. In an attempt to hide the losses of the previous four years, the Bank Board had reduced capital requirements further and further. Even worse, there was no discipline from the depositors. Some of the worst cases were supported "by an awful lot of money coming from every direction." Deposit brokers were chasing the highest interest rates around the country, relying only on the federal deposit insurance for their safety net. "All of a sudden," said Gray, "I found myself in this miserable situation of realizing that this policy was severely flawed."

Gray decided to target the money brokers as the root of the evil. He found a strong ally in FDIC Chairman Isaac—too strong, in fact, for the taste of some of his own Bank Board colleagues. "The FDIC and the Bank Board had always been at loggerheads," said Gray, "and here I was conniving with the enemy, in common cause to deal with the problem." After laborious negotiations, the two agencies issued regulations on January 16, 1984 that would have severely restricted brokered deposits. (Basically, the deposit funds would have treated a deposit broker as if all the accounts came from a single depositor, thus limiting the insurance coverage to $100,000.) One of the largest of the brokers, the Miami-based FAIC Securities Inc., promptly challenged the rule in court. To the amazement of Gray's attorneys, the judge in the United States Court of Appeals, D.C. Circuit, ruled that the regulation exceeded the authority of the FSLIC and the FDIC. The next step would be to draft legislation to provide that authority, but Gray and Isaac knew that step was hopeless. "The very day we lost, we had drafted a bill," said Gray. "But there was no way Congress was going to help."

Gray and Isaac were turning against a tide that was still running strong. The Bank Board had opened the flood gates for brokered deposits in 1980 when it repealed a rule limiting the "hot money" to no more than five percent of a thrift's total. More important, the industry now riding on this tide had an extremely important supporter at the top of Reagan's cabinet.

Donald Regan, then secretary of the Treasury, had previously been chairman of Merrill Lynch, the giant securities firm. His "thundering herd" of salesmen had been bullish indeed on brokered deposits. According to the FDIC, Merrill had become far and away the largest supplier of hot money to troubled banks and thrifts. By 1985, it had handled more than $770 million in fully insured jumbo CDs.

Regan was mindful of an apparent conflict of interest and personally stayed out of the fray. But Gray maintains that Treasury underlings took up the slack. Gray said that Treasury Deputy Secretary Tim McNamar spent seven hours on the phone with Gray before the brokered funds regulation came out, trying to talk him out of it.

Treasury and others argued that the brokers increased the efficiency of the capital markets, sending money to the regions that needed it. Need was indicated by high interest rates—in market terms, the price of the money. In rejecting this argument, Gray appeared to be an unsophisticated "re-regulator;" the issue was his first major break with Regan, and the beginning of a virulent feud that lasted for both their tenures. Gray's gut argument was that sooner or later, "the taxpayer would get stuck with the bill." His visceral reaction also made more sense than Treasury's sophisms. The thrifts hadn't been deregulated at all. The more than doubling of deposit insurance coverage had insulated them even further from the pressures of a truly free market. Congress and the Bank Board had given thrift owners a practically unlimited government subsidy and asked very little in return.

In chasing high interest rates, the brokers were cashing in on the "risk premium." Investors know, or should know, that when you get a higher than average interest rate, you accept a higher than average risk that you won't get your money back. Since the brokers could reap the higher interest and let FSLIC or FDIC take the risk, they channeled vast sums to the thrifts that had to pay the most to get their deposits, meaning to the thrifts making the riskiest investments, meaning to the crooks.

Ed Gray was soon to learn just how crooked the riskier thrifts had become. The details of that day are burned into his memory. It was March 14, 1984. Gray woke up at 4:00 or 5:00 A.M. to type the summary remarks, as he always did, for congressional testimony later that morning. He was going to tell the Barnard subcommittee once more about the horrors of brokered deposits. Before his testimony, he attended a director's meeting at the Bank Board building across the street from the White House compound. There he saw the video. It was a 20-minute tape played on a VCR in the Bank

Board's sixth floor conference room. Officers of the Ninth District Home Loan Bank had commissioned a local appraiser to shoot the video to show what was going on in Dallas. It may well have been the most effective audiovisual presentation in the annals of bank and thrift regulation.

The video opened like a home movie, with a hand pointing to a road map with a ballpoint pen. The narrator gave the itinerary, a corridor along the superhighway segment northeast of Dallas, and especially Route I-30 between Dallas and the huge manmade Lake Ray Hubbard in Mesquite. By air and then by highway, the hand-held camera traced this route, showing acres of built and half-built condos, densely packed and virtually unoccupied. His voice occasionally trembling with indignation, the narrator pointed to stockpiles of unused wallboard and ceiling joists; mounds of building scraps; and fire-gutted, vandalized rowhouses. "Complete lack of contractor control," the narrator exclaimed. "Tremendous waste everywhere." Contruction was shoddy; balconies leaned slightly out of plumb; sideboards buckled. There were no shops, schools, or amenities, "no sales effort, no leasing effort," and no people. Even the occasional well-built, heavily promoted project had only 20 to 40 percent occupancy. And still the crews kept on building. Commenting dryly on "contractor sensitivity," the filmmaker remarked, "They followed our vehicle and stopped us on the highway."

This film introduced Ed Gray to the real world of Empire Savings and Loan of Mesquite, the thrift run by the same Spencer Blain who had driven him to dinner in a blue Rolls Royce. The condos were built with no regard to the market or economic feasibility, but simply for the sake of building and generating loans. The densely packed sites had been financed by Empire and a group of related thrifts in one of the biggest land frauds on record. "I had to turn my head away," said Gray. "I couldn't look at it. It was so shameful."

When the lights came on, the three Bank Board directors voted to close Empire. Gray drove up Capitol Hill to deliver a statement whose harsh phrasing conveyed his shock. "The list of horror stories resulting from the misuse of brokered funds by desperate financial institutions," he intoned, "is growing as the weeks and months go on." In the coming weeks, Gray and his staff agonized over Empire S&L, reading documents into the evening to figure out what had gone wrong, and preparing for a congressional investigation.

□ 3 □

GRAY BELATEDLY LEARNED WHAT HIS HOST IN DALLAS, Spencer Hayward Blain, Jr., was really all about. The story was archetypal. Blain, the formerly solid, respectable banker, had been suddenly transformed into a financial swinger under the influence of the vulgar, ostentatious builder Danny Faulkner, a sixth-grade dropout who claimed to be unable to read or write. Until 1982, Blain had a distinguished career running a conservative thrift in Austin. He compiled a long list of industry credentials: vice-chairman of the board of the Federal Home Loan Bank in Little Rock; chairman of the advisory council of the Federal Home Loan Mortgage Corporation in Washington; member of the legislative committee of the United States League, president of the Texas Savings and Loan League. He was a patron of the arts and attended a White House luncheon honoring the President's Commission on the Arts and Humanities. Then something snapped, and he met Danny Faulkner.

David Lamar Faulkner was born in Mississippi on Christmas Day, 1932, the son of sharecroppers. Dyslexic in school, he said that other children taunted him because he couldn't learn to read or write (although on documents his signature, in script, seems firm enough). When he was 12, his lawyer recounted the tale, his teacher asked him to leave the class for a minute. At the door, Faulkner heard her tell his classmates, "Don't make fun of him because he's dumb and stupid. He can't help it." That was his last day in school.

Faulkner came to Dallas as a house painter and got his big break when he worked on the house of a local insurance man. Faulkner told an interviewer that he made a good impression by treating the businessman's wife with respect. When she came into the room where he was painting, he always put his shirt on. Doors opened to him, and as a painting contractor, he prospered. But Faulkner wanted more, and once Blain became his financier and figurehead, he was in a position to get it. Faulkner claimed that Blain first came to see him to check out his first condo development, Faulkner Point. Their partnership allowed him to replicate that project endlessly. Empire and other related thrifts gathered brokered deposits and lent the money to Faulkner's companies. With the cash, they could live the life they saw on television's "Dallas."

Faulkner drew more than casual inspiration from the TV soap opera. His Faulkner Point condos appeared in the show's opening credits. His celebrations matched Hollywood's imagination of Texan behavior. The entire Oklahoma Symphony played during his son's wedding, seated in the church choir section; as guests entered, the orchestra struck up the theme from "Dallas." A fleet of 18 Rolls Royces took the guests to a reception where a chocolate cake in the shape of the Faulkner Point condos occupied one table, and the candy dish featured a large chocolate Lear jet.

Every Saturday morning, Faulkner presided over a breakfast at the Wise Circle Grill on I-30, showering friends with gifts and business deals. His son said that Danny, Sr., may have given away as many as 30 Rolex watches in his career, worth $5,000 each. His land deals made instant millionaires of associates, such as an ex-gym teacher, pilots of his air fleet, and his son's former babysitter, although his beneficiaries often had to plow back their profits into Faulkner's investments. Faulkner also showered his largesse on politicians. Democratic Governor Mark White showed up at his Circle Grill breakfasts and met with him at the Capitol. After the collapse of Empire S&L, Faulkner and White had a falling out; Danny changed his registration to Republican and gave heavily to Republican Governor William Clements. But Faulkner was closest to Dallas Democrat Jim Mattox, formerly congressman with a seat on the House Banking Committee, then Texas Attorney General and, in 1990, candidate for governor.

A Dallas Morning News society writer caught up with Faulkner and Attorney General Mattox at the Southfork Ranch (yes, there is a real Southfork Ranch), where the two were attending the 1985 Cattle Barons Ball. Amid the sea of women in suede and diamonds and men in red plaid shirts and Rolexes, Faulkner and Mattox spent the evening together. "He flew here in my helicopter," explained Faulkner. "I had two helicopters that were supposed to bring in my family and friends, but one of them got broke. So we had to bring half in the helicopter and half in the Rolls Royce."

The two had been close friends since Faulkner moved into Mattox's congressional district in 1977, and in 1979, they were business partners. On December 6, 1982, Danny took their friendship one step further. During a political fund raiser at the home of Dallas banker Jess Hay, Faulkner looked on as his sidekick handed Mattox two checks, totalling $200,000. A witness in Faulkner's 1989 fraud trial testified that Faulkner originally meant for Mattox to earn the money in a "land flip," but then decided not to involve him. Shortly after the fund raiser, Mattox and Governor-elect Mark White showed up at the weekly Circle Grill breakfast. Led by Faulkner, the Circle Grill regulars pitched in between $50,000 and $60,000 in campaign contributions. "Why did you want to pay Mattox $200,000?" Faulkner was asked in a deposition. "Because I'm a nice man," Faulkner replied.

One of Faulkner's associates, testifying against him at his 1989 trial, gave a different view of Danny's personality. Clifford Sinclair, a crucial figure in the land fraud who had turned state's witness, described a conversation at Faulkner's heliport. Danny wanted to funnel $1.1 million to another of his partners. On the witness stand, Sinclair blurted out that Faulkner said something else interesting. "He was laughing about it," said Sinclair, "and made the remark that he had already bought himself a governor, an attorney general, and now he was buying himself a United States attorney." (All the incumbents that Faulkner had in mind have denied the insinuation.)

Faulkner's broad circle of friends helped him in many ways with his central occupation, conducting what Ed Gray later called, "one of the most reckless and fraudulent land investment schemes we have ever encountered." A central part of the scheme was the "land flip." Faulkner would line up his cronies and take a piece of vacant land worth maybe $125,000. A first set of buyers would pay $200,000 and then turn around and sell it for $400,000. The second buyer would immediately resell for $600,000, and so on until, by the end of the day, the parcel may have gone through six sales and wind up with a "market" value, supported by courthouse records, of $2 million or so. If Faulkner needed backup, he could always go to a friendly appraiser. With this documented value, he could now approach one of his controlled thrifts and borrow $2.2 million. The loan might be used to support the frenetic building captured on the Bank Board video, or it might simply go in someone's pocket.

In Faulkner's hands, the flip was also a supple device for rewarding friends or for providing them money to put where Faulkner wanted it to go. His partners testified that he planned how much of a profit he wanted each stage of the flip to generate. On December 2, 1982, for instance, Sinclair, the turncoat, started a flip by paying about $1 million for a tract. By midday, the third sale had jacked the price to $5.5 million. By the end of the day, the tract provided the collateral for a $7 million loan from an affiliated S&L. The flip was supposed to provide the payment for Mattox, until Danny decided to keep the Attorney General's name off the records. Loans on these inflated values enriched both Faulkner and Blain. These men and their cohorts made $136 million in the twelve months after September 1982. In the same period, Empire S&L grew from $40 million in assets to $320 million. Brokered deposits, nearly $200 million of the assets, made this rapid growth possible. (More than half of Empire's total deposits came from Mario Renda's tainted First United Fund of Garden City, Long Island. The runner-up, with 12 percent of the total, was the Miami-based FAIC Securities, Inc., which would later take the FSLIC and the FDIC to court over the brokered deposit regs and kill the project.) When the Bank Board shut down the thrift on March 14, 1984, FSLIC faced a payout of nearly $300 million to cover the insured deposits. Around 100 partners in the land flips were convicted of fraud. And Faulkner's condos were built so shoddily that the town bulldozed them. Faulkner, Blain and several other major figures finally went to trial in Lubbock during the summer of 1989. The jury was still out at this writing.

When Gray and his Bank Board colleagues watched the video tour of the I-30 projects, they had to ask how they had let this disaster happen. The blame couldn't be pinned on the examiners. In reviewing their reports, Gray found they had warned about the land deals since October 1982. The failure came from higher up.

□ 4 □

WHEN FSLIC EXAMINED EMPIRE IN 1982, the Bank Board followed up with a letter and nothing more. Empire didn't bother to reply until April, 1983 and then sent what the Barnard subcommittee called "a bland and nonresponsive 'kiss-off.' " In the meantime, the Texas Savings and Loan section began to worry about the I-30 land flips. On May 19, 1983, it signed a "supervisory agreement" with Empire, the details of which have not been released. But the Bank Board wasn't involved in working it out and may not even have known it existed. One other problem was well known to both bureaucracies. When Spencer Blain took over Empire from May to August 1982, he failed to file a Change of Control notice, a direct violation of the law. This breach in procedure bothered the regulators a lot, but they let him off with some minor restrictions. Up until December 31, 1982, Blain was still vice chairman of the regional Federal Home Loan Bank.

All this supervisory thrashing had been going on before Ed Gray accepted the invitation to the June 7 convention of the Texas S&L League, of which Blain was president, and wound up in Durward Curlee's bedroom hearing how Linton Bowman got his job. Bowman, the Texas S&L commissioner, later told the Barnard subcommittee, "At this meeting, the Empire problem was discussed in its entirety." Gray can certainly be faulted for not picking up on whatever Bowman had to tell him. Gray had no business in accepting dinner, or even a ride in a Rolls Royce, from a man who was tweaking his nose at Gray's staff. But one also has to wonder how Bowman could make a serious warning about Blain and then spend the evening pickin' and grinnin' in his penthouse.

Bowman claims that in his "briefing," he agonized over one of Empire's anomalies. In spite of its flaws, it appeared to be the most successful thrift in the industry. In hindsight, the paper profits aren't surprising. Empire was a pioneer in structuring its loans to give its own books a short-term boost. It not only lent Faulkner's crew the full amount of their grossly inflated appraisals, it threw in an extra 10 percent to cover a year or two of interest payments and its own excessive fees. Empire could demand a lending fee of up to 18 points and get it, because both lender and borrower knew that the loan was a fraud. In his April 1984 congressional testimony, Bowman claimed he had caught on to this game by the time Empire closed, but it ran rampant in the Texas thrifts for two more years.

Gray's people had another excuse. In moving the Home Loan Bank from Little Rock to Dallas, they had almost completely wiped out their supervisory staff. According to the Bank Board, only 10 or 12 of the 40 people in Little Rock relocated to Texas. Through the end of 1983, the regional office virtually gave up on controlling the Texas thrifts. Gray was perfectly willing to acknowledge that he was stretched to the limit. It was true. The demoralizing frustration set in, however, when he tried to do something about it.

Gray's first reaction to the Empire S&L crash course was to fire Joseph Settle, the chief supervisor in the Dallas Home Loan Bank. Gray had gone with Settle and some Texas thrift owners to fish for trout in New Mexico, and he didn't like what he saw. "He was like one of the good ol' boys," said Gray. In mid-April, Gray brought in a veteran from the San Francisco Home Loan Bank to discipline the Texas thrifts. Then Gray tried to beef up his examination staff. After the Empire S&L hearings, he said, he fired off orders to all 12 Home Loan Banks to hire more supervisors. He ran headlong into the Office of Management and Budget. OMB was more concerned with its hiring freeze, and unlike the FDIC, FSLIC was under its thumb. Gray recounted angry exchanges accusing him of missing the point of the Reagan Revolution, of resisting the effort to reduce the bureaucracy and get the government off the back of business. Gray threw up his hands at the "ideological loonies."

And in truth, Gray's gut instincts made better free-market economics than did OMB's "deregulation." As Gray and FDIC Chairman Isaac argued, banks and thrifts were only partly deregulated. The insurance funds had less control over what they did but still had to pay for their mistakes. This situation created the familiar problem that depositors had little reason to shop around to put their money in less risky thrifts, just as some of them became very risky indeed. But there was a more subtle failure of market discipline, as well.

The public simply had little way of knowing what a thrift was up to. Its loans and investments were shrounded by the bank secrecy laws. There were some red flags, to be sure. A wary depositor merely had to walk through the executive parking lot to see what kind of cars the bank officers drove. Too many Rolls Royces and Alfa Romeos, and you could brace for trouble. But only the examiners had the power to penetrate to the details of the thrift's management. Their flow of information was far too restricted, but it was a partial compensation for the lack of public scrutiny. Remove the examiners, and the thrifts ran totally unchecked.

Gray finally hit on a device to restore these eyes and ears. William McKenna, a director of the San Francisco Home Loan Bank and one of the most experienced S&L lawyers in the country, noticed a loophole in the Garn-St Germain Act. Possibly the examiners could be moved from the Bank Board staff in Washington to the staffs of the 12 privately financed Home Loan Banks. They would no longer be subject to OMB limits, and their salaries could be raised. The examination staff resisted at first, harboring old suspicions that the supervisory staff of the regional banks were too close to the industry. But by mid-1985, the move was well under way. FSLIC enforcement was beginning to emerge from utter chaos.

Then Gray and FSLIC encountered the most bitter irony. The more effective they became, the greater the resistance they provoked. Their failures were no longer simply from internal disarray. Powerful outside forces kept them from doing their jobs, with disastrous results.

CHAPTER TWELVE

□ □ □

Two, Three, Many Empires

□ 1 □

"I WAS TAUGHT TO BELIEVE THAT THERE ARE ABSOLUTES," Ed Gray says unapologetically. "There is right and wrong and no gray area." He relied more on this boyhood training than on economic instincts in the ordeal that lay ahead. When the Bank Board closed Empire Savings & Loan and replaced the Dallas supervisor, almost no one suspected how wrong things in Texas had become. Jack W. Pullen, a veteran of the San Francisco Home Loan Bank, took over the Dallas region as well. During the next six months, he alerted Gray that Empire was not unique, that many other thrifts had adopted its reckless behavior. "It was only through him," said Gray, "that I began to find out what a disaster we had on our hands."

Even so, it took years to appreciate how vast an economic crime had been committed. Federal probes are still unravelling the networks that bound together no fewer than 40 of the Texas thrifts. The pattern at Empire—rapid growth with brokered funds, illusory strong performance and very real looting—became a cliché. At the time it seemed as if the most reckless owners had been trained in the technique of busting a thrift. Previous bank scandals took on urgent interest when it emerged that some of their main figures were at it again. The web spread wide, from Florida to California, intersecting often enough with strands from organized crime. But all of this was unsuspected in the summer of 1984, when the Bank Board set out to discover what sort of problem it faced,

□ 2 □

BEFORE COMING TO GRIPS WITH THE REALITY OF TEXAS, the supervisors had to work through one sham argument. Texas lobbyists like Durward Curlee were vigorously blaming the S&L problems on the sharp drop in oil prices and the regional recession. National S&L groups, such as the United States League, gladly echoed the excuse. But Empire of Mesquite had collapsed without help from the petroleum market. As Bill Black of FSLIC observed in his famous suppressed testimony, 40 other Texas thrifts with similar management were insolvent in real-world bookkeeping by the end of 1984, well before the 1986 break in the oil market. The Oil Patch recession didn't help, to be sure, but consider one thing before allowing the thrifts to cast themselves as its victims.

Remember the video of Danny Faulkner's empire, the acres on acres of vacant condos, the tremendous waste, the lack of any economic rationale. Faulkner's crews built frenetically as the thrifts pumped out loan after loan, and then the thrifts were closed. The I-30 corridor was left with a 12½ year oversupply of housing, destroying the market for legitimate projects. Now consider that Empire of Mesquite did this mischief with $300 million in loans. What would be the effect if one multiplied this case a hundredfold? You would have a few years of boom and then a sudden collapse. Entire cities would be overbuilt, and half-built. The market would disintegrate because the construction had nothing to do with market demand in the first place.

This was exactly the pattern that at least one economist discovered when he turned his computer loose on the S&Ls. Ray Perryman, an economist with Baylor University, reported for the "Dallas Morning News" on the impact of the "excessive" lending. He started by figuring normal S&L lending on the basis of the previous decade. The change after 1982 produced more than $11 billion in additional loans. This "excessive" financing, said Perryman, stimulated nearly $30 billion in extra construction, cushioning the impact of the 1982 national recession. But the stimulus left behind "an enormous excess supply of real estate." When it ended, Texas suffered its own unique recession, while the rest of the country plugged happily along. Without the Mesquite-style shot in the arm, Texas would have gone through the 1982 recession, which helped purge the national economy of many ills, and would have grown steadily throughout 1987. At a normal, uninflated course, the Texas workforce would have wound up with 180,000 more jobs than it actually did. Perry summed it up in economist's talk; thrift lending, he concluded, "resulted in significant artificial stimulation," followed by "a substantial drag on aggregate growth." To put it simply, his study concluded that economic disaster didn't cause the thrift failures. The thrifts caused the economic disaster.

There were ironies and undercurrents in Texas history that had helped bring it to this pass, and they greatly complicated relations with the Washington regulators. The Lone Star State may have become more vulnerable than most to the financial looters precisely because of its deeply ingrained suspicion of financial institutions. When the Republic of Texas carved itself out of Mexico's northern domain in 1836, it was more deeply· under the influence of the politics of Andrew Jackson than any other region in America, and the most visible manifestation was the new country's hostility to banks. Not only were bankers symbols of undemocratic economic power, but many settlers had come to Texas to flee from bankruptcy. A visiting journalist in the 1830s found that when he crossed the border, "he was invariably surrounded and accosted sans ceremonie by numbers of the citizens, enquiring what he had done in the United States, that made it necessary for him to seek refuge among them? . . . when a new-comer averred that he had ran away from his creditors ONLY, he was regarded as a gentleman of the first water, and welcomed on all hands." In 1844, the Texas Congress passed "an Act to Suppress Private Banks."

This prejudice persisted until recently in the form of prohibitions on branch banking that were meant to protect small community banks that frequently owned too little capital to be viable. As a result, they were gobbled up by giant bank holding companies that became a prominent feature of the Texas landscape. Texas regulators also emphasized state's rights. Even now, the dual banking system is a highly emotional issue.

Financial manipulators have played on this history with great effect. One of the state's most celebrated political scandals, the 1969 Sharpstown case, revolved around an attempt to shield a politically connected bank from the federal regulators. Frank W. Sharp, the center of this storm, would have fit comfortably into Danny Faulkner's circle. Texas has seen quite a few wheeler-dealer developers of his type, who build an empire on paper, with substantial political help, and then go bust without suffering oppressive social opprobrium. In a state settled by fugitives from bank debts, tolerance is high for a good life lived on credit. The key to maintaining such a "highly leveraged position," the current euphemism, is to keep the examiners off your back.

Sharp flourished in the late 1960s, building the posh Sharpstown development in Houston as well as taking control of several banks and insurance companies. But federal examiners were giving him trouble at the FDIC-insured Sharpstown State Bank. He hit on a scheme that would cut out federal supervision entirely as well as appeal to Texan state sovereignty. He proposed a state law that would authorize private associations to insure bank deposits; these organizations would replace the FDIC in conducting examinations of their members. This sort of state-chartered private corporation resembled Ohio's ODGF and Maryland's MSSIC, which both collapsed in 1985, setting off bank holidays in both states.

In spite of its state's rights overtones, Sharp's idea didn't get very far on its own. So, in 1969, he gave it a boost by arranging a highly profitable stock deal for the governor, the chairman of the state Democratic party, the Speaker of the State House of Representatives and several influential aides. The politicians bought shares in one of Sharp's insurance companies, using loans from his Sharpstown State Bank. Within two months, they unloaded the stock at a price well above the market in a private sale arranged by Sharp.

In the meantime, Governor Preston Smith had added Sharp's banking bills to his call for a special session of the state legislature. Driven by House Speaker Gus Mutscher, the bills cleared both chambers with only 13 negative votes and landed on the governor's desk in 48 hours. By this time, the state's bank lobby had caught whiff of the game and raised a cry about the bills' major flaws. Governor Smith cashed in his stock, clearing an estimated $60,000, and, in a final twist, vetoed the bills.

The story broke in 1971 on the day of Governor Smith's reinauguration, when the Securities and Exchange Commission filed suit over the stock manipulation. The Dirty Thirty, a strange House coalition of liberal Democrats and conservative Republicans, made it a political cause célèbre. By the 1972 election, political careers had ended for officials even remotely connected with Frank Sharp, and reformers controlled the legislature.

One of the most prominent names in the Sharpstown case was that of the bright, young Lieutenant Governor Ben Barnes, not because he was a central figure, but because his career had previously seemed so promising. Barnes was sophisticated and well educated. A protégé of former Governor John Connally, he represented a new breed of enlightened southern politicians. Political columnists, Rowland Evans and Robert Novak, loved him. Barnes was never charged with wrongdoing, but just the association with Sharp was enough to drive him from public life. He devoted himself to business.

The real beginning of the Texas thrift debacle lies in the mid-1970s, in the so-called "Rent-a-Bank" case. The failure of the Citizens State Bank in dusty Carrizo Springs near the Rio Grande attracted the attention of San Antonio Congressman Henry Gonzalez. He sponsored a congressional investigation that turned up a network of investors who had bought and sold at least 20 small Texas banks in the preceding four years. In a foreshadowing of the Butchers' loan shuffle, banks in this web would swap shaky assets, eluding the examiners. Allen Pusey of the "Dallas Morning News," a superb investigator who uncovered the I-30 scandal, wrote, "A network of insider loans, self-dealing transactions and stock purchases . . . allowed them to float bad loans through the regulatory system." The most astonishing discovery, however, was the continuity between the Rent-a-Bank crew and the perpetrators of the later S&L disaster. "The same schemes, the same problems and many of the same people," exclaimed Pusey.

When the story broke, one of the characters prominently named was the same Ben Barnes. Once again he appeared by association, as the partner of a central Louisiana native named Herman Kendrith Beebe. Neither was directly accused of wrongdoing, but Beebe was omnipresent behind the scenes, providing financing for many of the bank acquisitions. It was a role he played to the hilt after Garn-St Germain, when the go-go types and high-flyers infiltrated the Texas thrift industry.

Beebe was born in 1927 in a rural Rapides Parish family. He joined the Navy toward the end of World War II. As a veteran, he went to Louisiana State University, graduating in 1949 with a major in agricultural education. He promptly got married. He worked as an assistant county agent until the Korean War. Called back to the Navy reserves, he got the idea of selling life insurance.

Beebe was tall and gregarious, with a wry sense of humor. (He named one daughter Easter Bunny Beebe.) He apparently did well as a salesman. By 1961, he had accumulated enough capital to start his own company, AMI, Inc., which originally invested in Holiday Inns. In 1966, he bought his first bank, Bossier Bank and Trust in a suburb of Shreveport. Beebe soon became one of the largest employers in Shreveport, a bloody, business-minded city that combines the worst features of Louisiana and Texas. In spite of an early run-in with the SEC, he developed close ties with some of Lousiana's most powerful figures.

At the peak of his career, in 1983, Beebe may have directly or indirectly controlled over 100 banks and thrifts. According to the fascinating study *Inside Job* by three reporters for the *National Thrift News*, "His influence in banking circles was so pervasive by the mid-1980s that he could be connected in some way to almost every dying bank or savings and loan in Texas and Louisiana." In 1985, the Office of the Comptroller of the Currency prepared a report outlining some of his intricate network of associates. It included some of the most prominent figures in the impending thrift debacle. The list overlapped with the political contributors on whose behalf House Speaker Jim Wright pressured the Federal Home Loan Bank Board. Investigators also claimed that Beebe had another set of connections, which he and his lawyers vehemently denied. Federal agents described him as a financier and business associate of organized crime.

According to testimony in several civil suits, Carlos Marcello, the legendary head of the New Orleans Mafia, had an account in one of Beebe's banks. (A congressional report singled out Marcello, born in 1910, as the most prestigious Cosa Nostra leader, partly because his "family" was the first to be established in the New World in the 1890s.) Marcello and his relatives were borrowers at Beebe-controlled banks. Perhaps just as telling, Beebe kept close ties to former Louisiana Governor Edwin Edwards, a Cajun charmer who parlayed his candor about borderline ethics into a political asset. ("In Louisiana, we don't just expect corruption of our public officials," explained one of his voters, "we demand it of them.") In 1981, the FBI's BRILAB sting resulted in the conviction of Marcello for his dealings with Charles Roemer, Edwards's commissioner of administration and father of Louisiana's current reform governor. Roemer and Marcello are still serving time. Edwards drew an annual $100,000 retainer from Beebe during two years when he was out of office. A lawyer for Marcello and the commissioner of financial institutions for Edwards (the regulator of state-chartered banks and thrifts) were both directors of a life insurance company headquartered in Beebe's Shreveport office.

Interpretations differ about Beebe's Mafia connections. The authors of *Inside Job* credited organized crime with a multistate cabal to "bust out" vulnerable thrifts. The authors have plenty of evidence to work with. Pusey of the "Dallas News" is less emphatic; he said that Beebe's dealings with Marcello show that he would do business with anyone. Hard-core mafiosi have been relatively rare in the thrift crisis. The types that do abound come instead from the sleazy buffer between grossly romanticized Sicilians and legitimate business. Loosely coordinated con artists, hustlers, and crooks flock to the easy marks. As a world-class swindler once told me, "When they hear there's a pot of money they all gather around." But for once the professional looters may have been outdone by the homegrown hotshots who moved into the thrifts around 1982. There is little doubt about Beebe's relations with them.

Pusey of the "Dallas Morning News" reported that Beebe operated through "a quiet pattern of quid-pro-quo lending." Institutions that needed cash could get it through his web of influence provided they did some favor for him. Loans might exceed the borrower's real needs, but the excess money would be earmarked for some other purpose. It might go for a stock issue, for the purchase of problem real estate from another bank's portfolio, or for a loan participation.

Beebe had this system well worked out by the time he started doing business with an ambitious young Dallas developer named Don Ray Dixon. Sometime during 1976, Dixon had been introduced to Beebe by Ben Barnes. Dixon became a close family friend, addressing Beebe as "Papaw." A former employee of Beebe told Pusey that Dixon had borrowed heavily from Continental Savings Association, one of the thrifts in the network. When in 1981 Beebe needed to float a Continental stock issue, he suggested to Dixon that he buy a substantial amount.

"Herman told Don that he could benefit by becoming one in our family of borrowers," said Pusey's source, "and to properly display that attitude, he should purchase some stock. And Dixon, being the intelligent man he is, said 'How much?' "

□ 3 □

DON RAY DIXON, A SHORT, DRIVEN FIGURE who resembles the actor Richard Dreyfuss in his moustached phase, was a hometown boy from Vernon, Texas. With a population just over 12,000, Vernon was the seat of Willbarger County, a center for oil and irrigated cotton fields set in rolling plains along the Red River, the state border with Oklahoma. Dixon was born on November 20, 1938. In high school, he had already made a name as an overachiever, and after two years at Rice University in Houston, he went away to UCLA. In 1960, he received a B.S. in business. After a stint in outdoor advertising in Milwaukee, Wisconsin, he came back to Dallas in 1962. He kicked around in several companies, making a modest success of home building until the market collapsed in the 1974 recession and the banks called his loans. By 1975, he said in one deposition, he was "unemployed, or self-employed would be a better description." Then he met Beebe, and his fortunes improved sharply.

From 1976 to 1979, Dixon worked in a company called Diman Corporation. Then in another permutation of his name, he started Dondi Construction Company, a prospering builder of Spanish-style homes with red roofs. With Beebe backing him and deregulation on the way, he started looking for a thrift to acquire and found one in his hometown. *Texas Monthly* writer Byron Harris reported Dixon's visit to the homespun R. B. Tanner, a former bank examiner who had founded the Vernon Savings and Loan in 1960 and run it with frugal care ever since. Dixon bought it outright in January, 1982 and asked Tanner to stay on the board of directors. At its first meeting, the new owner asked for approval for a $125,000 purchase of "a bronze sculpture of a squatting Indian." Tanner realized that things were going to change around the office, and he resigned from the board.

Dixon was indeed a man of expensive tastes. He liked exotic cars, Western art, $2 million beach houses and three-star restaurants in France. "That first night in Paris we had dinner at Castel's, the 'in', very chic private club in St. Germain," wrote Dana Dixon, Don's wife, in a paper later found by federal examiners in the files of Dixon's Vernon Savings and Loan. Under the title "Gastronomique— Fantastique!," Mrs. Dixon gushed about an October 1983 tour of the ritziest restaurants in France. Ostensibly "a bit of market study" for a "world-class restaurant" for Dallas, the Dixons and another Vernon couple toured by private plane and 1954 Silver Dawn Rolls Royce in the company of Yolande and Jean Castel, owners of that " 'in,' very chic" club. Ushered by their "charming," "witty," "twinkling" escorts, the Dixons hopped from La Tour d'Argent and Brasserie Lipp in Paris to the Troisgros in Roanne to the restaurant of

Paul Bocuse in Lyon to Moulin de Mougins in Nice. On the Riviera, they lunched with "a famous French artist, Cesar, and also a movie script writer."

"It was truly a dream trip," exclaimed Mrs. Dixon, "a trip hardly to be imagined by most, and barely to be believed even by those of us who experienced it at first hand." The trip was also paid for by the Vernon Savings and Loan.

Over the next two years, Dixon took further dream trips to France, England, Ireland, Denmark, and Italy, with frequent side trips to Geneva on undisclosed business. On his 1985 jaunt to Italy, Dixon squeezed in stops at both the Bulgari Spa and the Gucci Spa. Overall, according to FSLIC examiners, the Vernon thrift picked up a travel tab of $68,036.98. At one point Dixon submitted a one-month American Express Card bill (including overdue balance) of $34,444.42.

Vernon Savings owned a subsidiary called Vernon Capital Corporation, which in turn owned a California company called Symbolic Cars of La Jolla, Inc., devoted to Dixon's passion of buying and selling classic autos. In July 1986, Symbolic held an auction that sold eight of Dixon's cars for $1.8 million. The auction still managed to lose $200,000. Dixon even had the Vernon subsidiary absorb a $200 charge for towing his classic Hispano-Suiza.

When Dixon desired a pied-à-terre in California, Vernon obligingly put up $2 million for a beach house in Del Mar. The Dixons moved in, rent free, during June 1985 and spent nearly $200,000 from a special Vernon account to furnish it. A separate bill for flowers came to $36,780. When the Dixons built another house in Rancho Santa Fe, California, they flew to London to consult an interior decorator and buy $489,000 of furnishings. A Vernon subsidiary covered the trip by issuing a $500,000 note. Dixon covered his walls with Western art, listed on Vernon's books as an asset worth $5.5 million. The feds are still looking for 40 missing pieces, one of which, according to *Inside Job,* Dixon may have given to the Pope.

But even Dixon couldn't have spent all of Vernon's money on himself. The big losses came on Vernon's new brand of business. Abandoning traditional mortgages and moving from the town of Vernon to a North Dallas high-rise, the thrift plunged into the commercial loans, direct investments, and real estate acquisitions that Garn-St Germain and the even more liberal state deregulation had opened to it. These losses weren't simply from poor underwriting. Dixon tapped into a national network of thrift-busters. Vernon's loan portfolio reads like an index of corruption. When the thrift collapsed, 96 percent of these loans were uncollectible.

Owners of other thrifts lined up to borrow from Dixon, often handing over their own stock as collateral. They were charter members of the "Texas 40," the high-flying state-chartered thrifts later singled out by FSLIC's Bill Black as the source of the biggest losses. The thrifts would swap loans or take participations, or shares, in big loans, depending on their need to clean up their books. Sometimes, like the Butchers, they were one step ahead of the examiners; sometimes they just wanted to pump up their earnings reports. In one maneuver, called "swapping dead cows for dead horses," the thrift would ship out a loan that was starting to go delinquent in return for another bad loan. Both would get a fresh asset that they wouldn't have to write down for another six months. "A list was circulated at a meeting," testified Vernon officer Gregory McCormick about one such cleanup. "Friendly lending institutions were thrown out on the table, or tabled as to who might take what and how much they may buy."

The friendly institutions made quite a roster:

☐ Western Savings Association, headed by the frumpy Jarrett Woods. Dixon took a $23.6 million loan participation from Western, which crawled with alumni of the Rent-a-Bank scandal. Its top lending officer, Kenneth C. Hood, was indicted in 1984 on a charge of bank fraud at another institution and pleaded guilty in 1985; he had also once worked for Herman Beebe. Woods and Western wound up losing even more money, $1.4 billion, than Dixon did, although Woods has not been charged with a crime.

☐ Paris Savings and Loan Association, run from Dallas by Harvey D. McLean, Jr. McLean received $6.6 million in loans from Vernon, and his Paris Service Corporation received more than $10 million without board approval. FSLIC dates the deterioration of Paris Savings to its acquisition by McLean in 1983. But there are no criminal charges against McLean.

☐ Tyrell G. Barker, owner of State Savings and Loan of Lubbock. Barker, an old friend of Dixon, took a personal loan of $4 million. *Inside Job* reported that Barker bought State of Lubbock with financing from Herman Beebe and promptly moved its headquarters to North Dallas, flying back and forth in one of its two corporate jets, accompanied by his two pet dogs. Barker is now serving time on a federal bank fraud conviction in Lubbock for misapplication of funds.

☐ Charles Bazarian, a rotund Connecticut Armenian turned Oklahoman who busted banks as far away as Florida. A small personal loan to Bazarian showed up on Vernon's delinquent list, but Vernon had more than $1.2 million debt outstanding from Bazarian's CB Financial. Bazarian was convicted of mail fraud in connection with a scheme to defraud the Florida Center Bank of Orlando. A confederate in the case was a former Wall Street swindler, Michael Hellerman, living in the Federal Witness Protection Program under an assumed name. Bazarian also owned stock, and an $8.4 million loan, in Tampa's Freedom Savings and Loan, the fevered thrift that Marvin Warner and Juan Vicente Perez Sandoval had squabbled over.

☐ Tom Nevis, a developer with projects in New Mexico, Kentucky and Florida and, according to civil suits, some nasty business habits. Nevis owed Vernon more than $15 million on loans for a condominium and hotel project in Destin, Florida, on the Panhandle's "Redneck Riviera." He was later convicted for bank fraud involving State Savings and Loan of Corvallis, Oregon, another hub of the network.

☐ Jack Franks, Nevis's partner in the Corvallis loan. Franks was also a partner of Dixon, acting through Dixon's Dondi Group, Inc., in a $1.4 million loan on an office building at the airport that served North Dallas. Reporter Pusey turned up an interesting statement about Franks's fund-raising technique in a California lawsuit. One of his former partners said, "Franks and his associates would find institutional lenders with either government regulatory problems or officials who would be willing to deviate from sound financial practices." One California developer testified that he continued doing business with this set only after one of these associates cracked his ribs. In September 1988, Franks worked out a plea bargain with United States attorneys in north Texas and Oregon. He pled guilty in Dallas to helping a Vernon officer siphon off a kickback from an unrelated loan. His own borrowing at Vernon wasn't an issue.

The names go on and on. Frank Domingues of San Diego, California, with his partner Jack Bona, was a central figure in the 1984 failure of San Marino Savings and Loan in San Diego, at the time the largest thrift collapse on record. Vernon renewed a loan to Domingues less than two weeks after San Marino closed. Another prominent borrower from Vernon was John B. Anderson, a six-foot-three-inch-tall tomato grower from Davis, California, who took a loan for at least $14.3 million. Anderson also borrowed at least $16 million from Corvallis and many more millions from other thrifts on the national web. Anderson and Bona had one more thing in common: both bought casinos from Morris Shenker.

Writers and investigators have speculated for years about Shenker, a St. Louis lawyer who represented Teamster President Jimmy Hoffa and the Teamsters' notorious Central States Pension Fund. After Shenker filed for bankruptcy in 1984, Anderson, already a casino owner, bought the controlling interest in Shenker's Dunes Hotel and Casino in Las Vegas. Shenker stayed on as a board member. Bona, under his full name Bonacorte, picked up Shenker's half-finished Atlantic City Dunes Casino and Hotel project. (Bona went bankrupt in 1985. In 1988, the bankruptcy trustee sold the project to Royale Group, Ltd., run by Leonard Pellulo, whom we met in the chapter on Sunshine State.) While in financial collapse, Shenker courted many figures on the S&L network, including Charles Bazarian; he even provided them suites at the Las Vegas Dunes to make their deals. *Inside Job* speculated that his interest came from his loss of access to the Central States Pension Fund, which was put into Labor Department trusteeship in 1983; deregulation of the thrifts gave him access to a fresh pot of money. Like much else in that book, the thesis deserves serious consideration.

□ 4 □

AFTER THIS FLIGHT INTO DARKNESS, it's almost refreshing to get back to familar figures. Durward Curlee, the lobbyist, shows up on Vernon's ledgers with more than $73,000 in delinquent personal loans. At the end of 1985, he borrowed nearly $500,000. On February 20, 1986, the Vernon board approved a loan of $686,547 to Lawrence W. Taggart, former savings and loan commissioner for the State of California. Vernon Savings also gave substantial financing to the ubiquitous Ben Barnes and his partner John Connally, Nixon's Secretary of the Treasury. As the two slid into bankruptcy, the Vernon board, now with a state regulator sitting in on meetings, tried to foreclose on $13 million of Connally's and Barnes's projects. They warned "it was a bad business move because it ruins their business relationship," and the thrift backed off.

The list hardly exhausts Vernon's connections. One thrift officer pleaded guilty to making illegal campaign contributions to a string of Republican candidates, including Congressman Jack Kemp. And Vernon was only one nexus in an endless mesh. The doings of the high-flyers, the North Dallas 40 and their friends, have been vividly chronicled in the magazine and television reporting of Dallas journalist Byron Harris. Harris brought to light figures such as Stanley E. Adams, chairman of Austin's Lamar Savings and Loan Association, who once filed an application to open a branch on the moon (in the Sea of Tranquillity, to be precise). Harris's cameras caught the huge, sloppy figure of Thomas Gaubert, owner of Independent American Savings Association, looming over House Government Operations Committee Chairman Jack Brooks (D-Texas) at a Democratic fund-raising function like Bluto next to Popeye.

But the most colorful, and sleaziest, of them all was Edwin T. ("Fast Eddy") McBirney, who became chairman of Dallas-based Sunbelt Savings Association at the age of 31. McBirney ran his thrift so recklessly that locals called it "Gunbelt." His parties were famous. On Halloween, 1984, guests at his North Dallas mansion feted on lion, antelope, and pheasant meat while McBirney, dressed as King Henry the Eighth, stalked through a fog provided by smoke machines. (Sunbelt, Gaubert's Independent American, and Jarrett Woods's Western Savings developed such intricate financial links that FSLIC finally merged them into one institution, rather than try to sort out the loan swaps.)

Dixon and McBirney pioneered another method to bind this network—a means of corruption almost as powerful as money—namely, sex. Dixon used prostitutes lavishly to divert his borrowers and his board of directors. Jack Brenner, one of Dixon's employees, told Harris on camera about one party at Dixon's Del Mar beach house. Brenner said he excused himself from the affair after five minutes. "We left," he said, "because the place was full of a maze of hookers." A Vernon officer confessed to federal prosecutors that he had shipped two women from a Dallas topless bar to a board of directors meeting in California that lasted three days. The entertainment was supplemented by another six to ten women working out of San Diego escort services.

But it was McBirney's last party that carried this tactic to an extreme. According to several accounts, it took place in early March 1986 at the Las Vegas Dunes Hotel, Morris Shenker's old headquarters. McBirney flew 50 of Sunbelt's friends and customers for a weekend stay and invited them to a stag cocktail party at his penthouse suite. Four attractive women entered the room. They did a striptease, but to the shock of the party, they didn't stop there. After "an enthusiastic Lesbian romp," they moved through the crowd and performed fellatio on targetted guests. McBirney grinned widely throughout, but it may not have been just at the show. Psychologically, the scene was the financier's Jonestown. The borrowers who had helped him take corrupt advantage of his thrift were now visibly corrupted themselves, unobjecting participants in a spectacle of public shame.

It would indeed be a surprise for such an exhibitionist network to escape the notice of the regulators. And of course it didn't. The understaffed, underpaid Texas Savings and Loan Department noticed early on that people like Beebe, Dixon, and Tyrell Barker were in cahoots. "We knew what was going on as early as 1983," said Art Leiser, at the time the department's chief of examinations. Now stewing in retirement in Austin, the plain-spoken Leiser recalled doing a flowchart in June 1983 "that showed everything." These charts are still confidential, but Leiser defended his examiners vehemently. "These people did their job," he stated. Then they gave their information to the upper echelons "who didn't know what the Hell to do with it."

While Leiser inked in his first flowchart, his boss Linton Bowman was strumming a guitar with Durward Curlee in Spencer Blain's Registry Hotel penthouse. Bowman had been the state savings and loan commissioner since January 1983. As Curlee told Ed Gray earlier in the evening, the Texas industry had gone to great lengths to get him the job. Bowman's ties to the "Texas 40" ran beyond the social. In 1980, as deputy commissioner, he had formed a private development corporation, Cottonwood Investments, Inc., with his director of supervision, Patrick G. King, Leiser's immediate superior. When Bowman got the top job in 1983, King became deputy commissioner. A year later King left to join Don Dixon's Vernon Savings and Loan at a salary of $120,000. As the regulators closed in during mid-1986, King served as chairman of the board for over six weeks. In his two-and-a-half years at Vernon, King earned nearly $274,000 in bonuses, money that FSLIC charged in a civil suit had been obtained by fraudulently inflating earnings reports.

On September 5, 1989, King was convicted in federal court of conspiring to defraud Vernon, and of twelve other criminal charges together carrying a maximum possible sentence of 65 years. Courtroom testimony provided embarrassing detail about King's use of Vernon's money to procure a prostitute for his former boss, Commissioner Bowman.

Bowman has tried to downplay his ties to King. He claimed that Cottonwood had become inactive and that he never took loans, directly or indirectly, "from a state-chartered S&L in this state." He added, "My only Vernon connection was to Pat King, and that was in 1980." Bowman resigned as commissioner in the early fall of 1987 after the *Dallas Times Herald* reported that his financial records had been subpoenaed by the federal grand jury working with the Justice Department's North Dallas Task Force. Bowman has not been charged with any crime.

As the move from Little Rock to Dallas shut down FSLIC's southwest examination force, the high-flyers had little need to worry about neutralizing the feds. But they tried it anyway. Stanley Adams of Lamar Savings, the man who wanted to bring Texas finance to the moon, briefly employed Joseph Settle, former president of the Dallas Home Loan Bank, right after Gray fired him. There are even hints of outright corruption in the Dallas Home Loan Bank, although no federal employees have been charged with anything.

□ 5 □

THIS WAS THE SITUATION WHEN EMPIRE OF MESQUITE shocked Ed Gray into finding out what was happening in Texas. The high-flyers had gone suborbital. Supervision, both state and federal, was toothless, although the field examiners knew something was wrong. The "Texas 40" were growing at astounding rates, up to 1250 percent a year, thanks to brokered funds, but they were also rapidly going insolvent. Soon they would be the Texas 120. The leaders of the Texas Savings and Loan League realized, however, that an awakened Bank Board could cause them serious trouble, and they began to devote substantial energy to winning and keeping political friends.

The expansive developer Tom Gaubert was the first to feel the pressure. In January 1983, he had taken over a small thrift in Grand Prairie that quintupled in assets in a year. But examiners caught wind of a complex series of deals he had been working with a thrift in Mt. Pleasant, Iowa and noticed that they involved alumni, and possibly the technique, of the I-30 scandal. In mid-1984, with Congressman Barnard's committee on its back, the Bank Board's Enforcement Division started to investigate and by November decided to "neutralize" Gaubert's influence on his thrift until the issue was resolved. (Gaubert asked for a delay in the "neutralization" agreement until after the presidential election, because of his heavy fund raising for Walter Mondale.) But in a contradictory move, the Bank Board approved a merger between Gaubert's Independent American and a small failing thrift. (The Board may well have been trying to save the $40 million that closing the small thrift would have cost the rapidly dwindling FSLIC reserve.) Claiming that his thrift couldn't make the merger work without him, Gaubert lobbied heavily to regain control.

In May of 1985, he saw a chance to make a difference. Reagan had crushed Mondale, and Republican strategists bragged that party realignment was at hand. The president gave a federal judgeship to the incumbent Democrat from the First Congressional District of Texas to allow a special election. A Republican win in the East Texas district, a Dixiecrat stronghold and Sam Rayburn's old seat, would have been the final blow for southern Democrats. Gaubert organized an independent PAC (political action committee) to oppose the Republican candidate. He raised around $100,000, enough to claim that he provided the margin of victory when Democrat Jim Chapman narrowly won the special election.

The victory delighted Tony Coelho, chairman of the Democratic Congressional Campaign Committee, who made it a holy crusade to prevent a Republican surge into the House. It helped seal the Speakership for House Majority Leader Jim Wright. And it vastly increased the leverage of the S&L high-flyers. Gaubert's East Texas First PAC was a virtual catalogue of the Sunbelt-Vernon-Independent American network, accompanied by several smaller thrifts such as Commodore Savings and North Park. (The North Park president Bob Franks had helped Gaubert obtain his thrift back in 1983.) Almost all the funds in the PAC came from officers and borrowers of those five thrifts. And they didn't give out of civic duty.

Well after the special election, the North Dallas Task Force indicted former Commodore Savings chairman, Robert H. Hopkins, Jr., his brother, the thrift president, E. Morten Hopkins, and John W. Harrell, Commodore chairman after Hopkins, for channeling the thrift's money to the East Texas First PAC. The Hopkins brothers were convicted on all 47 counts, and Harrell was convicted on two counts of false entry. The three told their employees to give $1,000 contributions and then made it up by raising their salaries. Their trial took place just as Jim Wright was preparing his last-ditch defense before the House Ethics Committee, and it didn't help him any. One of the conduit employees testified about a conversation with his boss, explaining the contributions. Speaker Wright had agreed to kill a bill hostile to the S&Ls, said the thrift chairman, if they could raise $250,000 for East Texas First. Said David Farmer, Commodore's former chief financial officer, "In return for the contributions, Jim Wright guaranteed the legislation would not get out of committee." Farmer said both he and his boss "were amazed that as high ranking an individual in the Congress as he would be involved in something like this." The boss, Commodore Chairman John Harrell, said in his turn that he funneled $25,000 to the PAC without even knowing who the Democratic candidate was. Harrell said that Durward Curlee, the lobbyist, had told him to do it, citing his "golden rule." That precept, said Harrell, was "he who has the gold, makes the rules."

Wright vehemently denied that he made any promise, and, in truth, that charge was based on a second-hand conversation, but organizers of the PAC could count on help from the Speaker.

Gaubert's dispute with the Enforcement Division dragged on through 1986. In November, as Wright held the first FSLIC recapitalization bill hostage, he asked Bank Board Chairman Gray to give Gaubert an audience. Wright insisted that Gray exclude his director of enforcement from the talk, a direct blow at that office. In an effort to accommodate, Gray proposed that he appoint a special counsel to review the case. More than two years later, said Gray, he was startled to learn from the Phelan Report that the name of the counsel had come from Gaubert's attorneys. He was even further surprised to be told that the counsel's law partner had been defense attorney for both Jake Butcher and Marvin Warner.

(Credit, however, should be given to the special counsel, Nashville lawyer Aubrey Harwell, a courtly and accessible gentleman. His judicious report found no major abuse on the part of FSLIC but made fair-minded criticism of some of its conduct.)

In the end, Gaubert's Independent American was one of the first thrifts to be merged in the Bank Board's Southwest Plan. It had grown 4,600 percent since he bought it, and it wound up with a loss of nearly $900 million. Gaubert was indicted by a federal grand jury in Iowa, ironically for a land deal explored at length in the Harwell Report, but, after a hastily prepared prosecution, he won acquittal.

Don Dixon took a different approach toward winning friends. He wanted a yacht, so he bought the 112-foot *High Spirits*, launched in 1928 as the sister ship to the *Sequoia*, the presidential yacht of the Nixon years. It was one of his most sensible investments. Dixon brought the richly appointed ship to a mooring on the Potomac near Washington's soft-shell crab boats, and he placed it at the disposal of the Democratic Congressional Campaign Committee.

The "D-triple-C" was the personal creation and nationwide Tammany of California Congressman Tony Coelho, who, before his sudden resignation in June 1989, had parlayed his fund-raising prowess into the third-ranking position in the House of Representative's Democratic hierarchy. Coelho used the yacht at least 11 times in 1985 and 1986 to entertain D-triple-C contributors, but he claimed not to have noticed that the *High Spirits* captain never billed him for the $2,000 half-day charter fee or for the additional costs for food and drink, often running upwards of $1,300. Other congressmen could use the yacht on similar terms, for a time making arrangements through Martin Franks, Coelho's chief of staff. The bills went straight to Vernon S&L, in violation of the federal campaign finance law.

These congressional party-givers, who, along with Coelho, included Texas Congressmen J. J. Pickle and Jim Chapman, may not have realized how deep a swamp they were entering. As they poured champagne on their dinner cruises down the Potomac, the yacht was the center of one of Dixon's typically shady business deals. After buying the *High Spirits,* Dixon sold partnership shares to cronies, Vernon officers and borrowers, some of whom grumbled that they didn't want them. (One partner was lobbyist Durward Curlee, who lived on the yacht when he came to Washington. When Brooks Jackson of the *Wall Street Journal* questioned Rep. Chapman's parties on the *High Spirits,* the congressman's staff replied that election law allowed Curlee, as a volunteer, to donate the use of his residence.)

This partnership looked bad on Vernon's books, and some partners refused to pay on their notes, so Dixon decided to unload the yacht on two reluctant businessmen who were desperate for a loan. "I continually balked at doing the boat loan," said one of these victims, describing a talk with Dixon, "and he said that's the only way we are going to get the shopping center loan done." In mid-1986, as congressmen feted their donors in the yacht's salon, the two very unhappy borrowers bought it with part of a loan intended to refurbish a San Antonio mall. But they refused to register the title, causing months of aggravation when FSLIC foreclosed on the boat a year later.

Even though Dixon avoided taking direct ownership of the *High Spirits,* he wielded it effectively in his long fight against the regulators. From the moment Dixon bought Vernon S&L in January 1982, Bank Board regulators were trying to bring the S&L under control. In August 1984, FSLIC slapped Vernon with a "supervisory agreement" to correct its sloppy loan procedures. But judging from FSLIC's fraud suit and Vernon's own business records, these warnings didn't slow it down a step. From 1982 to 1986, Vernon's deposits grew from $80 million to nearly $1.6 billion, an increase of nearly 2,000 percent.

The Bank Board tried to get serious in early 1986 and, shortly afterward, the *High Spirits* showed up on the Potomac. In April a federal examination forced out Vernon's top officers (one of whom gave himself a $200,000 loan on the way out the door and was later charged with unlawful receipt of funds and bank fraud in an ongoing case). Coelho started using the *High Spirits* in May.

In July, the Bank Board imposed a cease and desist order on Vernon. In September, Dixon's surviving board sought "voluntary supervision" by the Texas Commissioner of Savings and Loan Associations, hoping for a "less confined environment." In August and September, Coelho used Dixon's planes for trips to California. And now the shoe dropped. Speaker Wright started calling Bank Board Chairman Edwin Gray with personal attacks on the most able of the Bank Board examiners. He made his point by freezing the bill to recapitalize the insolvent FSLIC. Congress would spare no more than $5 billion.

□ 6 □

BY THIS TIME, THE "HIGH-FLYERS" HAD THE EAR OF CONGRESS, and they had plenty to complain about. FSLIC was beginning to rebuild in Dallas after its disastrous move. Gray was pushing new procedures that had some bite, including a system for classifying loans according to their creditworthiness. Until this method was adopted in December 1985, FSLIC was the only federal regulator without loan classification. In early 1986, the Bank Board and its Dallas outpost felt strong enough, and worried enough, to catch up on its examinations. Many of the thrifts hadn't been visited in three years. The Dallas Home Loan Bank began a massive examination of almost everything in its jurisdiction, calling in reserves from ten of the 11 other districts.

In May, Ed Gray pulled off a real coup. He hired H. Joe Selby to become chief regulator in District Nine. Selby was only 55, but he was taking early retirement after a distinguished 32-year career in the Office of the Comptroller of the Currency. He had been the man in Washington, for instance, with direct responsibility for closing Hernandez-Cartaya's National Bank of South Florida. As a stand-in for the Comptroller, he sat on the FDIC board when it rolled up the Butchers' bank chain. Although he looked plump and avuncular, with pink cheeks and white hair, he delighted in his reputation for toughness. One interviewer noticed that he kept a Rambo doll on his desk.

The Dixons, Gauberts, and McBirneys found this all very unsettling. As the Phelan Report put it, "the 'high-flyers' were the most threatened by the strict enforcement regime, and they had the resources to make their voices heard. It was their complaints which apparently reached Wright's offices." A crucial intermediary was Wright's good friend George Mallick. Born in Fort Worth in 1932 of Lebanese descent, Mallick prospered as a real estate developer but remained an outsider to the city's clannish business elite. He met Wright in 1962, when Wright cut the ribbon to open one of his shopping center developments. In 1978, the Wrights and the Mallicks formed a joint investment company called Mallightco. When complaints from the thrift industry started to reach Wright's office in the fall of 1986, he asked Mallick to set up a meeting with some people from the industry. Mallick arranged a luncheon at Fort Worth's Ridgelea Country Club on October 21. He expected about 15 friends, but 150 showed up. In the question and answer period, about 15 of them took turns recounting what an aide to Wright called "horror story after horror story about the capricious and arbitrary manner that the Bank Board was treating savings and loans in the Southwest." At the lunch, Wright asked Mallick to prepare a report on the industry in the Southwest. At a later meeting with Gray, Wright suggested that Mallick act as an arbitrator between the Bank Board and the Texas thrifts.

The results were devastating. With complete disregard for the character of his petitioners and for the public mission of the Bank Board, Wright delayed recapitalization for a year and then allowed only a grossly inadequate amount. At the same time, the bill took some pressure off the high-flyers by rescinding some of Ed Gray's reforms, such as the loan classification system. The delay turned a $30 billion problem into a $300 billion problem, with consequences we are just beginning to feel. Yet when Congress turned against Speaker Wright, it seized on the most trivial of the possible issues, his business deals with his friend George Mallick. The House evidently feared raising the issue of his pressures on Gray and the Bank

Board. Too many in Congress were accomplices. But the tacit acceptance of this political interference created a baleful precedent. The Ethics Committee turned its back on the warning of the late Senator Paul Douglas, repeated several times in the Phelan Report:

> A legislator should not immediately conclude that the constituent is always right and the administrator is always wrong, but as far as possible should try to find out the merits of each case and only make such representations as the situation permits.

In forgetting this warning, Congress prepared the way for abuses even worse than those of Wright. Even before Wright's story had run its course, Gray discovered that the congressional capacity for mischief ran unabated and that the Senate was capable of setting political precedents as scandalous and damaging as anything done by the House.

CHAPTER THIRTEEN

□□□

Nemesis

□ 1 □

ED GRAY FELT HUMILIATED AND DIRTIED by his compromise with Speaker Wright. A deep depression settled over his staff. Not only had they sacrificed their principles to placate the Speaker, but the compromise hadn't worked. The recapitalization bill was far too stingy to deal with the problem, which was the industry's intention in the first place, and its fine print presented the examiners with one booby trap after another. At the point that Wright withdrew from the debate, leaving Coelho to carry on, the true cost of the debacle was conservatively estimated at $30 billion, three times the amount of the bonds that FSLIC was now authorized to sell. And the meter was ticking at the rate of $10 million a day. Yet with all this hanging over his head, Gray had an even more pressing and debilitating problem. The sword of Damocles was less immediate than the dagger between his shoulder blades.

Even now, Gray can't discuss it for more than a few minutes without erupting into a cold fury, at odds with his otherwise genial character. He reserves his greatest vehemence not for Jim Wright or Tony Coelho, or any Democrat in Congress, but for the second most powerful man in his own administration, White House Chief of Staff Donald Regan.

□ 2 □

GRAY SAID THAT REGAN CALLED HIM right after his appointment, asking if he was going to be "a team player." Gray answered yes, not understanding what Regan had in mind. He promptly offended the former Merrill Lynch chairman by his campaign against brokered deposits. Through early 1985, as Gray pleaded with the budget office for more examiners, he began to see Regan's hand behind the scene. Gray had won that round by transferring examiners to the regional Home Loan Banks but not before one last word from OMB. A senior budget official invited him to lunch at the White House mess, a clubby wood-panelled hideaway decorated with naval pictures. Instead of conciliation, the OMB official delivered a threat. The budget staff had caught Gray in what looked like a violation of a budgetary statute. "They wanted to send me to jail," said Gray. "It was absolutely ludicrous."

That episode ended when the Justice Department refused to handle the case, and the violation turned out to be merely a clerical error. But Gray crossed Regan even more directly in regard to a plan to issue preferred stock for the Federal Home Loan Mortgage Corporation, known on Wall Street as Freddie Mac. Money from the stock issue was meant to recapitalize Freddie Mac, but Gray said, "OMB and Don Regan wanted to use it to balance the budget." Gray thoroughly antagonized them at a meeting in the fall of 1984, when he called their plan a confiscation of private property. "This is what they do in Russia," he remembered saying. "This isn't Russia."

The remark wasn't tactful, but by this time Gray's relations with the Executive Office Building were beyond repair. During his lunch at the White House mess, he said, the budget official told him, "You're an old member of the administration, but you don't understand what the purpose of the administration is. We want to get government off the back of business. We ought to be reducing the number of examiners, not increasing them." At this point, said Gray, he concluded that these people were loony, "ideology had so blinded them."

Unlike the dispute with OMB, however, Gray suspected that more than ideology poisoned his relations with Regan. During President Reagan's first term, Don Regan had been ensconced in the massive Treasury Building on the other side of the White House compound; as secretary of the Treasury, he had been a leading voice, but not the only one, on economic policy. After the 1984 election, Regan and White House Chief of Staff James Baker worked out a highly unusual deal. They would swap jobs. On February 4, 1985, Regan moved into the southwest corner of the White House. Since President Reagan had little interest in the details of economic policy, Don Regan became, or imagined himself to be, the surrogate president in that area.

Regan didn't like Gray's attempts to crack down on the thrifts, and Regan had become a formidable opponent. Gray began to learn just how formidable in mid-July 1985. Gray remembered that he had just returned from a successful trip in Europe selling Freddie Mac paper when he heard that a California friend on the White House staff was trying to reach him. His friend said, "Look, I've got to tell you something. You've got to keep your head up." His friend had heard Don Regan say at a staff meeting, "I want Ed Gray out of his job."

Regan was asked why. His answer, Gary recounted, was simply, "There's too much turmoil." Not turmoil in the Bank Board, Gray added, but turmoil in the industry. Gray said that it was ironic that just that April his wife had reminded him he had promised not to stay in the job for more than two years. He wanted to leave at the end of the summer. But he wasn't going to leave now.

On September 30—Gray remembers the date—another White House friend, Ed Rollins, asked to see him. It was Rollins's last day in the White House, and Gray walked the block to the West Wing to visit him in his office. As Gray remembers it, "He said, 'Look, you and I have been friends for a long time. We both think the same way about Don Regan.'" But Regan had a message for Gray that Rollins had volunteered to deliver.

"Regan wants his own team," continued Rollins.

"His own team!" Gray exploded. "He's not the president! I'm on Ronald Reagan's team."

"But Regan thinks he's the president," replied Rollins.

Gray asked a question he had asked before. Should he try to talk to the real President? Rollins said no and gave him an argument he had already heard. "Don Regan will badmouth you before you go in. He'll sit in the meeting and interrupt. After the meeting, he'll badmouth you some more."

Gray never tried it. Instead, in October, he thought briefly about throwing in the towel. He asked for a totally confidential meeting, just himself, his friend Edwin Meese, and Don Regan. If the three could work out terms in total privacy, he might leave the ring. The message went through. That Friday, said Gray, he received a call from Monica Langley of the *Wall Street Journal* asking about his impending resignation. In a fury, Gray wrote a note to Meese. "I told you he was a liar and a good-for-nothing bastard." Gray summarized its contents. "I'm going to fight him every step of the way."

Gray often asks himself a chilling question, "What might have happened if I had left?" He is convinced, based on later developments, that Regan would have replaced him with an industry stooge. The FSLIC bankruptcy that Gray labored so hard to bring to light might have been concealed until the last minute. The collapse would have involved not just 500 corrupt thrifts but the entire financial system. The general run that Treasury feared in January 1989 would have been inevitable and entirely rational. Gray had his faults and may have stumbled in his fight, but the country should be grateful that he could summon the courage to remain so blunt and pigheaded.

□ 3 □

GRAY'S RESOLVE WAS STRENGTHENED by the strong suspicion that outside forces were acting through Regan, forces who cared less about ideology than about their dividends. When Gray heard from Regan, he often detected the tones of Charles H. Keating, Jr. A beanpole of a man, the six-foot-five Keating was easily Gray's most formidable enemy in the industry.

Keating, the owner of Lincoln Savings and Loan of Irvine, California, was born in 1924 in Cincinnati, Ohio, and his Queen City connections figure strangely in his story. A national championship swimmer, Keating attended the University of Cincinnati on an athletic scholarship and continued in law school. He and his brother William, later a United States congressman, founded the prominent Cincinnati law firm of Keating, Muething and Klekamp. This firm later handled securities work for Marvin Warner and his Home State Savings. Keating left the law practice in 1972 to work for the publicity-shy multimillionaire Carl Lindner. Keating's biographers trace many similarities between his business style and his mentor's; preeminently, they both built their empires on a savings and loan. Lindner, who drove an ice cream truck during the depression, based his conglomerate American Financial Corporation (with nearly $12 billion in assets) on the Hunter Savings Association. The state-chartered Lincoln Savings was the linchpin of Keating's American Continental Corporation, originally a homebuilding division in Lindner's empire. Keating also learned from Lindner's deft use of political contributions.

Political pull helped Lindner clean up after the Ohio Bank Crisis in 1985. Months after Home State closed, Chemical Bank of New York was about to purchase its remains when Lindner's Hunter Savings swooped in with a surprise last-minute bid. Lindner picked up Home State under a state law giving Ohio institutions the right to top any out-of-state offers with a final bid. This unusual provision was in part the work of Cincinnati's Republican state Senator Stanley J. Aronoff. In 1984, Senator Aronoff received a $6,000 contribution from Carl Lindner. After closing on Home State in a deal heavily subsidized by the state, Lindner recouped much of his cash investment by immediately selling two-thirds of its branches.

Keating left Lindner's shadow in 1976, when he moved to Phoenix. He was sent to manage Lindner's homebuilding arm, American Continental Homes. In 1979, the SEC charged Lindner, Keating, and Donald Klekamp of the Keating law firm with arranging millions

of dollars in improper loans to Lindner's employees. In the same
year, Keating struck out on his own, buying Lindner's subsidiary and
changing its name to American Continental Corporation. In 1984,
he bought Lincoln Savings and Loan. In his first three years at the
thrift, Keating excited controversy by his attempts to rebuild its
balance sheet. Keating led the thrift into a large stake in "junk
bonds," high-yield corporate bonds. He invested aggressively in real
estate projects, raw land, and corporate subsidiaries. Keating also
made a name for himself as a straitlaced moralist and militant conservative. He campaigned nationally against pornography. He insisted on careful dress and grooming for his employees, to the point
that Phoenix locals called his firm "the Stepford Company."

Keating's overriding character trait seems to have been an absolute conviction of his own righteousness and a habit of defining
the right as his own self-interest. He also believed firmly in advancing his vision through political contributions. His donations in
Phoenix, driven by issues such as water development, became so
notorious that the city passed an ordinance limiting all campaign
giving. The *Los Angeles Times* toted up $700,000 that Keating and
his associates had given to 36 state and national candidates. Keating
replied that he had given to far more than 36. It later emerged that
he had given at least an equal amount to supposedly nonpartisan
"get-out-the-vote" drives and foundations linked to individual politicians. In 1980, Keating briefly ran John Connally's presidential
campaign. He later hired Connally's son Mark as his press spokesman.

His political involvement and his devotion to deregulation put
Keating on a collision course with Ed Gray. Keating took personal
affront to Gray's complaints about the California thrift law, the Nolan Act, which gave the state's S&Ls, Lincoln included, a carte
blanche for direct investments. They faced the issue squarely in
congressional hearings at the end of February 1985. The Barnard
subcommittee had called Ed Gray on the carpet to defend a recent
Bank Board package of regulations to control thrift investments and
impose higher capital standards on those taking greater risks. The
package was a coherent attempt to deal with the high-flyers, whose

rapid growth already posed a clear threat to the insurance fund. Gray singled out the California law in his opening statement.

Keating took the stand to rebut Gray. "To reregulate today," he said, "is burning the house to roast the pig." After Keating came Robert Hopkins of Commodore, speaking for a group of Texas thrifts organized by Durward Curlee, Hopkins made a mock apology for his rapid growth, to appreciative laughter from the committee. Two academics rounded out the opposition, George J. Benston, an extreme proponent of deregulation, and Alan Greenspan, former chairman of the President's Council of Economic Advisors. Both said the direct investment rule would do more harm than good. Greenspan added that the solvency of the FSLIC insurance fund shouldn't be the main concern since Congress would bail out the depositors anyway. Both Benston and Greenspan acknowledged that they were speaking on behalf of Lincoln Savings and Loan. (Hopkins, Durward Curlee's spokesman, was convicted in 1989 for illegal campaign contributions. His thrift went insolvent in March 1986, with a loss of nearly $700 million. Alan Greenspan is now chairman of the Federal Reserve.)

Through 1985, industry complaints about Gray became more insistent, the congressional hearings grew more hostile, and negative articles cropped up in the press. Gray was convinced that Keating and his allies leaked the stories. (One March 1985 piece by the *Wall Street Journal*'s Monica Langley said Gray catered to the large conservative California thrifts and slighted the fast-growing, less conventional ones. The heavily slanted piece quoted only one critic by name, the owner of a California thrift that went bankrupt two years later.) Gray still sees the public criticism and Regan's campaign to oust him as part of the same axis, with Charles Keating at one pole.

At the end of 1985, Keating took more direct action. It began with a series of "very clandestine" telephone calls to another member of the Bank Board. The caller, a lobbyist for the United States League of Savings Institutions, wanted to pass on the word that a client was interested in offering a job to Ed Gray. "It was public knowledge he was in debt," said one of Gray's staff. "He was unpopular with many in the industry and he wasn't likely to find a Happy Hunting Home.'' But the nature of the call, on behalf of an unidentified client, alerted Gray's defenses. He asked Shannon Fairbanks, his chief of staff, to smoke out his would-be benefactor. Fairbanks called and asked who was making the offer. It turned out to be Charles Keating. She set up a breakfast to learn more. Keating showed up, along with James Grogan, Lincoln Savings' general counsel, formerly an aide to Senator John Glenn. Fairbanks recalled that Keating "said maybe Gray could do something positive for him in his organization because Mr. Keating was not having a very good time with him where he was now.'' She says it was a pleasant meal, but, on behalf of Gray, she firmly turned him down. Gray later learned that other regulators had received similar offers and that some had accepted.

One of the regulators who did go over to the other side was Lawrence W. Taggart, former California savings and loan commissioner. Taggart, member of a family well connected in state Republican politics, held that post from 1983 through 1984, just after the Nolan Act deregulated state thrifts. During his brief tenure, by his own account, he processed or tried to process 210 applications for new state charters. FSLIC refused to grant them insurance because at the time Taggart had only 43 examiners on his staff. After resigning, he took the job of president of TCS Financial, a San Diego consulting firm financed by Charles Keating. Through 1985 and part of 1986, Taggart worked with Lincoln Savings. During the rest of 1986, he consulted for several Texas thrifts, including Don Dixon's Vernon S&L. (We've already noted that Vernon gave Taggart a $687,000 loan.) Taggart may be one of the least repentant figures in the entire S&L disaster.

Taggart later testified that during his time in Texas, the thrift industry, meaning Dixon and his friends, felt threatened by the revival of FSLIC supervision. "There had been one or two individuals placed in the Dallas bank," he said, "which were causing havoc within the industry in Texas." So Taggart sat down on August 4, 1986, and wrote a letter to "the Honorable Donald Regan, Chief of Staff, White House." The seven-page single-spaced letter complained in detail about "re-regulation" by FSLIC, about the 250 examiners poised in Texas to close thrifts in the event of recapitalization, about the federal attempts to preempt the liberal thrift laws in Texas and California. In the first paragraph, Taggart warned, "these actions being done to the industry by the current chief regulator of the Federal Home Loan Bank Board are likely to have a very adverse impact on the ability of our Party to raise needed campaign funds in the upcoming elections."

It's not known how Regan responded, if at all, but on one point Taggart and Keating had their way. By the summer of 1986, both of Gray's Bank Board colleagues had resigned. As the only member of the board, Gray was effectively paralyzed. Many decisions, including the closing of a thrift, couldn't be made without a majority vote. Gray had been asking Regan for months to make appointments, but nothing happened. Now the thrifts themselves, as represented by Taggart, were asking for new directors, as a check on Gray. Taggart asked Regan to end the "monarchist agency" by appointing "two individuals who are both knowledgeable about the real problems which plague the industry today, and who have the 'backbone' to stand up to a strong-willed Chairman if differences should arise." (According to Gray, one of the candidates on the "short list" was Durward Curlee.)

On November 8, right after the election, Regan granted Taggart's wish. The White House named two new directors in recess appointments, a procedure detested by Congress. (During the frequent congressional vacations, the president can put someone in place to serve at his pleasure for up to a year without Senate confirmation.) One, Professor Lawrence White of New York University, was uncontroversial, but the other was big trouble. This was an Atlanta lawyer and real estate investor named Lee H. Henkel, Jr. Charles Keating later claimed credit for advancing Henkel, "with Don Regan being the main guy that we lobbied."

The trouble began during Henkel's first board meeting, on December 18. Gray proposed a two-year extension for his rule limiting direct real estate investments, one of the "pig roast" rules Keating had testified against. The new majority voted him down. Then Henkel proposed a new version with an interesting exemption. As Bill Black, the FSLIC director of litigation, thought it over in the back of the room, he realized that it was tailor-made to exclude Lincoln Savings. Gray and White voted it down. Black told Gray his suspicion, and Gray notified Senator William Proxmire, chairman of the Senate Banking Committee, who by now was his only court of appeal.

As Proxmire dug deeper, he discovered that over the past three years Henkel and his businesses had received more than $133 million in loans from Lincoln Savings. According to a leak to the *New York Times,* at least $86 million were still outstanding by June 1986, and some were in default. The Justice Department opened an investigation. Faced with the hostility of Senator Proxmire and long-delayed confirmation hearings, Henkel resigned from the board on April 1, 1987. The investigation was apparently dropped.

□ 4 □

WHILE KEATING WAS PULLING STRINGS WITH DON REGAN, he was feeling a pinch at home. On March 12, 1986, the Home Loan Bank of San Francisco began a routine examination of Lincoln. By the fall, the examiners had found serious problems. Its appraisals were hiding $131 million in losses, loan swaps were generating paper profits, and direct investments exceeded Bank Board regulations by $615 million. (It was this last rule that Henkel had tried to change at the December 18 board meeting.) Keating made his customary response to the pressure. He pulled political wires.

On April 2, 1987, the day after Henkel's resignation, Gray underwent the first of two lobbying sessions later known to his staff as "the four-senator meeting" and the "five-senator meeting." Gray remembers being called, alone, to the office of Senator Dennis DeConcini, Democrat of Arizona, in the lavishly marbled Hart Office Building. He arrived at 6:00 PM and found three other senators waiting as well. John McCain, a Republican and the other senator from Arizona, was there, as were Alan Cranston, Democrat of California, and John Glenn, Democrat of Ohio. "We want to discuss with you some concerns we have about Lincoln Savings," said DeConcini. "Our friend at Lincoln Savings had relayed these concerns to us." Gray noticed that the senators always said "our friend"; they never used Keating's name. As Gray remembers it, and as usual his memories are vivid, DeConcini offered a quid pro quo. A few weeks earlier the Bank Board had adopted another, stricter limit on direct investment and broadened its scope to include loans on undeveloped land. As a developer with extensive land holdings, Keating was very worried about their impact, worried enough to challenge them in a court suit.

DeConcini asked Gray to withdraw the regulation. In return, said Gray, the senators offered to help him with a problem they thought he was having with Lincoln, "namely my [alleged] concern that Lincoln wasn't making enough home loans." Gray was perplexed and astonished. He hadn't mentioned anything about home loans and had made a point of staying away from the Lincoln case. Beyond that, the idea of a quid pro quo was bizarre. As he wrote later to Senator McCain, "I had never been asked until this meeting with you and your colleagues—by any United States senator—to withdraw a regulation for any reason, particularly on behalf of a friend, and especially in the privacy of a senatorial office."

The meeting continued for a full hour. Gray defended the direct investment regulation. DeConcini said it should be withdrawn because it might be unconstitutional. Gray replied that only the courts could decide that (and later they did, allowing it to stand). The senators came back again and again to the ongoing examination of Lincoln. They kept asking why it was "taking so long." They asked about appraisal standards "which the Senators understood (presumably from the 'friend') were allegedly harsh and unfairly applied on Lincoln." And they asked why Gray didn't know more about the financial condition of Lincoln. Senator Glenn in particular was upset about Gray's unfamiliarity with the case, although Gray explained that in light of the frequent accusations of vendetta from their "friend," he preferred to leave it to the "first-rate team" from the San Francisco Home Loan Bank. He offered to put them in touch with the Eleventh District regulators.

After the meeting, Gray went back to his office and gave a full account to three members of his staff, including Bill Black, by now promoted to deputy director of FSLIC. This caution didn't prevent an ugly dispute later, when his summary began to circulate. The senators denied that anyone had asked Gray to withdraw the regulation. DeConcini wrote to Gray, "I am surprised and disappointed that a former high administration official would stoop to this kind of duplicity." Gray remarked that that is why they had him come alone to DeConcini's office, to provide "deniability" if he ever decided to talk. When the senators called later that week for a meeting with the San Francisco team, Bill Black decided not to make the same mistake. Three officers from San Francisco, including James Cirona, president of the Home Loan Bank, flew to Washington for the April 9 conference, and Black escorted them to Senator De-Concini's office. This time, Black took notes throughout, as close to verbatim as he could make them.

The same four senators were there, along with Senator Donald W. Riegle, Jr., Democrat of Michigan, soon to be chairman of the Senate Banking Committee. DeConcini started, around 6:00 PM, with a strong defense of Lincoln S&L. "Lincoln is a viable organization," he said. "It made $49 million last year, even more the year before." DeConcini said Lincoln had two disagreements with the Bank Board: the lawsuit on the direct investment regulation and the appraisals. He took the thrift's side on both.

"We suggest that the lawsuit be accelerated and that you grant them forbearance while the suit is pending," he said. "I know something about the appraisal values of the Federal Home Loan Bank Board. They appear to be grossly unfair."

Cranston popped in to say he shared the senators' concerns. McCain said he didn't want to be improper. Glenn asked, "Why has the exam dragged on and on?"

Riegle, introduced as an expert from the Banking Committee, added, "The appearance from a distance is that this thing is out of control and had become a struggle between Keating and Gray, two people I gather who have never even met. The appearance is that it's a fight to the death. This discredits everyone if it becomes the perception."

All of them in one form or another threw in a disclaimer. "If there are fundamental problems at Lincoln," said Riegle, "OK."

The regulators started to explain. Appraisals had been bad in the 1984 exam. Keating promised to correct them, but in the 1986 exam they were worse. Underwriting was bad. None of the loan files that were examined had credit reports on the borrowers.

"I have trouble with this discussion," DeConcini interjected. "Are you saying that their underwriting practices were illegal or just not the best practice?"

"These underwriting practices violate our regulatory guidelines," replied Cirona.

"They are also an unsafe and unsound practice," added Black, using the legal language that justifies a bank closing.

The senators continued to hammer away. "Some people don't do the kind of underwriting you want," said Glenn. "Is their judgment good?" Michael Patriarca, director of District Eleven supervision, fielded that one. "That approach might be okay if they were doing it with their own money. They aren't; they're using federally insured deposits."

"Where's the smoking gun?" objected Riegle. "Where are the losses?"

"What's wrong with this if they're willing to clean up their act?" said DeConcini.

Cirona took the offensive. "This is a ticking time bomb," he said. The Senators continued to defend Lincoln, but the regulators had the dirt. The following exchange altered the entire tone of the meeting.

PATRIARCA: I'm relatively new to the savings and loan industry but I've never seen any bank or S&L that's anything like this. This isn't even close. You can ask any banker you know about these practices. They violate the law and regulations and common sense.

GLENN: What violates the law?

PATRIARCA: Their direct investments violate the regulation. Then
              there's the file stuffing. They took undated documents
              purporting to show underwriting efforts and put them
              into the files sometimes more than a year after they
              made the investment.

GLENN: Have you done anything about these violations of law?

PATRIARCA: We're sending a criminal referral to the Department
              of Justice. Not maybe: we're sending one. This is an
              extraordinarily serious matter. It involves a whole
              range of imprudent actions. I can't tell you strongly
              enough how serious this is.

DeConcini made one last objection. Why do Lincoln's auditors
continue to vouch for their books? "You believe they'd prostitute
themselves for a client?" he exclaimed.

"Absolutely," said Patriarca. "It happens all the time."

The senators left for a vote on the floor. When they returned,
uncharacteristically subdued, the focus shifted from berating the
regulators to saving Lincoln. "Is this institution so far gone that it
can't be salvaged?" asked Riegle. "I don't know," said Patriarca:

> "I think my colleague Mr. Black put it right when he said that
> it's like these guys put it all on 16 black in roulette. Maybe
> they'll win, but I can guarantee you that if an institution con-
> tinues such behavior it will eventually go bankrupt."

"Well, I guess that's pretty definitive," said Riegle, and the meeting broke up.

□ 5 □

IN THE "FIVE-SENATOR MEETING," the regulators from San Francisco
said not only that they were making a criminal referral, but that the
Lincoln examination would be finished in seven to ten days. What
followed is considered by some highly competent observers to be

the biggest scandal of all, an even worse precedent than anything done by Jim Wright and his whole corrupt Texas crew.

Sometime in May 1987, a month after the meetings, San Francisco sent two recommendations to Bank Board headquarters: put Lincoln Savings in either a conservatorship or a receivership. Lincoln was so badly run, concluded the examination, that it should be taken out of Keating's hands. The first plan would appoint a conservator to run it and try to turn it around. The second, the receivership, would close it and pay off the depositors. There was one problem. Of the three grounds for closing a thrift, insolvency was by far the easiest to prove, and, so far, Lincoln Savings was not insolvent. San Francisco's recommendation was based on the two other grounds, dissipation of assets and operation in "an unsafe and unsound" manner.

Following routine, the notice went to ORPOS, the Bank Board's Office of Regulatory Policy, Oversight, and Supervision. From there, the case went to the office of the general counsel. The legal staff agonized for weeks, since Keating would be certain to take them to court. (As *Business Week* later put it in a headline, "For Charlie Keating, the Best Defense is a Lawsuit.") Finally, toward the end of June, the recommendation arrived on the desk of Shannon Fairbanks, Gray's chief of staff.

Ed Gray had eight days left in office. He had served four years, three months and eight days, a full term and more. After his brief honeymoon he had been under constant attack, but he had outlasted his enemies. Don Regan resigned at the end of February, swallowed up by the Iran hostage debacle. (When he heard the news, Gray sent an aide downstairs to a liquor store, and his staff celebrated with California champagne. He doesn't remember how many bottles.) An explosive new controversy, the closing of Lincoln, was not high on his "To Do" list.

He had good reason to let the issue ride. His staff warned him that it might "appear that I was somehow trying to 'get' Charlie Keating in a sort of 'last gasp act of revenge.' " He was told, says Gray, "that this might somehow give credence to Mr. Keating's nevertheless absurd allegations that I had 'a vendetta' against him."

Congress was finally about to pass FSLIC recapitalization; bad as the bill was, no one wanted to upset that applecart. And furthermore, Gray didn't think he'd get board approval. "The only other board member, at the time, Larry White, had made it very clear—to me," said Gray, "that he did not want to take up major matters until after the new board (under Danny Wall) took office." So Gray left Keating to his successor and began a drawn-out search for a job. (His job hunt gave a negative confirmation to Professor Kane's caustic argument that regulators collect deferred compensation after they leave office. Gray's reward for attempting to restore supervision was a cold shoulder from the industry and the crack from a House Banking Committee staffer that he would wind up sleeping on the heating grates with the homeless. He finally became president of a mid-sized thrift in Miami.)

Under Gray's successor, however, the Keating affair took a sinister turn. The new Bank Board chairman was M. Danny Wall, who had as many friends on Capitol Hill as Gray had enemies. Wall had been staff director of the Senate Banking Committee during the Reagan era's six years of Republican control, and his ties with Senator Jake Garn, committee chairman then and now ranking Republican, were far older. Wall was the head of urban renewal in Salt Lake City, Utah when Garn was city councilman and mayor. He came to Washington with Garn, and his wife was the Utah senator's personal secretary. Wall's immediate job was to restore relations with Congress and pass the recap bill.

Wall started meeting with crucial figures. He paid a courtesy call on Speaker Wright. And, according to the Home Loan Bank of San Francisco, he met with Charles Keating. In a confidential report to the Bank Board's Enforcement Review Committee, the San Francisco bank said the meeting occurred just after Keating had a breakfast with Speaker Wright. The report said that Keating told Wall "that firing the general counsel of the FHLB San Francisco would please Jim Wright." The general counsel was now Wright's old antagonist Bill Black. The *Arizona Tribune,* in breaking the story, said the meeting may have occurred either in July or September. Wall acknowledged a September meeting with Keating. But he denied there was one in July, and for good reason. If it took place, as other regulators have said it did, then Wall committed a serious impropriety. In the traditional view of ethics, judges, or quasi-judges such as a Bank Board director, should not be having ex parte contacts, private meetings with only one party, in a dispute they may be called on to judge.

We don't know what else went on in those meetings, or in other of Wall's contacts on the Hill, but strange things happened to the Lincoln Savings case. The criminal referral mentioned by Patriarca dropped from sight. Though the staff recommended supervisory action, nothing happened for months. Leaks about the examination appeared in some papers. Lincoln sued the Bank Board for the alleged breach of confidentiality. On September 2, 1987, lawyers for Lincoln met with senior regulators at the Bank Board. The Eleventh District wasn't notified and didn't participate. The Bank Board referred the case to its Enforcement Review Committee. The San Francisco Bank renewed its recommendation for a conservatorship and submitted a 700-page report with four boxes of documents as exhibits. From February to May, 1988 the Bank Board committee held 23 hours of hearings to review the evidence. Lincoln offered to drop its suit and sign a Memorandum of Understanding if it could transfer its headquarters to the jurisdiction of the Seattle Home Loan Bank. The Review Committee, in a curious report, deplored the "seriously adversarial relationship" between Lincoln and the San Francisco Bank.The Bank Board voted to take supervision of Lincoln away from the Eleventh District and handle it with its own staff. The vote was two to one. Chairman Wall and new member Roger Martin voted for the transfer. At the end of May, Lincoln worked out a new deal with the Bank Board. The thrift would raise new capital and sign a supervisory agreement, while Bank Board personnel would give it a fresh examination. The new exam started shortly afterward. The supervisory agreement was so favorable to Lincoln that the "Stepford Company" celebrated with Dom Perignon champagne. According to one story, the party grew so raucous that someone threw a typewriter out a window.

This regulator-swapping continues to appall the professionals. "That sends an absolutely terrible message to the industry at exactly the time that you need to be saying, 'We need stronger regulation,' " said Frederick D. Wolf, assistant Comptroller General of the United States General Accounting Office in unusually blunt testimony in February 1989. The message was even worse in the context of the "five-senator" meeting. The senators were told damaging details from the Lincoln examination, and they were informed about a criminal referral even before Lincoln had been notified. Yet if any of them pressed the Bank Board to act on San Francisco's findings, it certainly doesn't show up in the record. The political pressure worked in favor of Lincoln Savings, and, although the senators deny there is any connection, any onlooker has to be struck by the lavish contributions they all received from Keating.

In early 1988, the *Detroit News* added up the most visible donations. During the 1980s, Senator DeConcini, the host of the meetings, received $43,000 from Keating and his associates. His Republican colleague from Arizona, Senator John McCain, received $112,000. Senator John Glenn got $34,000; Senator Cranston, $41,000, and Senator Riegle, $66,130. After the story appeared, Senator Riegle, the expert witness, returned $76,100 to Keating and his employees. The others kept the money. It later emerged that Cranston was even deeper in Keating's debt. A get-out-the-vote fund that employed Cranston's son received $400,000 from Keating's American Continental Corporation. The California Democratic Committee received another $85,000. Cranston also solicited $450,000 from Keating for two other voter registration groups. Their activity undoubtedly helped Cranston win a narrow contest for re-election.

Another of these back-door contributions, $200,000 worth, went to Senator John Glenn, the former astronaut. The syndicated columnist Warren Brookes reported that this batch was arranged by the Lincoln Savings corporation counsel James Grogan, a former aide to Senator Glenn. According to Brookes, Grogan also roped Glenn into the four- and five-senator meetings. These outside contributions poured through a gaping loophole in the federal campaign contribution law. Since they went to nonprofit, supposedly nonpartisan organizations, they didn't count as political donations and were also tax-deductible.

The legality didn't stop the contributions, or the political intervention, from becoming a major embarrassment in early 1989, when it turned out that the San Francisco examiners had been right all along. In his year of bought time, Keating struggled with a declining real estate market; with his auditors, whom he changed several times; and with short sellers on the stock market, who gambled on his company's imminent demise. (Two financial writers compared the latter struggle to "mud wrestling, in which both sides are so obnoxious that it is hard for the spectators to root for either.") In April 1989, Keating lost his footing in the muck and declared a Chapter 11 bankruptcy for his American Continental Corporation. In a last maneuver, he pulled $400 million in assets out of Lincoln Savings and Loan and sheltered them in 11 subsidiaries that fell under the protection of bankruptcy court. The Bank Board slammed the barn door the next day, on April 13, placing Lincoln in a federal conservatorship.

It quickly emerged that Lincoln was a disaster even worse than its most severe critics had imagined. The five senators had the impression that Keating had rescued a failing thrift; the truth was that he had taken a healthy thrift and bled it dry. The accountants Kenneth Leventhal & Company analyzed 15 of Lincoln's real estate deals and concluded that they were "sham" transactions, using "accounting gimmickry" to produce artificial profits. These deals turned $135 million in paper profits, "more than 50 percent of all pre-tax income ($238,633,000) reported by Lincoln since it was acquired by American Continental Corporation." But, said Leventhal, Lincoln gave the other parties side deals that cost itself $50 million more than it booked. The report concluded with language that for auditors is as blunt as a kick in the face:

> Seldom in our experience as accountants have we encountered a more egregious example of the misapplication of generally accepted accounting principles. This Association was made to function as an engine designed to funnel insured deposits to its

parent in tax allocation payments and dividends. To do this, it had to generate reported earnings, and it generated earnings by making loans or other transfers of cash or property to facilitate sham sales of land. It created profits by making loans. Many of the loans were bad. Lincoln was manufacturing profits by giving its money away.

Within weeks after the seizure of Lincoln Savings, the Bank Board estimated it would cost FSLIC at least $2.5 billion to liquidate it, not counting the $400 million in assets that the thrift transferred out at the last minute. The Federal Reserve had to lend cash to cope with a run on the thrift. The cost ranked among the largest in the history of either FSLIC or the FDIC.

The pain of this failure was also greater than that of many others. In the year after the five-senator meeting, Keating tried to boost Lincoln's capital by selling junk notes that masqueraded as certificates of deposit. That is the charge of lawyers for many of the 23,000 customers who bought some $250 million of these subordinated debentures. "Subordinated" means that these note-holders are way down the line in collecting from a bankrupt Lincoln. The notes had no federal guarantee and in fact no substantial backing of any kind. Yet, claims the class action fraud suit, Lincoln sold them in its 29 branch offices to clients who thought they were the equivalent of an FSLIC-insured CD. The junk notes carried a higher interest rate than did the insured CDs, but not so high that it signalled their extreme riskiness. The possibility for confusion about the federal guarantee is so prevalent that it is a good question whether thrifts should ever be allowed to sell subordinated debentures directly to depositors. Even Keating himself was skeptical of these notes at one point. In the 1985 hearings on direct investment, he said, "I do not happen to think subordinated debenture is viable capital; I think it is a sham. So, I do not really care, but everybody else was doing it."

With cries of fraud echoing from 23,000 constituents, many of them elderly, Senator Cranston slowly realized that he might have blundered. But the realization came late. As late as April 1989, Cranston was hectoring the Bank Board to approve the sale of Lincoln Savings to a group of Keating's employees headed by former Congressman John H. Rousselot. (Cranston abandoned all ideological barriers in his help for Lincoln Savings. A liberal with credentials so ancient that he was once sued by Hitler,* Cranston gladly endorsed the very right wing Rousselot, a former employee of the John Birch Society.) On June 7, 1989, stung by Ed Gray's account of their meeting, Cranston wrote an angry note claiming that his message had been, "Don't keep Keating twisting in the limbo of your bureaucrats' malicious indecision." A month later, he released a statement saying, "looking back from the view of the current climate, I did a pretty stupid thing, politically."

In the last week of July 1989, as House and Senate conferees hammered out the last details of the S&L rescue bill, observers wondered why Senator Cranston insisted so strongly on a minor point. Supported by Senator Riegle, he was willing to compromise major issues, such as the source of funding for $50 billion, so that Danny Wall could stay in his job without renewed confirmation hearings. The *Wall Street Journal* finally concluded that Riegle and Cranston didn't want Wall to go on a stand under oath in front of television cameras. They were afraid it would bring out the whole story of their interference on behalf of Lincoln Savings and Charlie Keating.

With the S&L rescue bill on the way to President Bush, the Bank Board declared Lincoln Savings insolvent and placed it in receivership. The books closed on Lincoln on August 3, 1989. But months earlier, Charles Keating gave it a suitable epitaph. After American Continental went to bankruptcy court in mid-April, he held a combative press conference. "One question, among the many raised in recent weeks," he told reporters, "had to do with whether my financial support in any way influenced several political figures to take up my cause. I want to say in the most forceful way I can: I certainly hope so."

---

*The case, brought in a Connecticut civil court, involved an unauthorized translation of *Mein Kampf* that Cranston published to alert the American public to the true nature of the Nazi movement.

PART FIVE

The Big Fix

CHAPTER FOURTEEN

□□□

The Seamless Web (II)

□ 1 □

THE NETWORK WE SAW IN FLORIDA spins its way west. The cliques in Texas have their own local history; we've seen the continuity in the Rent-a-Bank crew. But there are also fascinating national tendrils, attached to the latticework of national political fund-raising. Some of these were uncovered in the investigation of House Speaker Jim Wright, although their significance wasn't appreciated at the time.

□ 2 □

SPEAKER WRIGHT AND RICHARD SWANN

ONE REAL SURPRISE IN THE HOUSE ETHICS COMMITTEE INVESTIGATION of Speaker Wright was the reemergence of Richard Swann, a crucial figure in the Tallahassee junta. When Brooks Jackson and Edward Pound broke the story in the middle of the hearings, they emphasized Swann's role as owner of a troubled thrift. Wright earned $50,000 in an Orlando land deal with Swann that was actually arranged by Wright's friend George Mallick through their jointly owned investment company, Mallightco. The Ethics Committee found no evidence that Swann had tried to influence Wright's position on thrift legislation, so it concluded that the deal was proper.

The business deal was less interesting, however, than the connection between Swann's highly developed Florida fund-raising network and the congressional campaign committee. Wright was a houseguest and featured celebrity at Swann's home during a July 1985 barbecue that Swann hosted for the Democratic Congressional Campaign Committee. According to a former associate, Swann was also close to Congressman Tony Coelho, chairman of the DCCC.

Preoccupied by losses at his American Pioneer Savings Bank, Swann has reduced his political work, said a spokesman. But his influence has survived Wright's downfall. He was a major fund raiser for the presidential campaign of Missouri Democrat Richard Gephardt, now the House majority leader.

□ 3 □

SPEAKER WRIGHT AND HERMAN BEEBE

AT THE END OF THE ETHICS COMMITTEE INVESTIGATION, tantalizing hints emerged of a link between Speaker Wright and Herman Beebe, the eminence grise of the high-flying gang. This connection could have been political dynamite, but after Wright's resignation most of the press lost interest. Ironically, the revelation came from Wright himself.

Stung by the accusation that his wife Betty had been a mere conduit for payoffs from Mallick, Wright released affidavits to show that she had indeed earned her keep. Her work for Mallightco, he said, included researching a bank deal with a Dallas businessman named Louis Farris. During his resignation speech, he produced an affidavit from Farris, one of several that he inserted into the congressional record. (No one in the press seems to have picked up the record later to read what the affidavits said.)

Farris stated that he met with Mallick, Speaker Wright, and Betty Wright in the summer of 1983 in his search for partners in "various investment proposals." He paid $25,000 to buy out their stock in the tiny First National Bank of Weatherford, a West Texas town of 8,000, where Wright served two terms as mayor in the early 1950s. Farris met several more times with George and Betty. "At the time," Farris said, "I was attempting to assemble a chain of banks in several states, and I was looking for partners and investors."

The alert Dallas reporter Byron Harris noticed that shortly before these meetings, Farris had been employed by Herman Beebe "as his so-called deal man." In one of these deals, as described by *Dallas Morning News* reporter Allen Pusey, Farris was involved in selling a partnership in the Dallas-Fort Worth Airport Bank, then owned by Herman Beebe and Dallas businessman Clint Murchison. Murchison wanted to end his partnership, and Beebe wanted to replace him with Don Dixon, later of Vernon S&L fame. Pusey described Farris as Murchison's partner, and nothing indicated that Beebe was involved in his effort to assemble a chain of banks. In any event, as Farris testified, "George and Betty reviewed my proposal but decided not to participate." If Betty Wright saved her husband from even that indirect a link with Beebe, then she did deserve her pay.

Another affidavit came from Fort Worth investor John A. Freeman, whose name emerged in the 1977 Rent-a-Bank hearings. Freeman was a partner with Herman Beebe and Ben Barnes in buying an insurance company in 1976.

Wright had other second- or third-step associations with the shady Louisianan. In 1985 he had free use of a Falcon 20 twin-engine jet owned by Kenneth C. Hood, the former employee of Beebe who became top lending officer at Jarrett Woods's Western Savings Association until Hood's conviction for bank fraud at a Dallas bank.

Breaking the story during the Ethics Committee hearings, the *Wall Street Journal* observed that Hood had agreed to plead guilty to the charge at the time of Wright's trip. The bill for the three-day excursion to eight Texas cities came to more than $8,000. Hood picked it up in apparent violation of federal campaign law. Wright repaid him four years later, after the *Journal* started asking questions.

The trip tied Wright to the high-flyers more closely than previously realized. House Ethics Committee Special Counsel Richard Phelan missed it in his report, and it may not have come to light if one of Hood's former employees hadn't talked to the *Journal*. Wright's office said the tour was meant to prepare for a fund-raising "Cowtown Jamboree" held several months later in Fort Worth. But it brought Wright in contact with the thrift owners whom Thomas Gaubert was organizing into the supposedly independent East Texas First PAC for the special congressional election in the First District.

Vickie Rosell, Hood's former chief financial officer, told the *Journal* that Hood complained he lent out the plane because Edwin McBirney, chairman of Sunbelt S&L, told him to. "McBirney said I have to let Jim Wright use the plane this week," she said he told her. Tom Gaubert of Independent American Savings flew along with Wright and several aides. During the dates of the trip, July 1 and 2, Gaubert's East Texas First PAC reported several $1,000 donations from Harvey McLean of Paris S&L, his wife, and at least eight employees of Sunbelt Savings. It would have broken federal campaign law for Gaubert to coordinate his independent PAC with congressional leaders. After the trip, Wright presented Hood with a small gavel on a plaque. Said Rosell, "Ken had it mounted right next to his phone on the plane."

Another of Wright's plane trips raised questions. In July 1984, a Lear jet provided by Vernon Savings and Loan flew Wright, an aide, and Congressman Tony Coelho, then head of the Democratic Congressional Campaign Committee, from Santa Ana, California through Addison, Texas (the North Dallas airport favored by the high-flyers) to Shreveport, Louisiana, Beebe's hometown. The DCCC told reporter Byron Harris that the visit to Shreveport was personal. Harris noted in his broadcast, however, that within 90 days, Beebe contributed $5,000 to the Democratic Senatorial Campaign Committee and $5,000 to Coelho's DCCC.

□ 4 □

BETTY WRIGHT AND JAMES LING

THE FREEMAN AFFIDAVIT IN THE CONGRESSIONAL RECORD gives an interesting picture of the way the web worked, tying together the great and the famous. Freeman said he knew Jim Wright from 1968 and met Betty Wright at a reception shortly after their marriage. In 1979 he cut the congressman in on oil wells. At the Wrights' anniversary party that year, Betty introduced him to George Mallick and said they should meet sometime "to discuss business opportunities." Shortly after, in a meeting in Mallick's office, she told Freeman, in his words, "that she would appreciate the chance to look at opportunities I might be interested in and that they in turn would do the same for me."

Subsequently, continued Freeman, "I was having dinner with Mr. Jim Ling in Fort Worth and discussing the formation of a company to acquire interests in the energy field. Mr. Mallick and Betty Wright were dining at the same club and came by the table and were introduced to Mr. Ling. The following day I called Betty and told her that I was discussing an investment in Matrix Energy with Mr. Ling and it might be something that Mr. Mallick might be interested in." The Mr. Ling at this dinner was the legendary James J. Ling, one of the foremost corporate raiders of the late 1960s. Ling, credited with pioneering the hostile takeover, was making a modest comeback.

Ling now became more interesting than the Wrights. Six months after the meeting at the Fort Worth club, Betty called Freeman and said she wasn't interested in Matrix. But another investor had a great deal of interest, the redoubtable Marvin Warner. On July 21, 1981, Warner's Home State Financial Services, Inc., the holding company for his Cincinnati thrift, lent Ling and a partner $2.5 million each to purchase 2,750,000 shares of Matrix Energy, Inc. Warner sold most of the loan as a participation to ComBanks/Winter Park, soon to merge in Freedom Savings and Loan of Tampa. Warner also bought nearly 15 percent of the shares of Xenerex Corp., the parent of Matrix.

The link between Warner and Ling, by Ling's own account, was his partner, Jack W. Bertoglio, from Coral Gables, Florida. Ling and Bertoglio guaranteed each other's $2.5 million loan from Home State Financial. Bertoglio was involved with Warner in at least one other big deal, a 1982 attempt to take over Global Natural Resources. Global, an oil and gas leaseholder based in Jersey, the English Channel island, was a remnant of Bernard Cornfield's collapsed Investors Overseas Services, one of the biggest financial scandals of the 1960s. Bertoglio also owned a partnership in the United States Football League team, the Tampa Bay Bandits, along with Stephen Arky and Ron Ewton, of E. S. M. Government Securities. (In 1985, Bertoglio had a falling out with Arky over the venture and took him to court in Tampa.) Bertoglio outlasted Warner and showed up with a new set of associates. His name appeared on the books of Don Dixon's Vernon Savings and Loan as a coguarantor of a $17.6 million letter of credit to Gold Crown, Inc., a Delaware corporation. In 1981, Marvin Warner owned $2.5 million worth of Gold Crown stock.

□ 5 □

THE BOTTOM FISHERS

JAMES LING INTRODUCED ME to the Southmark Corporation in 1986. I was interviewing him for a brief profile. He talked about the opportunities for constructing a fast-growing conglomerate from the wreckage of the Texas economy. His example was Southmark and its chief executive Gene Phillips. "He's a nice guy," said Ling. "Not many of them here are." Neither of us realized what a tangle of connections we would stumble into at that rapidly growing, indescribably complicated outfit, whose holdings ran from real estate syndications (its core business) to a thrift, a casino company, retirement homes, and time-share resorts. Phillips and his partner, New York lawyer William Friedman, appeared in one of the earliest of our webs and at the end were busily spinning one of the last and most wide-ranging. "They're bottom fishers," said one of their chroniclers. "That's why they show up in so many of the failing thrifts." But they move the thrift story into the realm of Drexel Burnham and Michael Milken, one of the most masterful web makers of them all.

Gene Phillips, who for the hub of a major network is remarkably shy and withdrawn, was born in North Carolina in 1938. He met his alter ego, New York lawyer William Friedman, during his first bankruptcy in South Carolina in 1973. Friedman was impressed by Phillips's resilience, and the two formed an investment company to deal in real estate and anything else that came along. In 1978, they happened on a national bank in Marietta, Georgia, a booming suburb of Atlanta. Their stormy attempt at a takeover produced a strange alliance.

The president of their target, the First National Bank of Cobb County, was Emmett J. Foster, who previously had worked in Atlanta's National Bank of Georgia as the right-hand man of Bert Lance. When Phillips and Friedman showed up at Cobb County, Foster decided to throw in with them. According to a suit by the United States Comptroller of the Currency, Foster helped them with financing and suppressed good news about the bank's financial condition until after they made a tender offer for the bank's stock. After a drawn-out legal battle, Phillips dropped his attempt to buy the bank, and the suit was dismissed. He and Friedman sold their stock at a profit of $2 million and moved their operations to Dallas. Foster left Georgia for Knoxville, Tennessee where he became the president for 11 of C. H. Butcher, Jr.'s banks. None of the Butchers' regulators seemed aware of Foster's run-in with the OCC.

In Dallas, Phillips paid a courtesy call on Jim Ling and adopted his strategy of conglomeration, buying a wide variety of enterprises with no apparent connection. One acquisition that did make sense, however, was a thrift, the San Jacinto Savings and Loan of Houston. Phillips bought the thrift in 1984 to help finance his real estate syndications. His main business remained the marketing of partnerships in these syndicates, designed to hold real estate and provide tax shelters. Through San Jacinto, he built ties with the North Dallas high-flyers. The thrift lent $22 million to fellow Dallas syndicator Craig Hall, the first to use Jim Wright to fix the Bank Board. Don Dixon's Vernon S&L worked out a loan participation agreement with Southmark and its thrift to help circumvent growth restrictions imposed by the Bank Board. According to former regulators, substantial financing also went to Charles Keating of Lincoln Savings and Loan.

As usual, some of the strangest connections revolved around Herman Beebe. In 1982, at the urging of the junk bond brokers Drexel Burnham Lambert, Phillips bought stock in Novus Property Company, the descendant of a real estate investment trust formed by the First Wisconsin National Bank of Milwaukee. Phillips, Friedman, and two Southmark employees went on its board of trustees, along with an officer of Energy Bank in Dallas, identified by the OCC as one of Beebe's satellites.

Novus was the landlord of a Las Vegas shopping center containing the Silver City Casino, which is operated by Circus Circus Casinos, Inc., another Drexel Burnham client. (A managing director of Drexel sits on the Circus Circus board of directors.) At one point Circus Circus owned $10 million of Southmark's preferred stock. The casino connection brought Southmark in shoulder-rubbing distance of notorious characters such as Anthony Spilotro, a murderous mafioso who ended his career in a shallow grave in an Illinois cornfield. Phillips told investigators for the New Jersey Casino Commission that he didn't know Spilotro or any of the other bad types associated with Circus Circus.

(On December 31, 1985, a Southmark subsidiary made another Las Vegas investment, a $19 million package of real estate and stock in the Dunes Hotels and Casinos, Inc. This deal put Phillips cheek-to-jowl with Morris Shenker, the notorious Teamster lawyer discussed earlier. Phillips also started dealing with John Anderson, the California tomato grower who borrowed heavily at Vernon.)

In the same month that the Southmark subsidiary shelled out $19 million, Phillips and Friedman personally bought control of Herman Beebe's Bossier Bank and Trust for $10 million. Bossier, a Louisiana state bank, was a heavy lender to high-flyers Harvey

McLean and Don Dixon. Phillips and Friedman bought the stock through their personally owned Syntek Finance Corporation, which already held 49 percent of the Bossier common stock as collateral on a loan. They were sued over the deal by a Southmark shareholder, who claimed they had taken personal advantage of a deal that should have been made available to the publicly owned company. The advantage can't have been that great, however, since Bossier was closed by regulators six months later.

Earlier that year, Beebe bought a large chunk of Southmark's preferred stock. After federal indictments crimped his business activities, Southmark returned the favor. Southmark bought Beebe's string of nursing homes and, to prop him up until the deal could be completed, lent him nearly $30 million.

By this time, Southmark was well on its way to establishing a network as intricate as Beebe's own. When the Bank Board restricted its ability to finance its deals through the San Jacinto thrift in 1986, it cast around for another cash cow, for a time trying to break into the Atlantic City casino scene. It even thought of trying to take over Resorts International, a bottomless pit of intrigue. But the savior turned out to be the junk bond market. From 1986 on, Drexel Burnham floated more than $2 billion in Southmark issues, allowing the company to grow like a supernova. Southmark reached nearly $9 billion in assets before it collapsed. A large amount of these bonds went into Drexel's network of thrifts, just as Southmark picked up large chunks of Drexel's other issues. One major holder was Charles Keating's Lincoln Savings, which carried on a myriad of deals with Southmark, details of which were just coming to light by the late summer of 1989.

Some of the deals revolved around three-cornered ties between Southmark, Keating's American Continental Corp., and the MDC Company of Denver, Colorado. Some of Keating's transactions criticized in the Leventhal report took place with MDC, which in turn purchased a homebuilding subsidiary of Southmark, when Phillips had to sell assets. Curiously, each corporation had a common structure. Originally a real estate holding company, each had ties with a thrift for internal financing. MDC's thrift was Silverado Savings and

Loan of Denver, which was seized in late 1988. (President-elect
Bush's son Neil had been on its board of directors until his resignation that summer. When Bank Board lawyers took over the thrift,
they found a personally inscribed picture of George Bush on the
thrift president's desk.)

The collapse of one in this trio sealed the doom for the others.
By the spring of 1989, Southmark was headed for disaster. Phillips
and Friedman had been ousted by disgruntled stockholders. Their
successor had little corporate experience. (An accountant in Marietta, Georgia, he had been hired by Phillips in 1978 as an agent to
buy stock in the Cobb County bank takeover.) That quarter, Southmark posted a loss of more than $1 billion, a staggering achieve-
ment. But the final push into bankruptcy, said a lawyer involved in
the aftermath, came from Charles Keating. With Lincoln heading
into its own disaster, Keating attempted to collect on Southmark's
junk paper.

The junk bond—thrift network rapidly became an important fac-
tor in the industry, supplanting Beebe and the high-flyers as a source
of political influence. In May 1986, Congressman Tony Coelho decided to try a junk bond investment. His friend Thomas Spiegel,
president of Columbia Savings and Loan in Beverly Hills, obliged
by cutting him into an oversubscribed Drexel Burnham issue. Spiegel
lent Coelho money for the purchase and even held it for a month
until Coelho could complete the financing.* At the time, Bank Board
lawyers were trying to talk Spiegel into rescinding a $9 million bonus
he had given himself, on the grounds that it would look bad in Congress.

Spiegel kept his bonus and mollified Congress by donating large
amounts to Coelho's Democratic Congressional Campaign Committee. He also helped out Senator Cranston's voter registration
campaign. Just as Congress attempted to deal with an existing thrift
debacle, the junk bond network was laying the groundwork for a
new one. In debating the 1989 S&L rescue, the FIRREA (The Fi-

---

*A spate of news articles on this deal, on the eve of Speaker Wright's departure from
Congress, helped lead to Coelho's resignation.

nancial Institutions Reform, Recovery and Enforcement Act), the House added a provision prohibiting thrifts from holding junk bonds. The Senate weakened it by allowing S&Ls to transfer their holdings to a subsidiary, thus setting up a "firewall" to prevent them from becoming a claim on the deposit insurance fund. Yet the damage may have already been done. The collapse of Southmark's junk bonds was already rippling through the system, and other defaults were on their way.

□ 6 □

So THE WEBS KEPT SPINNING. As one appeared to dissolve, another took its place, incorporating loose strands. It sometimes seems futile to try to master their details, but we must try because unless we understand these connections we will not understand the fix.

THE SEAMLESS WEB

The charts on the following pages present in visual form part of the network of business, political, and other relationships among various individuals who have played some role in the developing story of the S&L crisis. Names in boldface type are individuals whose main area of activity is within the state(s) covered by the charts. Those names not in boldface are out-of-state individuals with significant connections inside the state.

The charts have been designed to be as accurate as possible. However, please note that the relationships depicted here can be fully understood only through a careful reading of the chapters in this book that explain those relationships. In short, these charts illustrate and complement but in no way substitute for the complete text of *The Big Fix*.

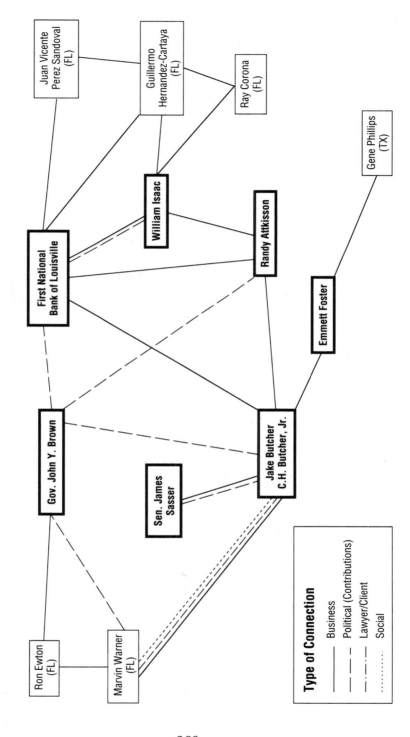

THE TEXAS CONNECTIONS

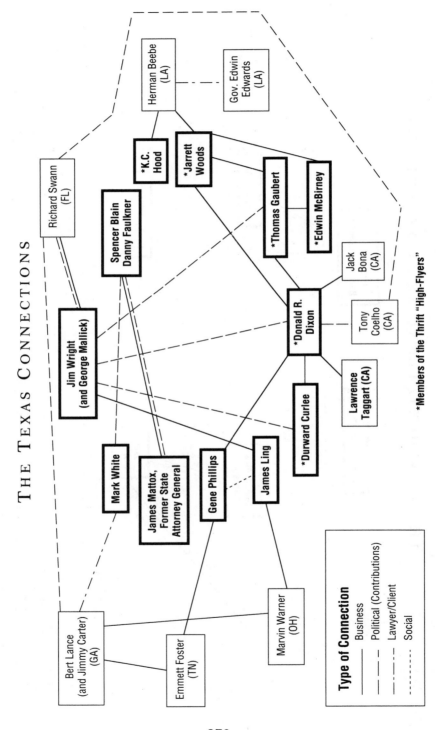

*Members of the Thrift "High-Flyers"

Herman Beebe (LA)

Gov. Edwin Edwards (LA)

*K.C. Hood

*Jarrett Woods

Richard Swann (FL)

Spencer Blain Danny Faulkner

*Thomas Gaubert

*Edwin McBirney

Jack Bona (CA)

Jim Wright (and George Mallick)

Donald R. Dixon

Tony Coelho (CA)

Lawrence Taggart (CA)

Mark White

James Mattox, Former State Attorney General

Gene Phillips

James Ling

*Durward Curlee

Marvin Warner (OH)

Bert Lance (and Jimmy Carter) (GA)

Emmett Foster (TN)

Type of Connection

——— Business

— — — Political (Contributions)

—··—··— Lawyer/Client

············ Social

270

THE FLORIDA CONNECTIONS

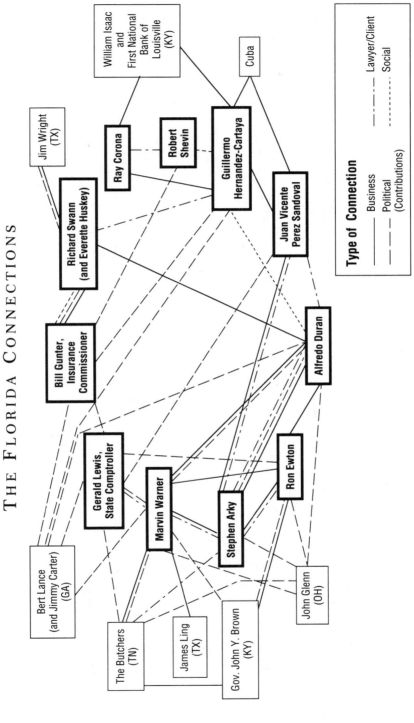

Type of Connection

— Business
—·— Political (Contributions)
—·—·— Lawyer/Client
·········· Social

Boxes: William Isaac and First National Bank of Louisville (KY); Jim Wright (TX); Ray Corona; Robert Shevin; Guillermo Hernandez-Cartaya; Cuba; Richard Swann (and Everette Huskey); Juan Vicente Perez Sandoval; Bill Gunter, Insurance Commissioner; Alfredo Duran; Gerald Lewis, State Comptroller; Marvin Warner; Stephen Arky; Ron Ewton; Bert Lance (and Jimmy Carter) (GA); The Butchers (TN); James Ling (TX); Gov. John Y. Brown (KY); John Glenn (OH)

THE NATIONAL NETWORK

Jake Butcher
C.H. Butcher, Jr.
(TN)

Richard Swann
(FL)

Bert Lance
(Jimmy Carter)
(GA)

Gov. John Y. Brown
(KY)

Herman Beebe
(LA)

Gov. Edwin Edwards
(LA)

Marvin Warner
(OH)

Jim Wright
(TX)

Don Dixon
The "High-Flyers"
(TX)

Charles Keating
(OH)

Lawrence Taggart
(CA)

Tony Coelho
(CA)

"The Five Senators"
DeConcini
Glenn
McCain
Cranston
Riegle

Don Regan
(DC)

Type of Connection

——— Business
– – – Political (Contributions)
–·–·– Lawyer/Client
·········· Social

272

CHAPTER FIFTEEN

□ □ □

The Greatest Crime

□ 1 □

FOR MORE THAN THREE YEARS, the American financial system has careened along the edge of a precipice. Officials in the Treasury, the Bank Board, and elsewhere in Washington worried constantly that one little twitch of the wheel, some pessimistic report, some stray comment or uncontrolled bank or thrift failure, might send the bus over the side. It's a wonder we escaped the crash long enough for the thrift rescue bill, The Financial Institutions Reform, Recovery, and Enforcement Act, to become law on August 9, 1989. But the road still isn't out of the mountains. A collapse of confidence may be less imminent in a system backed by $300 billion in federal bailout money than it was when Congress thought it could dole out $5 billion at a time. But basic flaws have remained unaddressed and grow even more serious.

It is crime enough that the economy was exposed to the irresponsible congressional dallying of 1986 and 1987. The threat of widespread thrift runs, a not altogether irrational reaction to the circumstances, could have plunged the country into a recession—or worse, if poorly handled. But the crime here is more than a figure of speech. The great bulk of the losses in the S&L industry were caused by acts that should be judged in a court of law.

The General Accounting Office gave impressive testimony about the extent of the illegality. We referred earlier to its report on 26 failed thrifts. The man in charge of the study, Frederick D. Wolf, wrote a biting summary of the results, which the GAO delayed a long time in releasing. Wolf, the former Assistant Comptroller General for accounting and financial management and now a private citizen, read his summary to Congressman Gonzalez's House Banking Committee last January:

> GAO found that extensive, repeated and blatant violations of laws and regulations characterized the failed thrifts that we reviewed in each and every case. Virtually every one of the thrifts was operating in an unsafe and unsound manner and was exposed to risks far beyond what was prudent. Under the Bank Board's definitions alone, fraud or insider abuse existed at each and every one of the failed thrifts and allegations of criminal misconduct abounded.
>
> Economic downturns in some sectors of the economy were beyond management's controls and affected all of the thrifts. The failed thrifts, with their illegal and unsafe practices coupled with high-risk investments were unable to withstand the downturns. On the other hand, many thrifts who were operated prudently withstood the same economic conditions in the same areas.
>
> Lastly, despite the fact that examination reports revealed critical problems at the failed thrifts, federal regulators did not always obtain agreements for corrective action. When they obtained them, they were in many cases violated, ignored, and in many cases it was years before resolutions were taken. The failed thrifts were not responsive to the concerns of the regulators.

Wolf confirmed what we have seen over and over again. The examiners saw what was happening. Their reports laid out the problems so clearly that the upper echelons had no excuse not to act. But the supervisors did not act, or their efforts were easily frustrated. The GAO did not, and could not, explain the cause of this frustration, but we have seen the pattern in heartbreaking detail. Political pull reined in the regulators. Corrupt thrift owners and bankers discovered how easy it was to beat the system with a call from a friendly congressman, and congressional friendships were easily purchased. The fix was in.

The 1989 resignations of House Speaker Jim Wright and his number three man Tony Coelho came so quickly, we suspect, because the rest of Congress knew it couldn't stand a prolonged scrutiny of its responsibility for the thrift crisis. The political interventions weren't limited to Wright and his Texans. But even Congress might be surprised at the extent of the fix. It spanned the country in a tangled, shifting, but enduring network of campaign contributors, political movers, and unsavory business deals. It followed power, not ideology, and cut across all partisan lines, so that any of its principal figures could exclaim, as Preston Sturgess's Great McGinty once heard his mentor say, "I'm all the parties." The corruption reached the White House, anyone's White House. And it ruined the careers of many who opposed it.

One of the saddest features of the fix was the toll it took on the state and federal bureaucracy. I have personally encountered at least a dozen admirable people, former examiners, regulators, or law enforcement agents, who left their jobs because of the cynical miasma that came to envelop them. They may have been lucky compared to those left behind. The morale of regulators under political pressure has sunk to a shocking low. Personal corruption is widely reported. As Professor Kane wrote, many endure the low pay because they expect to make up for it when they leave public service and work for the people they have been regulating. In some cases, the demoralization may have taken the ultimate toll. I know of two of President Carter's United States attorneys who took their own lives shortly after leaving their posts. This elite group of lawyers chosen for their high character and legal skill has suffered a suicide rate one thousand times greater than that of terminal AIDS patients. I can't look into the hearts of the two suicides I know of, but it chills me that both were in charge of investigations discussed in this book, and that it was on their watch that criminal referrals were ignored and promising leads cut short.

□ 2 □

WE HAVE ENCOUNTERED THE FIX IN A NUMBER OF CASES, running into characters we have met earlier. It's hard to tell how much is conscious planning and how much is natural selection. (As one former regulator observed, "These people tend to sort themselves out.") A progression emerges, however. Each case is bolder, more destructive, and more accepted than the last. The Coronas manipulated a split between state and federal regulators, until the publicity grew too intense. The Butchers managed to neuter the FDIC, but their collapse was a national scandal. Marvin Warner embarrassed Ohio Governor Richard Celeste, but Celeste won a handy reelection. Jim Wright and his leadership circle protected some of the sleaziest characters in the thrift debacle, yet the House Ethics Committee found the Speaker's conduct "consistent" with congressional standards. Five senators stepped in for Charles Keating, who had donated more than a million dollars at their behest, and when the press asked them point blank, most of them saw no need to return the money. Keating bragged about the influence it bought him. After all the reports about fraud in the thrift debacle, some of them suppressed by the likes of Fernand St Germain, former chairman of the House Banking Committee, Congress still refused to accelerate a Justice Department appropriation to prosecute some of the crime.

The depositors have to wonder how many more scandals there are out there. And, since Congress often won't let the regulators protect them, depositors have to be able to protect themselves. Customers should choose a thrift at least as carefully as they select shoes. Fortunately, it's not too difficult to tell which thrifts to avoid. Even though bank secrecy shrouds their financial innards, certain external signs warn of their character. Here, prepared with the help of Jesse Barr, the man who helped the Butchers execute their fraud, are eight Warning Signs Of A Failing Thrift:

1. *Change of ownership between 1982 and 1985.* Thrift supervision was at its weakest then and many people entered the industry who should never have been let in. The character of management is absolutely crucial.

2. *Extremely rapid growth since 1982.* The worst failures have been thrifts that grew at four-digit rates and were sometimes highly touted by analysts.

3. *Risky nature of asset portfolio.* Traditional loans have been relatively safe. Unconventional investments, ADC (acquisition, development, and construction) loans, and real estate acquisitions have not. Speculations in government securities market and junk bonds remain to be tested, if you want to stay for the ride.

4. *Weak structure of loans.* If possible, find out how commercial loans have been structured. How much equity is required? What percentage of appraisals are lendable? A loan for 100 percent of appraisal, plus interest payment reserve, with high fees for frequent renewals is the tipoff of a Ponzi scheme.

5. *Impressive architecture and art collections.* Lavish new buildings are a tried and true funnel of thrift funds to the owner's pocket. Ask if his wife does the interior decorating, and for how much. When the thrift management likes art, you have to wonder whether that's your deposit hanging on the wall. The high-flyers went for cowboy and Indian paintings, but tastes vary. One thrift owner put $13 million of his institution's money into a Rembrandt. Sometimes, however, the art work holds its value better than the loan portfolio.

6. *Opulent means of transportation.* Researchable by a walk through the executive parking lot. If the officers drive Mercedes, Porsches, or Rolls Royces, watch out. Even worse are corporate jets or helicopters. If the owner has a yacht, take the life boat.

7. *Luxurious lifestyle of management.* Beware a well stocked winecellar. The better it is, the more likely the proprietor is to be drinking your deposit. Lavish parties should give you the willies. Do you really want your banker strutting around as King Henry the Eighth? Your head could be the next to roll. Jesse Barr warns against "a little too much flash and good life," and he should know. If a banker spends like there's

no tomorrow, maybe it's because he knows he doesn't have one.

8. *Political contributions.* Someone who gives politicians more than he can write off on his income taxes must want something, ranging from prestige to protection. The more he gives, the more likely he wants protection. Here is where the network can be seen in its widest extent. The campaign reports of some candidates read like a directory of potential regulatory problems. These reports often reveal that a number of a company's executives were moved to contribute the same amount on the same day. This coincidence sends the message that the company as a whole needs something.

□ 3 □

PERHAPS THESE WARNING SIGNS will help protect the individual depositor. What can be done to protect the system? We focused on a few recommendations that haven't gone far in spite of, or because of, their merit. A first step would be to improve the status of the examiners. They deserve the pay, here and now, to make them forget about future compensation in the private sector. They also deserve protection. Some regulators, such as the Comptroller of the Currency, have lobbied hard to have their people covered by the law punishing interference with federal officials. Others, such as the old Home Loan Bank Board, have not even provided procedures for reporting threats or intimidation. Above all, the examiners deserve respect. A great many have worked courageously against impossible odds. They deserve better than to be made the scapegoats for the debacle, especially when they know better than anyone where the real failure lies.

The structure of the thrift and banking system could still use work, even though the 1989 Act is easily the most significant change since the depression. Deposit insurance still presents the same temptation. Treasury officials disparage the argument that lower insurance will force depositors to pick their thrifts carefully, an attitude that makes one worry about Treasury's stewardship of the insurance fund. For a truly basic reform that shows how half-hearted the current measures have been, consider allowing each individual to insure only $100,000 of his savings anywhere in the country. One Social Security number, one insurance policy. This measure would reduce the potential exposure of both insurance funds by a factor of 16,000 (for the 16,000 banks and thrifts where an individual can open an insured account, and receive the $100,000 guaranty at each). Such a measure would satisfy the original intent of deposit insurance, to protect the small depositor. It would certainly restore market discipline to the industry. Then you could have deregulation, true deregulation. There might still be Don Dixons and Charlie Keatings who want to make reckless loans or plunge into the junk bond market, but they wouldn't be able to make their institutions grow by 4,000 percent on brokered deposits. Skeptical depositors would starve them out quickly enough.

This proposal is what is sometimes called "politically unfeasible," on the grounds that the voters would rather pay $300 billion in taxes and bank fees than subject the rich to a measure of insecurity. So how about a measure that should have immense popular support, namely, ending unnecessary bank secrecy. If we are spending more money to strengthen the bank and thrift examiners' corps, as we should, why not share their findings with the depositors? After a great deal of technical analysis, the examiners boil their results down to one number, the institution's rating. On a scale of one to five, one is the best; five the worst. This number is very easy to understand. Yet it is one of the most closely guarded secrets in the federal government. The regulators are afraid that the number is *too* easy to understand. The public would pull its funds from a bank or thrift with a "five" rating. That would be a run. The institution would probably fail. And that, the regulators say, would be bad.

It may not be obvious to the public why a poorly managed outfit should be protected as it continues to collect their money. Since a "five" rating usually results from a large measure of fraud and management misconduct, the regulators in a very real sense are covering up for criminal behavior. (This theme has been raised in a number of interesting law suits.) The explanation has been that a run on a sick bank might lead to a panic at healthy banks, thus endangering the economy and collapsing the financial system. Again, why would depositors stage a run at a healthy bank unless they doubt its true condition? A panic is far more likely to result from poor information or rumor.

The most important reforms, however, must come in a third area, in the political atmosphere. The examiners may be capable, and the financial structure may be reformed, but the politicians will still find a way to pervert the system. As long as the political culture tolerates the sort of interference we have seen in this book, trouble lies ahead. One approach, advanced by Ed Gray in the January 1989 San Francisco hearings, would simply make it a felony for a political figure to obstruct the legitimate work of a federal regulator. (One of his employees would go even further and proposes, only half in jest, that it should be a crime for a congressman to telephone a thrift or bank supervisor.) Chances are very slim, however, that Congress will deny itself such a lucrative source of campaign funds. The more feasible means of controlling this pressure may be to make it as public as possible. All political contacts, letters, telephone calls, meetings, should be recorded in a public file, with full transcripts. The press, political opponents, and the public itself, should be able to see just who is pulling wires, and for what. The fix comes at the expense of the public, and ultimately only the public can end it.

Three years ago, we could blame the regulators for letting these debacles develop. Now we have to blame elected officials. The next time around, we can only blame ourselves.

EPILOGUE

□ □ □

Paying the Price

□ 1 □

"THESE THINGS ARE ALWAYS WORSE than they seem at first," Paul Volcker remarked during the Ohio Bank Crisis of 1985. His words have held true at every stage of the savings and loan debacle. Although the disaster seemed as bad as it could get in November 1989, when this book first appeared, the crisis deepened in almost every respect—financially, administratively, politically, and morally—in the following year.

Serious discussions of the money it will take to clean up the savings and loans industry now use numbers more appropriate to astronomy. The highest estimate to date is $1.3 trillion. The "responsible" press shies from using this figure and prefers a U.S. Treasury estimate that is one-tenth the amount and is based on a dubious accounting principle. But the larger figure is supported by a detailed breakdown of principal and interest and appeared in a reputable academic forum, the *Stanford Law and Policy Review.* Even worse, the financial debacle has spread from the S&Ls and their bankrupt insurance fund to commercial banking. The Federal Deposit Insurance Corporation fund, now renamed the Bank Insurance Fund, looks ominously like the FSLIC (now defunct) of 1985.

So what happened to the "rescue" that passed Congress in August 1989? It seemed, for a few minutes anyway, that Washington had learned that delays in closing bankrupt thrifts added billions to the taxpayers' ultimate bill. (The meter runs at up to $20 million a day.) Yet the administration of the rescue quickly became mired in a morass of divided responsibility, indecisive "oversight" and bureaucratic jealousy. The "rescue" came in the form of the FIRREA, the Financial Institutions Reform, Recovery and Enforcement Act of 1989. It abolished the Federal Home Loan Bank Board, previously in charge of the savings and loan industry, and replaced it with several bodies. The Office of Thrift Supervision (OTS) took over regulation of the surviving S&Ls. The Resolution Trust Corporation (RTC) tried to cope with the failing thrifts, merging, selling or closing them down, disposing of their assets and, when necessary, paying off depositors. Layers of oversight boards tried to make policy for the structure. But halfway through its first year, the rescue stalled.

The respected chief executive of the RTC's Oversight Board resigned in February, 1990, complaining privately about interference from the Treasury Department. The career regulators complained that where final decisions under the old Bank Board were made by a panel of three, now they involved 34 members of several oversight boards. Responsibility was diffused because no one, including Congress, wanted to be in full charge of the disaster. Delays, and an accelerating recession exhausted the RTC's fund by the end of 1990, but Congress adjourned without authorizing more spending, thanks mainly to obstruction by Illinois Congressman Frank Annunzio. In January 1991, Treasury Secretary Nicholas Brady acknowledged that the rescue would cost an additional $80 billion.

M. Danny Wall kept his job through the transition thanks to his powerful friends in Congress. Some of his most disastrous decisions in dealing with Charles Keating and Lincoln Savings and Loan can be explained as attempts to maintain these friendships. When Wall finally left his post in March 1990, months after hearings on the Lincoln case had damaged his reputation so severely that he was forced to resign, he left behind an agency more demoralized by politics than it had been in the worst days of Speaker Jim Wright's extortions.

As Congress and the political system grappled with the enormity of the debacle, a new dimension of failure came into view. Bad policy had produced enormous losses, but this policy was tolerated because it helped to perpetuate a self-serving political establishment. The public was undeniably angry but seemed unable to react clearly. The savings and loan issue played a definite role in the 1990 midterm elections, and it should have an even more powerful influence in 1992. But the results to date have underscored the stagnation of Congress, the sources of which pose a broader moral danger to the governing of America.

□ 2 □

ACCORDING TO THE BEST CURRENT ESTIMATES, the total cost of the savings and loan disaster could well exceed $1.5 trillion. Figures of this magnitude fall so far beyond the scope of ordinary human experience that they are almost meaningless. But consider an exercise in time scales. It would take nearly two years to count off one million minutes. One billion minutes would take us back to the time of Christ. One trillion minutes would push us back to the dawn of human evolution. The difference between a million and a trillion is the difference between a trip to the moon and a trip to another galaxy. In more relevant terms, $1.5 trillion equals half of the annual gross national product and 40 percent of all the insured deposits now held by all the banks and thrifts in the country.

Faced with this figure, the public mind rebels and says it can't be true. Papers such as the *Wall Street Journal* and the *New York Times* stick to the safe side. As late as the fall of 1990 they were quoting the slightly less incomprehensible estimate of $180 billion "and up." This low-balling persisted even after the United States General Accounting Office informed Congress that a recession and continued high interest rates could easily push the S&L rescue cost to $500 billion, "excluding general Treasury financing costs," and in any case would exceed $325 billion.

The excuse for ignoring this authoritative statement was provided by an accounting technique called "present value," which considers the cost of paying off all the savings and loan losses right now. As we've seen in great detail, the cleanup costs have soared precisely because Congress refused to give the regulators the resources to handle the problem here and now. At the present moment, the United States government simply can't raise enough money to pay off the losses immediately. So for the foreseeable future, it will have to borrow. For the next three to five years, it will issue bonds earmarked for the S&Ls. After that, it will issue Treasury bonds and notes to pay the interest on the first bonds. Anyone carrying a home mortgage knows that you wind up paying the equivalent of two extra houses in 30 to 40 years of interest payments. If you take the conservative General Accounting Office cleanup cost of $325 billion and add an annual rate of 8 percent over 40 years, you will see that $1.5 trillion is a very reasonable estimate.

The country has already felt this pressure on the federal budget dramatically. The messy budget negotiations just before the 1990 midterm elections forced President Bush to break his "read my lips" pledge of no new taxes and severely damaged his political standing. Some $30 billion of the $130 billion gap to be closed was directly related to the S&L rescue. The cold wind of the thrift crisis has completely dissipated the *ignis fatuus* of the post–Cold War "peace dividend."

Even more ominously, the thrift debacle now looks like the beginning of a general financial crisis. The S&L crisis has entered a second phase that threatens to engulf half of the industry. In 1987, a typical defunct thrift was most likely to be a Texas "high-flier" that had wasted a billion or so dollars of depositors' money on looney real estate deals, insider lending, and high living for the owners. In 1989, a new rathole opened up, bigger and deeper than all the others. A network of larger thrifts had bet the farm on the junk bond market orchestrated by Michael Milken, the wonder boy of Drexel Burnham Lambert. In March 1989, a federal grand jury indicted Milken on 98 counts and nearly $2 billion worth of securities fraud. Drexel Burnham disgorged $650 million to settle similar charges, a payment that pushed it into abrupt and unlamented bankruptcy in mid-February 1990. No one in Washington or on Wall Street lifted a finger to prevent Drexel's crash. Aside from the world of junk bonds, and the S&Ls dependent on them, the major markets showed barely a ripple.

The fall of Drexel Burnham devastated Milken, however, and disintegrated his financial web. On April 24, 1990, the boyish former cheerleader with the dark curly hair pleaded guilty to six felony charges of securities fraud and conspiracy. He agreed to pay $600 million in fines and penalties. On the day before Thanksgiving, Federal District Judge Kimba Wood shocked the financial world by sentencing him to 10 years in prison.

Judge Wood declared that the sentence, the harshest to date in the 1980s Wall Street scandals, was required to deter others from committing "financial crimes that are particularly hard to detect." The *Wall Street Journal*'s editorial page, Milken's last unpaid defender, scoffed at the argument, but these obscure transgressions may well have been crucial in holding together Drexel's "daisy chain" of savings and loans. In a bankruptcy claim filed just a week before Milken's sentencing, thrift regulators charged that Drexel had helped disguise S&L junk bond losses by propping up "a market for junk that would not otherwise exist." The FDIC and the Resolution Trust Corporation (RTC) alleged that Drexel had helped others "plunder the S&Ls" through "bribery, coercion, extortion, fraud and other illegal means." After setting nearly 100 accountants and more than 50 lawyers to scouring Drexel's deals, the regulators blamed the firm for more than $2 billion in losses at 40 or more thrifts and said they could have expanded the list with more time.

Although this claim falls far short of charging Drexel with major responsibility for the thrift debacle, the junk bond collapse pushed some major S&Ls over the brink. Among the new casualties was Columbia Savings and Loan of Beverly Hills, California. Columbia, run by Milken's close friend Thomas Speigel, held a third of its nearly $13 billion asset base in junk bonds. This concentration of high-risk issues was said to be the largest in the country. Speigel, at one point one of the nation's highest-paid executives, held off the regulators with an apparently healthy balance sheet and the claim that he had unusual expertise in managing the risk. This illusion crumbled along with the junk bond market.

The junk bond collapse triggered another disaster so peculiar that it may eventually dwarf even Keating and Lincoln Savings as the symbol of everything wrong with the S&Ls. This was the case of Centrust Savings Bank of Miami, Florida. To the federal regulators, Centrust owner David L. Paul is the living epitome of "vanity and greed," and he indulged himself in epic style. Between 1984, when Paul took control of a sleepy, money-losing Miami thrift, and 1989, when his empire collapsed, he paid himself more than $16 million in salary and dividends. He built a $6 million estate for himself on an island in Biscayne Bay and hid salaries for his butler and servants on the Centrust payroll. He spent $1.4 million a year on a corporate jet and put it at the disposal of Florida State Comptroller Gerald Lewis for a campaign fund-raising trip. When he wanted to impress VIPs, including U.S. Senator John Kerry (D.-Massachusetts), he flew six chefs from Paris to prepare a dinner costing $122,000. (The diners ate and drank from Bacarrat crystal and wiped their lips with French linen that cost Centrust an additional $107,000.) Senator Kerry later wrote an article for the *New York Times* asking, "Where did all the S&L money go?" As one of 40 guests at Paul's Lucullan feast, Kerry personally consumed about $3,000 of the missing funds.

Paul passed all the bounds, however, when he paid out $7 million for his custom-built, 95-foot yacht, *Grand Cru*. The boat offered "many features never found on a yacht before," as the yacht broker marveled when it came time to sell it. Paul had instructed the boat builders to install gold-leaf ceilings with indirect lighting, a whirlpool in the master suite aft, and a working fireplace between the salon and the afterdeck.

Like other S&L owners with yachts, Paul also plunged heavily into political fund raising. As a mainstay of the Democratic Senatorial Campaign Committee, he grew close to Senator Kerry of Massachusetts, who headed the committee. He donated at least $1,000 each to senators Lloyd Bentsen of Texas, George Mitchell of Maine, Howard Metzenbaum of Ohio, Edward Kennedy of Massachusetts, Jim Sasser of Tennessee, Frank Lautenberg of New Jersey, and Terry Sanford of North Carolina. In the House, he supported Tony Coelho of California and Fernand St Germain of Rhode Island, the former Banking Committee chairman, as well as a mixed bag of candidates from Florida. Senator Joseph Biden of Delaware was a special favorite. Paul flew to Wilmington in 1987 to watch Biden announce his campaign for the presidency. Later, Paul gave $10,000 to Biden's re-election campaign for the Senate. With this generosity came access. Paul's schedule books show meetings with senators Reigle and Cranston. The senators are two of the "Keating Five."

Paul financed this opulence through balance sheet smoke and mirrors. "I periodically pick up his prospectus when I need a laugh," a local business reporter told a visitor in 1986, "as do many people." The biggest cloud of smoke veiled Paul's dealing in junk bonds. Defying periodic warnings from Federal Home Loan Bank examiners, Paul bought up to $1.4 billion in junk bonds through Drexel Burnham, which had helped finance his takeover of Centrust in the first place.

Paul had to pull heavy wires with the Florida state comptroller to get permission for these investments. The comptroller's legal staff argued in 1986 that unrated bonds violated state law on S&L holdings. State-chartered S&Ls were clearly limited to holding investment-grade bonds. Comptroller Lewis, who had been flying on Paul's airplane, fired the recalcitrant lawyers and gave the go-ahead. This decision proved to be momentous, both for Paul's Centrust and for Milken's ability to jimmy the junk bond market. Near the top of Paul's 47-story semicircular Centrust tower, which loomed over downtown Miami like a slightly tilting wedding cake, bond traders working under tight security swallowed bond issues so risky that even Milken couldn't sell them in the public market. Centrust became the major dumping ground for Drexel Burnham's private placements. By January 1988, Centrust held more than $1 billion of bonds so speculative they hadn't been rated by the bond-rating agencies. Nearly 90 percent of these bonds had been bought through Drexel Burnham.

Both state and federal examiners rang early warnings about Centrust's "dangerous dependence" on "the informal network of buyers and sellers controlled by Drexel." Cooperating in a 1986 joint examination, both sets of regulators told Centrust that "the absence (for any reason) of Drexel as the major market maker could have a serious negative impact on this market." But at the time, the Drexel network, later known to regulators as "the daisy chain," was flying high.

Milken's defenders overlook this phenomenon, and it didn't play a role in his criminal case, yet the federal S&L regulators charge that this daisy chain linked some of the most notorious S&L villains in a nationwide conspiracy for plunder. The FDIC and the Resolution Trust Corporation filed a $6.8 billion claim in the Drexel Burnham bankruptcy that provides the most damning overview of Milken's operation.

"Beginning at least in 1982," the regulators charged,

> Drexel and those acting in concert and conspiracy with it have willfully, deliberately and systematically plundered the S&Ls. . . . By bribery, coercion, extortion, fraud and other illegal means, they forced or induced the S&Ls to use money consisting primarily of federally insured deposits to purchase many billions of dollars of junk bonds underwritten by Drexel— many of them improperly issued without registration. The wide range of illegal conduct in which Drexel and its co-conspirators engaged included market manipulation, threats, bribes, agreements to control prices, and numerous fraudulent misrepresentations about the value and liquidity of junk bonds. At the same time, this group of predators knowingly attempted to and did monopolize the nationwide junk bond market or markets.
>
> As a result, Drexel and the other predators received billions of dollars in illegal profits, while federally insured savings and loan institutions have suffered and are continuing to suffer billions of dollars in losses. Drexel and its co-conspirators targeted the S&Ls because federal deposit insurance enabled the S&Ls to amass an enormous pool of capital. Ready, repeated, easy access to that pool of capital was a necessary part of Drexel's scheme to create the illusion that junk bonds had value and that such value could be realized in a liquid market.
>
> As part of the manipulation of the market and to promote the illusion of value and liquidity, Drexel's junk bond department developed a network of co-conspirators, including persons who controlled S&Ls, to purchase and sell junk bonds at the bidding of Drexel. The overarching goal of the co-conspirators

was to share in the plunder of their own institutions and to obtain other benefits—including assistance in evading regulatory discipline of their S&Ls—which Drexel provided to those who purchased large quantities of Drexel-underwritten junk bonds.

This vision of a global conspiracy, in which federal deposit insurance kept the junk bond market afloat, has only partly proved out. Lawyers for the RTC and FDIC worked under a tight filing deadline, which the bankruptcy judge refused to relax, and they emphasized that they gave only the first results from their massive study. Yet they presented the strongest confirmation yet that David Paul, Charles Keating, and the Texas high-flyers weren't acting alone.

□ 3 □

DREXEL BURNHAM LAMBERT UNDER MILKEN, it turns out, invested heavily in starting up both Centrust and Lincoln Savings and Loan. In August 1983, Drexel underwrote a $125 million junk bond issue for Keating's American Continental Corporation (ACC) and urged him to take over a savings and loan. In December, Keating set his sights on Lincoln and sold ACC preferred stock to raise the money to buy it. Drexel underwrote the $56 million issue and wound up holding 10 percent of American Continental's stock.

Strands of the Drexel web reached tangentially to the family of the U.S. president in the case of M.D.C. Holdings of Denver, Colorado. From October 1983, Drexel was the main underwriter for this Denver home builder's commercial paper, helping it grow to a $2.5 billion national corporation. In 1988, an M.D.C. subsidiary took a $10 million loss trying to keep the Silverado Savings and Loan afloat. Silverado became a national scandal in election year 1990 because one of its directors happened to be Neil Bush, son of the president. Neil Bush indisputably misused his position, approving loans to a business associate who was cutting him in on excessive profits, and thrift regulators sought to punish him with an order banning him from the thrift industry for life. An Administrative Law judge made his own recommendation, weakening the restrictions considerably. The final decision at this writing rested with OTS director Timothy Ryan. Bush announced that he would contest any discipline. The House Banking Committee raked Silverado over the coals, as a case study in the failure of regulators to control a politically connected thrift disaster. (According to one document from the hearings, Silverado officers bragged that two Federal Home Loan Bank Board examiners who had tried to crack down on the thrift in 1987 "had been run out of town.")

The case of Neil Bush and Silverado deserved to be taken seriously, certainly more seriously than the White House took it. Even after the onset of the debacle, President George Bush attended a Republican fund raiser in Colorado hosted by M.D.C. chairman Larry Mizel. But the fixation on presidential politics blinded the press to some truly fascinating links in the Drexel daisy chain. When Milken peddled M.D.C. bonds, he placed them in at least 11 thrifts, including some of the biggest disasters in the industry. Lincoln and Centrust were high on the list. Keating's extensive business deals with M.D.C. are noted on page 265, so perhaps it should not be a surprise to learn that as late as 1989, David Paul's Centrust was thinking of buying out the Denver developer.

M.D.C. itself had given a helping hand to the Southmark Corporation of North Dallas, buying out a home builder owned by Southmark's thrift subsidiary, San Jacinto Savings. This gesture, too, was hardly surprising, given Drexel's importance for Southmark (see page 264). This real estate syndicator was struggling in 1986 after federal tax law changes undercut its business of providing tax shelters, but Drexel's bond issues helped turn it into a $9 billion power. Milken sold large chunks of these issues to 12 of his major thrift clients. Eight of these, including Centrust and Lincoln, had also bought the M.D.C. issues.

Southmark anchored the daisy chain in Texas, where an astonishing number of the high-flyers intertwined with Drexel and with each other. Southmark's thrift, San Jacinto Savings Association of Houston, was crucial in ways not yet fully disclosed, since it stayed open until December 1990, years longer than its counterparts. Even though San Jacinto is known as a buyer of Milken's bonds, its holdings weren't analyzed in the RTC/FDIC filing because it wasn't then a failed thrift. We've already noted, however, than San Jacinto lent $22 million to Craig Hall and swapped loans with Don Dixon's Vernon Savings and Loan.

Southmark and San Jacinto also gave Charles Keating an entree into the world of the Texas S&Ls. In 1985, Keating, five family members, and 15 other friends formed a partnership to renovate the Hotel Pontchartrain in Detroit. Things didn't work out, and a year later the partners had to refinance their investment. They turned to San Jacinto, which loaned them $35 million. Within the preceding month, Lincoln had granted nearly $100 million in loans to Southmark. One of these deals made Keating's thrift a $20 million creditor of the notorious Edwin T. McBirney, the "Fast Eddy" of Sunbelt Savings and Loan. McBirney, the procurer of prostitutes, may have been strange company for Keating, the fighter against pornography, but Fast Eddy was finding his place in the Drexel daisy chain. When the feds had time to go through Sunbelt's books, they found that it was holding 19 Drexel bond issues, including M.D.C. and Southmark. (By the time of the RTC/FDIC filing, the reconstituted Sunbelt Savings also incorporated Tom Gaubert's Independent American S&L, Western S&L of the recently indicted Jarrett Woods, and a thrift run by Don Dixon-henchman Woody Lemons, who was since sentenced to 30 years for his role in Vernon S&L. It's not clear which of these thrifts had bought Drexel's stuff.)

Charles Keating had other roads to Texas, moreover. One of the broadest was his personal friendship with former Governor John Connally. Keating had been a finance chairman and, briefly, campaign manager of Connally's 1980 run for president. Four years later, he bankrolled one of Connally's abortive real estate developments in the "goat country" west of Austin. Connally and his business partner Ben Barnes, the tall, blond and charismatic protégé whose political career had ended in the Sharpstown scandal, were doing a grand tour of the high-flyers. "They were raising loans all over creation," said one observer. With Connally as a reference, Keating had all the access he needed in Texas. It's no wonder that

Lincoln and the Texas high-flyers appeared to be coordinating their political lobbying.

This joint effort reached a peak in 1985 when Lee Henkel, an Atlanta attorney, received an interim appointment to the Federal Home Loan Bank Board. Henkel, a former chief counsel for the IRS, commanded a relaxed good ol' boy style that deflected questions from the House Banking Committee, but his brief career on the Bank Board continues to raise eyebrows.

Henkel maintained at the House Banking Committee hearings on Lincoln that "every single minute of my public service was conducted properly, ethically, and without any thought whatsoever of either personal benefit or some benefit for a past associate." The "past associate" was Charles Keating. Henkel conducted more than $100 million of business with Keating. By his own account, they met through John Connally. When Henkel was appointed IRS chief counsel by President Nixon in 1971, he also served as ranking assistant general counsel of the U.S. Treasury under then Treasury Secretary Connally.* In 1979, Henkel volunteered to serve as East Coast finance chairman for Connally's presidential campaign. Keating was his West Coast counterpart, and the two met through the national finance committee.

As Keating took over Lincoln Savings, he funnelled more than $126 million in loans to partnerships involving Henkel. More than $90 million of these were still unpaid when Henkel joined the Bank Board, and examiners had classified several as substandard. Henkel maintained that he had paid off his line of credit and personal guarantees with Lincoln and put his other interests in a blind trust. But lawyers in a class action suit against Lincoln weren't impressed.

---

*John Connally's bribery indictment stems from this period, and ironically it involved the Federal Home Loan Bank Board. Bank Board regulators were bearing down on an old friend of Connally's named Jake Jacobsen. Jacobsen asked Treasury Secretary Connally to help him out by calling Bank Board Chairman Thruston Morton. Connally called twice, and the next day Jacobsen came to his office with $5,000 in $100 bills. Jacobsen testified that Connally took the wrappers from the bills into his private bathroom and flushed them down the toilet. Connally was tried and acquitted on the charges. Henkel wasn't mentioned in the incident, but he apparently hasn't held it against his former boss.

The attorneys for the thousands of "the weak, meek, and ignorant" who bought Keating's junk notes included Henkel as a defendant, presenting a scathing version of his conduct. Their suit alleged that Lincoln's loans to his partnerships were actually "disguised direct investments," since Lincoln took a large part of the profits and provided most of the financing. Just before Henkel's appointment, charges the suit, Henkel "undertook to conceal the true nature of his financial ties with Keating—ACC/Lincoln." In August 1986, he travelled to Phoenix with a lawyer for Keating named Margery Waxman and, says the suit, made "secret agreements" with Keating to tidy up his personal finances. Henkel set up a blind trust for his stock holdings in a company called Continental Southern, which had done a number of real estate deals with Lincoln. According to the suit, Keating agreed to buy the stock from the blind trust for $3.7 million, some 10 times its actual value, giving Henkel the funds to pay off his personal debts to Lincoln. Henkel denies the agreement, but at this writing he has been unsuccessful in getting discharged from the lawsuit.

Although the alleged meeting with Keating was private, Henkel's first major act on the Bank Board generated a very public controversy, described on page 242. He introduced an amendment to the direct investment rule, then the center of a $615 million controversy with Lincoln Savings. In the House Banking Committee hearings, Henkel insisted that his hastily drafted 11-point substitute was meant to address what he thought was a broad problem on which he'd been lobbied, not by Keating but by the U.S. League of Savings Institutions and the owner of another Phoenix thrift, Gary Driggs of Western Savings. (Driggs, by the way, had his own high-flying dealings with M.D.C. Holding and with Southmark.) An internal Bank Board memo, however, maintained that Henkel's version of the rule would have benefited just two S&Ls. One was Keating's Lincoln. The other was Southmark's San Jacinto.

Whatever the questions about Henkel's personal conduct, there's little doubt that his appointment was part of a bold attempt to wrest control of thrift supervision from the hands of Bank Board Chairman Edwin Gray. The class action suit and the "Keating Five" Senate Ethics Committee hearings starting in November 1990 revealed just how intensely Keating worked to stack the Bank Board. Keating kept detailed but not exhaustive logs of his political meetings. These logs show at least 22 meetings or phone calls with congressmen, White House officials, and Henkel himself about the Bank Board nominations. The logs specifically name not only Cranston, Reigle, McCain, and DeConcini, who were all Ethics Committee defendants, but also former Senator Paula Hawkins, former Congressman Chip Pashayan, and Congressman Doug Barnard, as well as White House Chief of Staff Don Regan.

Senator John Glenn reported that Keating's staff asked him to support Henkel as early as the spring of 1986, more than half a year before the seat on the board opened up. (Documents suggest that Henkel's predecessor delayed leaving the board until Congress adjourned so that the White House could make a "recess appointment" not immediately subject to Senate confirmation. Keating's logs show an August 12, 1986, breakfast with Bank Board member Don Hovde "re: recess appointment.") Glenn declined to help, but others of the Keating Five took up the task with gusto.

Donald Regan, in two of his rare statements on the S&Ls, told the House Banking Committee and Senate Ethics Committee Special Counsel Robert Bennett that Senator DeConcini lobbied him heavily on behalf of Henkel. The effort included a letter sent on June 6, a phone call on July 23, and a discussion, hotly denied by Senator DeConcini, about whether the senator would drop his opposition to a right-wing judicial nominee in return for the Henkel appointment. In his turn, Senator DeConcini reminded the ethics panel that fellow Arizona senator John McCain had accompanied Henkel on an August 1986, vacation flight to the Bahamas, paid for by Charles Keating. The ethics panel questioned Senator Cranston's chief aide on the Banking Committee, Carolyn D. Jordan, about an allegation that she tried to discourage a Banking Committee investigator from looking too deeply into Mr. Henkel's background. She said she couldn't remember the call, but she admitted, "I can't say it's false."

On September 10, Keating spent a day in Washington to advance his nominees; he started with breakfast with Ms. Waxman, his lawyer, and worked through appointments with Barnard, Cranston,

McCain, and Reigle. He wound up with a 3:30 session with Don
Regan. (Waxman, formerly a high-ranking official under Don Regan
at the Treasury, may have been key in lobbying for Henkel, but the
Senate Ethics Committee explored her role only lightly.) Henkel
testified that his name was first proposed by then Senator Mack
Mattingly of Georgia, who received $10,000 in donations from Keat-
ing's family and friends, and $2,000 from Henkel himself.

In the meantime, Keating was getting a two-for-one return on
his time and money. His logs show that from mid-August 1986, he
was also pushing George Benston for the other vacant seat on the
Bank Board. He took his September 10 swing through Washington
on behalf of both nominees. Benston was a paid consultant to Keating
and produced a report arguing that direct investments were harm-
less. The struggle to name Benston was in some ways as revealing
as the coup over Henkel. It showed that at least some Texas high-
flyers were taking a ride on Keating's back.

Before Benston emerged, the short list for the seat vacated by
Mary Grigsby included Durwood Curlee, the affable Austin lobbyist
for the Texas high-flyers. Curlee confirmed that he was interviewed
for the post, with the support of Senator Phil Gramm (R.-Texas).
But Curlee portrayed himself as more of a placeholder and said he
withdrew as soon as Professor Benston was recruited. Benston said
that Wendy Gramm, wife of the senator, talked him into it, against
his better judgment. The message, relayed, he believes, from Don
Regan, was, "We can't get rid of Ed Gray. This thing is in really
bad shape. We need help on the Bank Board." But Benston was
basically an academic, and his forceful free market views alienated
Senator Proxmire, then chairman of Senate Banking. With his nomination foredoomed, Benston withdrew, and Lawrence White took
his place.

What would the Bank Board have been like if this double coup
had succeeded? What if Henkel had moved to the chairmanship and
the second vote of three owed his position to Keating's lobby work?
In hindsight, the prospect of a Bank Board stacked by Keating seems
awful to contemplate, but in practice it probably would have worked
out like the board under Danny Wall.

□ 4 □

NONE OF THE SENATORS ON THE ETHICS COMMITTEE seemed to find it remarkable that their proceedings focused so much on Edwin Gray. They grilled him for three days, trying to find chinks in his account of the four- and five-senator meetings. DeConcini and Cranston and their lawyers attacked him personally and very nastily, both in and out of the committee room. Even Keating himself, in an earlier appearance on the C-Span call-in hour, reserved his most concentrated venom for the inoffensive, unpolished, former Bank Board chairman. Yet Gray had left office, gladly, while the Lincoln case was still in its early stages. The most damaging actions—the removal of jurisdiction from San Francisco; the giveaway memorandum of understanding; the second, Washington-directed, examination—all came in the tenure of M. Danny Wall. Under Wall, hints of the political interference that fertilized the thrift crisis piled up thicker than ever, just as the disaster reached full flower.

Wall may have escaped intense public scrutiny precisely because he didn't keep the detailed transcripts and memoranda that Gray produced with such devastating effect. A source close to the Ethics Committee investigation complained, with a reference to Star Trek, that Wall and the Senate seemed to communicate "by Vulcan mind meld."

But enough has emerged to show that thrift regulators under Danny Wall were deeply demoralized and battered by politics at the very moment they were supposed to be rescuing the industry. A story told at a House Budget Committee hearing illustrates the mood. Early in 1988, a group of senior thrift regulators gathered for a weekend conference at Airlie House in Airlie, Virginia. In a general meeting the chief regulator, Darrel Dochow, decided to sound the group out on its guess of the cost of the thrift disaster. He asked his staff to raise their hands and keep them up until he reached the number that corresponded to their best estimate. He started calling out $5 billion, $10 billion, $15 billion. At $30 billion, then the upper limit of the official estimates, most of the hands dropped. But a few brave souls kept them up and were prepared to keep them up until Dochow reached $100 billion or higher. Dochow cut his recital short and, according to some memories, said that there was no room for pessimists on the team. While acknowledging the incident, Dochow says he was just trying to say that the problem could be handled. His critics think he was orchestrating a cover-up for the presidential election.

Dochow, a surprisingly youthful career regulator with blond hair atop a fireplug physique, took over regulatory affairs at the Bank Board just after Danny Wall became chairman. He has received a public drubbing for a series of decisions in which Wall stayed in the background. "It's almost as if you were the official fall guy," said Congressman Charles Schumer, chairman of the Budget Committee hearing.

"Sometimes I feel that way," answered Dochow.

Dochow's trail answers the question that vexed some members of the Senate Ethics Committee: If the meetings with all of those senators didn't influence Gray's policy toward Lincoln, what's the fuss all about? The official attitude toward Lincoln changed dramatically as soon as Gray left. The San Francisco office had just wrapped up its examination of Lincoln and wanted to send its men back in to check on some anomalies. Bill Black, the counsel to the Home Loan Bank of San Francisco, told the Senate Ethics panel that he believed that the second visit would have exposed Lincoln's shady loans and led to its closing in the fall of 1987. But the examiners never had a chance to go back. Dochow's Office of Regulatory Affairs (ORA) vetoed the request.

When Keating saw that he couldn't shake the San Francisco examiners, he asked for a transfer to a friendlier jurisdiction. His first choice was the Seattle Home Loan Bank, where Dochow had worked before coming to Washington. In February 1988, Dochow called his former colleagues in Seattle to see if they would take on Lincoln. (Seattle smelled a hot potato and refused.) House Banking Committee chairman Gonzalez expressed amazement that Dochow would make such a move on his own. "I can't imagine that he would be doing this—doing free-lance on his own," he said.

Dochow eventually took charge, running a second examination of Lincoln through his own Office of Regulatory Affairs, using personnel drawn from most of the Bank Board's 12 districts. At first, the ORA project seemed designed to break down. From the beginning, an atmosphere close to paranoia engulfed the rank and file of the ORA team, now called, none too happily, the "13th District." The examiner-in-charge, J. Stephen Scott, a protégé of Dochow's from the Seattle District, led a disastrous orientation meeting in which he warned against a witch-hunt. Some in the audience thought he sounded like a cheerleader for Lincoln. Examiners started keeping their own private logs. (Said a horrified project supervisor, "That's what they do when they think something's wrong.")

But Lincoln was so far gone that a whitewash was impossible. By all accounts, the turning point in the exam came in August when William Crawford, the California commissioner of savings and loans told the feds that he sensed something fishy in Lincoln's "tax-sharing" arrangement with its holding company, American Continental Corporation. Two of Dochow's assistants flew to Phoenix for a dinner meeting with the leaders of the examination. The men from headquarters told the field workers they had to report accurately on Lincoln, "be it good, bad, or ugly." Dochow testified that the dinner meeting put the examination "back on the right course," a remarkable admission that it had been drifting for most of the summer. The rank and file complaints tapered off. Experienced investigators were added to the team and concluded that Keating and other insiders were draining cash from Lincoln into their own pockets. "Up to that point," admitted Dochow, "I had believed that the insiders were not illegally using Lincoln for personal benefit." By the end of December, 21 months and perhaps a billion dollars in losses after the San Francisco district wanted to take over Lincoln, the ORA concluded it would have to seize the thrift. The influence of the five senators and of Danny Wall, their former employee, remained far in the background, but it's hard to imagine any other reason for these delays.

Lincoln, however, was only one of the demoralizing incidents. Politics, both bureaucratic and congressional, continued to afflict examiners before and after FIRREA, the "rescue" bill, had abolished the Bank Board and substituted the Office of Thrift Supervision under the direct control of the Treasury. This revision returned examiners to the federal work force, removing the buffer of employment by the regional Home Loan Banks, which had protected Bill Black from the wrath of Speaker Jim Wright. By this time Black was too notorious a witness to be touched without an outcry, but other examiners now realized that Dochow and Danny Wall stood over them in the chain of command.

On the other hand, work for the regional, industry-owned Federal Home Loan Banks carried its own pressures. Presidents of thrifts under supervision sometimes sat on FHLB boards of directors and weren't shy about defending their private interests. (It was only after one egregious set of internal scandals that the Bank Board demanded the resignation of FHLB directors whose thrifts were under disciplinary orders.) The regional banks lived a schizophrenic life. One set of employees, the examiners, sat as watchdogs over their members and reported to Washington. Another, the supervisors, were supposed to act on the examination reports, but they answered to a regional board of directors, half of whom were S&L executives, some of them pretty bad ones. But examiners like Lisa Walleri and Trish Cosgrove learned that structure didn't make that much difference to people who told embarrassing truths. Either way, no good deed went unpunished.

Lisa Walleri charged that her former superiors at the Federal Home Loan Bank of Seattle ordered her to falsify one of her examination reports. As examiner-in-charge of the troubled Far West Federal Bank in Portland, Oregon, she concluded that the Seattle FHLB's experimental program to save the thrift wasn't working. She said her superiors told her to change her findings and in effect cover up the S&L's bad investments or lose her role in the examination. When she refused, her higher-ups forged her signature to the altered report. The stress of the conflict, she said, kept her from work for weeks, and she was finally discharged for absenteeism.

Walleri may be unusual in making her case public. (She filed a workers' compensation claim and a federal lawsuit, and she eventually testified at a congressional hearing.) But she was by no means the only one to charge that upper levels of the Federal Home Loan Banks harassed and even discharged examiners who made embarrassingly harsh findings about favored S&Ls.

A former commercial bank loan officer, Walleri joined the Seattle FHLB in 1986 and immediately drew the highest ratings for her work, including praise for her "enthusiasm." In April 1988, she was put in charge of the examination of Far West, a thrift that had nearly collapsed in 1985. Senior officials in the Seattle FHLB had used a new gimmick, "risk control arbitrage," to attract new owners. To help pay off Far West's losses, Seattle would lend its own funds for the thrift to invest. Earnings from the loan were supposed to match the amount of "good will" Far West had to write down each year. The program had fans in D.C. and acerbic critics in other districts.

Walleri evidently produced a highly negative review of Far West, the details of which are still cloaked by bank secrecy laws. Three months after she turned in her examination, her immediate superior, who had previously approved it, handed back a new version with her criticisms deleted on October 11, 1988. Walleri immediately said she wouldn't sign the new report. On October 12, she was removed as examiner-in-charge.

In late January 1989, a senior official met with Walleri for her annual review and gave her an unacceptable rating for her Far West job. The same day she went to a doctor who told her she suffered from "significant work-related stress" and told her to take time off to recuperate. The Seattle official was J. Stephen Scott, who a few months later was put in charge of the new examination of Keating's Lincoln Savings and Loan.

Walleri's story has a relatively happy ending. She managed to find an unusually persistent lawyer, Tomas Finnegan Ryan of Portland, Oregon, to take her case. On October 25, 1990, in a hearing before Congressman Charles Schumer's Budget Committee Task Force, an official of the Office of Thrift Supervision delivered what amounted to an unprecedented public apology. John F. Downey, deputy director for regional operations, reported that an independent "peer review" of the Seattle Bank had looked at Walleri's examination and the changes. "While it was agreed that the cosmetic editing and reorganization of the report were warranted," he said, "the deletion of substantive criticisms and the changing of the component rating factors were not."

Downy said as clearly as a bureaucrat could that Walleri was right and her superiors were wrong. Yet Far West responded to the hearings with a public attack on her mental condition. Even though the peer review was a year-and-a-half old, she has not yet been reinstated. At last report, she earned money by delivering telephone books.

Patricia Cosgrove of New York City wasn't as lucky. She offended her bosses at the Home Loan Bank of New York by her detective work at the mob-ridden Flushing Federal Savings and Loan in Queens. Trouble at this thrift burst into view when one of its major borrowers was slain, gangland style. Other borrowers, and subsequent defendants in civil and criminal suits, made up a regular rogues' gallery. They included a confessed penny-stock scam artist for the Mafia; two ex-convict con men who helped drag down 1984 Democratic vice-presidential nominee Geraldine Ferraro by involving her husband in a fraudulent loan application; and a restaurateur well known in the tabloids as Frank Sinatra's confidant and bodyguard. Yet in 1986 Cosgrove was reprimanded for being "too aggressive" toward Flushing Federal's management.

Unable to find an attorney willing to challenge the New York FHLB, she filed a *pro se* federal case, acting as her own lawyer, just before expiration of the statute of limitations. She has been eking out a living as a babysitter.

Walleri and Cosgrove are by no means isolated incidents; their experiences are close to becoming commonplace. In a further hearing, Schumer worked over the highly damaging peer review of the Dallas Home Loan Bank. A team from the Cincinnati Bank found that examiners had repeatedly been forced to downplay criticisms of thrifts managed by members of the Dallas FHLB board of directors. In one case, the cover-up extended to a stock shuffle that the review board referred to the Office of Enforcement in D.C. when it completed its work in 1988. A 1985 examination of the First Federal Savings of Arkansas found $200 million in problem assets and gave the thrift a rating of 4 on a scale where 5 is rock bottom. Several months later, the Dallas FHLB sent the chief examiner back for a limited "technical review" that found only $50 million in problems and raised the rating to a 2. With the more favorable result, the thrift converted from mutual ownership to stock ownership. A year later, another examiner counted $200 million in problem loans, the same as in the 1985 examination. The examiner was removed. He was told that he wasn't getting along well with the thrift owner, who happened to sit on the Dallas FHLB board.

The peer review continued with case after damning case of excessive "forbearance," extended to such people as the Dallas real estate operator Craig Hall. These complaints, along with a long list of administrative failures, sadly helped end the career of the Dallas chief regulator H. Joe Selby, who just a year earlier had been the target of Jim Wright's monumental abuse as a "gestapo" persecutor of the Texas high-flyers. The peer review didn't mention Wright's extreme pressure and gave short shrift to Selby's appeal to consider the chaotic condition in Dallas before he arrived.

The Schumer hearings weren't well publicized, but they gave possibly the most devastating glimpse the public was allowed into the inner workings of thrift regulation, covering as they did the Home Loan Banks under both Danny Wall and Edwin Gray. But other investigations showed how deeply politics continued to taint Danny Wall's rescue. The midnight sales of troubled thrifts in December 1988, at the tail end of the "Southwest Plan," provided ample grist for critics of the administration. Senator Howard Metzenbaum (D.-Ohio), by Keating's account the one senator who had asked him for money and been turned down, ran the sale and consolidation of 15 Texas thrifts into the Bluebonnet Savings through the mill of a Senate Judiciary Committee hearing, and he provided both wheat and chaff of his exposé exclusively to the *New York Times*. His hearings showed that a Phoenix, Arizona businessman named James M. Fail bought the thrifts with only $1,000 of his own money. He borrowed much of the rest of the $70 million purchase price from insurance companies he controlled and he received a promise of $1.85 billion in federal subsidies. In 1989 the first installment of this subsidy made Bluebonnet the most profitable large S&L in the country, even though it made only a handful of loans. One of the largest of these loans went to a Republican lobbyist named Robert Thompson who had worked as congressional liaison for then Vice

President Bush. Thompson worked for Fail in pulling off the Blue-bonnet deal and wrote several letters directly to Chairman Wall.

Wall was ultimately forced from his job by House Banking Committee hearings into the Lincoln Savings failure. Confounding the cynics, Banking Committee chairman Henry Gonzalez took a thorough look at the five-senator meetings. In sessions stretching through November 1989, he gave Keating-accusers Edwin Gray and William Black their first national forum. When hostile members of the committee, such as Jim Wright crony Carroll Hubbard of Kentucky, tried to discredit Gray, Gonzalez, long a supporter of the former Bank Board chairman, provided avuncular protection. But the attack on Danny Wall was withering. A panel of 10 employees from the D.C.-directed Lincoln examination recounted a number of instances in which their leaders seemed to be orchestrating a "white-wash." Wall and his supporters complained bitterly that Wall wasn't allowed to defend himself until the end of the series, yet his own appearance hurt more than it helped by making public the ferocious backbiting on the Bank Board.

In the end, however, a lawsuit involving Danny Wall came to symbolize all that was wrong with the rescue. The Olympic Federal Savings and Loan Association of Berwyn, Illinois, won a restraining order against a federal takeover with the argument that Wall's appointment to the Office of Thrift Supervision was unconstitutional. The FIRREA legislation that launched the rescue contained a rider keeping him in office without Senate confirmation. (Reports at the time said this rider was the work of senators Cranston and Reigle, who were trying to avoid the embarrassing hearings on Lincoln, which Gonzalez gave them anyway.) The Olympic suit argued that this breach of procedure rendered invalid all of Wall's acts in office, including his thrift seizures and new regulations. When a federal judge took it seriously enough to grant a stay, the White House was finally shocked into action. In March 1990, three months after Wall's resignation, the administration named T. Timothy Ryan, Jr., a 44-year-old labor lawyer, as his successor. Ryan was quickly confirmed by a large Senate vote, in spite of resistance from some senators apparently responding to thrift industry fears that he would be too hard to control.

□ 5 □

CONGRESSIONAL HEARINGS UNEARTHED much valuable information about the thrift debacle, yet most of them also aroused deeply mixed emotions. After having done so much to create the disaster, the members of Congress used these forums to berate the bureaucrats for yielding to the lawmakers' pressure. The attacks on the 1988 fire sales, a favorite congressional topic, ignored the Bank Board's need to attract private investors with taxbreaks and other sweeteners because Congress in 1987 had refused to give it sufficient capital to handle the failed thrifts itself. In the hearings on the Dallas Home Loan Bank, neither the Schumer committee nor its witnesses mentioned the extreme pressures that Speaker Wright and his leadership circle exerted on behalf of figures like Craig Hall. On being told that the examiners' manuals contained 47 pages of guidelines on granting "forbearance," Congressman James Slattery of Pennsylvania demanded with great indignation and a vacant stare to know who had written them. No one had the heart to tell him that forbearance was specifically mandated by the infamous CEBA legislation of 1987. In short, Congress wrote them.

The thrift crisis, it became increasingly clear, was part of an even more serious political crisis. In an article in the *Stanford Law and Policy Review*, former Securities and Exchange Commission member Joseph Grundfest listed four factors that had made the S&Ls so successful with Congress. One, they had a wide geographic base; two, they advanced a nonideological program, home ownership; three, they lobbied vigorously, and even ruthlessly; and four, the cost of doing them favors didn't show up on the budget until too late. And this pattern didn't fit only the S&Ls; farm financing, home mortgages, and student loans, to name a few, are also potential financial time bombs. As Grundfest summed it up,

> An industry that garners the support of a geographically dispersed, ideologically neutral, monied constituency that is not asking for a direct handout can cut through Congress like a hot knife through butter.

The most important of these factors, however, is money. Congressmen respond to large donors, perhaps more now than ever in living memory, for two reasons. The cost of mounting effective campaigns has grown so great that seven-digit budgets for House elections are no longer a rarity. And second, with enough money and the right technology, the incumbent almost certainly will win. After two elections in which 98 percent of the incumbents who chose to run again were reelected, anti-incumbent rhetoric flourished in 1990. It had some effect; only 96 percent of the running incumbents were returned. Campaign money not only buys technology, it deters serious opposition. The political scientist Gary Jacobson reported that only 40 seats were truly contested in 1990.

The tremendous advantage of incumbency, and of course the crosscurrents of many other issues, blunted attempts to hold congressmen accountable for their role in the S&L crisis. Opponents tried to pin the issue on several senior congressmen, such as Doug Barnard (D.-Georgia), chairman of the Government Operations subcommittee with oversight for the financial regulators; Frank Annunzio (D.-Illinois), second in seniority on House Banking; and Stephen L. Neal (D.-North Carolina), fourth in seniority. All of these were tarred by questionable deals with thrift owners, yet they won re-election (albeit by reduced margins). The congressmen who clearly lost because of the thrift issue—Denny Smith in Oregon, Chip Pashayan in California, and Stanley Parris in Virginia—were fairly vulnerable Republicans.

These anemic results revived ancient concerns about a weak link in representative government. What happens if elected representatives develop vested interests separate from, and even opposed to, the interests of the taxpayers who elected them? One of these interests, clearly, would be self-perpetuation in office. It's an ominous symptom that to some minds the main issue in the 1990 election was not abortion, not Iraqi aggression, not even the S&Ls, but redistricting. With no expectation of offending the public, party leaders and press pundits talked openly about the importance of manipulating election district boundaries for the sake of protecting party interests and their own incumbents.

The voters could see this legislative arrogance in the televised Senate Ethics Committee hearings, and it was appalling. The World's Greatest Deliberative Body turned out to have the ethics of a street gang. Its paramount concern was to protect its own members, no matter what damage they did to the public. Members of the panel made no effort to conceal their annoyance with the zeal and thoroughness of Special Counsel Robert Bennett, or with the most damaging witnesses against the five senators. Senator Terry Sanford (D.-North Carolina) testily lectured the regulators about the importance of campaign contributions, showing no repentance for his own $1,000 from David Paul. Senator Trent Lott (R.-Mississippi) delivered a naive screed about defending businessmen from the over-zealous federal government, as if the thrift owners had never plundered FSLIC and a $1.5 trillion charge on the next taxpaying generation didn't matter. Senator Warren Rudman (R.-New Hampshire) tried to clap his hands over his ears or over the mouths of embarrassing witnesses when they put the case of the Keating Five into a broader political context.

Senator David Pryor (D.-Arkansas) at least had the decency to look chagrined during the proceedings, since he could easily have been sharing the dock with the accused. Pryor, perhaps even more than Jim Wright, had delayed the recapitalization of FSLIC in 1986, adding untold hundreds of billions to the final cost. In October 1986, Speaker Wright cut his first deal with Bank Board chairman Gray over Craig Hall and let a $15 billion recapitalization bill pass the House. But in the Senate, David Pryor decided to settle a grievance over FSLIC's treatment of some well-connected thrifts in Arkansas and Texas.

In a letter of October 3, 1986, Pryor wrote to Gray, "I have put a 'hold' on the Senate recapitalization bill and am anxious to receive assurances from you that you will correct the abuses which have been taking place in Arkansas and other states." The hold killed recapitalization for a year and set the stage for Wright's far greater extortions in 1987.

Some of the witnesses, the staff aides, unintentionally lifted a curtain on the feudal mind of the "legocracy," the permanent network of legislative aides and committee personnel that runs Congress. The legocrats spend their days, and much of their nights, protecting their "principals," drafting their letters, scripting their meetings, and (in one case described by Cranston aide Carolyn Jordan) even inserting statements in their names in the *Congressional Record* without their knowledge. The aides are often brighter than their senators and mock them in private, but in the last resort they're expected to take the rap for their man. In return, the aides seem even less restricted than their senators in accepting favors from contributors and lobbyists, and their power to influence details of legislation makes them a far better buy. If anything ever comes of the political calls for a special investigation of Congress, it should examine the deeds of staff members as well as those of the senators and representatives.

Political scientists will retort that we have merely described the way Congress "really works." And we are in truth suffering more from a corrupt system than from corrupt senators. Yet the case of the savings and loans introduced a virulent element that no system can ultimately survive. The money that men like Keating were offering and that the senators so eagerly chased had not been earned by entrepreneurs, risk-takers, or captains of industry. It had been stolen. The campaign contributions came from the vaults of the S&Ls, which meant it came from the depositors, and ultimately from the deposit insurance fund and the taxpayers.

It's this twist, the source of the money, that the senators have been so determined to ignore. This insouciance was effectively described by the John Dean of the Ethics Committee hearing, the former staff aide to John Glenn and highly paid lobbyist for Keating named James J. Grogan. Recounting Keating's strategy of "buying access" to the senators, Grogan told of the greeting between Keating and Senator Cranston at a dinner at the luxury Bel Air Hotel in Los Angeles in early 1988. Said Grogan, "Senator Cranston came up and patted Mr. Keating on the back and said, 'Ah, the mutual aid society.' " This mutual aid kept Cranston in office, and it postponed Keating's day of judgment, but it came at the expense of Keating's depositors and the taxpayers.

The most telling moments before the Ethics Committee came when witnesses managed to break through the restricted ground rules of the panel and compare the senators' conduct to a higher standard. Edwin Gray had sent friends a column by former Senator William Proxmire that cut to the heart of the political crisis, and when a cross-examiner gave him an opening, he stubbornly insisted on reading it to the committee. This is some of what he read:

> After serving 31 years on the Senate, every day of that time on the Senate Banking Committee, eight years as chairman, I am convinced that good moral people serve on that committee.
>
> I am also convinced they are sincerely, honestly hypnotized by a system of thinly concealed bribery that not only buys their attention but frequently buys their vote.
>
> The special interests that make these contributions know exactly what they are doing. They know just what changes they want to make, for example, to free them from restrictions designed to keep insured bank deposits from being used for risky investment.
>
> A little change can make it possible for them to make or lose millions while the taxpayers make nothing but can lose billions.
>
> The S&L and bank lobbyists know that. Here is precisely why they raise millions of dollars for campaign contributions. Any senators or House members who believe they are getting this big money because the lobbyist admires their character or personality are kidding themselves.
>
> These contributions to members of committees with jurisdiction over the contributors' industry are bribes, pure and simple.

□ 6 □

GRAY'S READING OF PROXMIRE'S WORDS left the Ethics Committee in a momentary hush, not least because it mentioned "the B-word," bribery. For a reply, some weakly gave lip service to campaign finance reform, a buzz phrase that will very likely become the stock answer to the crisis. Yet the ugly decline in congressional conduct came very quickly at the heels of the earlier post-Watergate wave of reforms. The public has every right to equate congressionally drafted campaign reform with incumbent protection. Proposals for public financing of congressional campaigns ought to meet with a stony stare, unless linked to a limit on congressional terms.

The public is more likely to pursue its own remedies, such as initiatives for term limits along the lines of the measures passed in 1990 by Colorado and California. Disgust with the cost of the S&L mess may well revive the tax limitation movement that was neutralized by the Reagan years. Some may even consider striking at the cause of soaring campaign expenditures, namely political television commercials. A case could well be made for the European campaign model of nationalizing a chunk of prime-time television for serious political statements. But those who make this case will find themselves instant targets for the hostility of the television industry.

These structural changes, moreover, won't touch the moral dimension, the site of the real decay. Two documents illustrate the dramatic degeneration of standards in Congress. The currently prevailing attitude marks the pages of the House Ethics Committee report on Speaker Wright. While condemning the Speaker on a relatively trivial matter, the Committee refused to consider his wire-pulling for the Texas thrift owners. This behavior, said the committee, was "not inconsistent with congressional standards." Charging Wright on these counts, it said, would jeopardize "the ability of members effectively to represent persons and organizations having concern with the activities of executive agencies."

The older standard appears in the book *Ethics in Government* by the late Senator Paul Douglas, one of the last giants on Capitol Hill. The special counsels to both the House and Senate Ethics Committees used Douglas as their point of reference. He wrote, "A legislator should not immediately conclude that the constituent is always right and the administrator is always wrong, but as far as possible should try to find out the merits of each case and only make such representations as the situation permits." In other words, the legislator should exercise his independent judgment, with an eye not merely to the interest of his contributor, but to the public good. What does the Douglas standard embody that the congressional Ethics Committees have refused to acknowledge? The answer is an old-fashioned quality: statesmanship.

This term is not only old-fashioned, it's unfashionable. While academic political science hasn't forgotten the word outright, it dismisses this standard as a delusion of an earlier era. And the academic outlook, which reads politics as a mechanistic interplay of special interests, has contaminated the politics of the real world. One political science analysis of the thrift debacle concluded, "Congressional behavior in this case should be seen as fairly routine politics rather than an outrageous deviation." The Keating Five, Jim Wright and his cronies, and all the uncaught others say in their own way, "I was just doing what any congressman would do for a constituent." They have gladly abandoned the duty to worry about the moral character of the constituent who asks for a favor, or about the impact of the favor on the general welfare. The $1.5 trillion cost of the savings and loan disaster proves that this neglect is not trivial. The public will be acutely aware of this absence of statesmanship for years to come, since we have to pay for it.

The coming years hold much promise for our country. The moral collapse of communism and the teetering of the Soviet empire have greatly reduced our main external challenge. For the rest of our lives, the greatest threats to our republic will come from within. Yet the savings and loan crisis shows how easily these threats can become real.

Chapter Notes

PROLOGUE: *How to Start a Depression*

Page 1—"The crowd immediately entered . . .": Bray Hammond, *Banks and Politics in America from the Revolution to the Civil War* (Princeton: Princeton University Press, 1957), 610–11.

Page 2—From a high point of 29,211: *Statistical Abstract of the United States, 1929* (Washington, D.C.: Government Printing Office, 1929), Tables 269, 284, 285, 288.

Page 3—Conclusion of Raymond B. Vickers: Raymond B. Vickers, "Sleazy Banking in the '20s and Today," *Wall Street Journal*, May 23, 1989, A18.

Page 4—Failure of the Bank of the United States: M. R. Werner, *Little Napoleons and Dummy Directors: Being the Narrative of the Bank of United States* (New York: Harper, 1933), 210–11; and Susan Estabrook Kennedy, *The Banking Crisis of 1933* (Lexington, KY: University Press of Kentucky, 1973), 1–5.

Page 4—No less an authority than: Milton Friedman and Anna Jacobson Schwartz, *The Great Contraction, 1929–1933* (Princeton, NJ: Princeton University Press, 1965), 13–14.

Page 5—There is another version: Werner, *Little Napoleons*, 210.

Page 5—Second respite ended: Kennedy, *Banking Crisis*, 75–76, 133–35.

Page 6—Congress delivered an even heavier blow: Kennedy, *Banking Crisis*, 40–42.

Page 7—"It's incredible": Rexford G. Tugwell, *Roosevelt's Revolution: The First Year* (New York: MacMillan, 1977), 21; Kennedy, *Banking Crisis*, 153.

Page 8—According to one private analyst: Lowell L. Bryan, *Breaking Up the Bank, Rethinking an Industry Under Siege* (Homewood, IL: Dow Jones-Irwin, 1988), 44–45, Exhibit 4–5; cf. Frederick D. Wolf, Assistant Comptroller General, *Banks and Savings & Loan Insurance Funds: Financial Condition and Proposed Reforms*, Statement before Committee on Banking, Finance & Urban Affairs, House of Representatives, Washington, D.C., 101st Cong. 1st Sess., March 10, 1989, 21–26.

Page 9—Roosevelt knew: Kennedy, *Banking Crisis*, 161–63, 178–87.

Page 9—Harrumphed one of Roosevelt's advisers: Tugwell, *Roosevelt's Revolution*, 23.

Page 11—According to a National City Bank bulletin: Quoted in [Edward Stone], *Contemporary Legislative and Banking Problems* (New York: American Institute of Banking, 1934), 272.

Page 11—He said in his first press conference: Kennedy, *Banking Crisis*, 214–22.

Page 12—Foreclosures clogged banks: [Stone], *Banking Problems*, 44–45, 158–65.

Page 14—Wrote John Kenneth Galbraith: John Kenneth Galbraith, *The Great Crash* (Boston, MA: Houghton Mifflin, 1954), 196–97.

PART ONE—THE FIX IS IN

CHAPTER ONE: *The Biggest Scam in History*

Page 17—Says one thrift regulator: background interview, April 1989; John Liscio, "Anatomy of a Mess," *Barron's*, February 27, 1989, 15.

Page 19—An excited Edwin Gray: Testimony of Edwin Gray before the Subcommittee on Financial Institutions and Consumer Affairs, United States Senate Banking Committee, Washington, D.C., 99th Cong. 1st Sess., June 6, 1985; William Isaac, " A Statement on Brokered Deposits," presented to Subcommittee on General Oversight and Investigations, United States House Committee on Banking, Finance and Urban Affairs, 99th Cong. 1st Sess., July 16, 1985.

Page 19—Renda pleaded quilty: United States v. Martin Schwimmer and Mario Renda (United States District Court, Eastern District of New York), CR-87-423.

Page 20—According to one study: Lowell Bryan, Frank Tourreilles, Mark Shapiro, "Perspective on the Current Thrift Crisis" Report by McKinsey & Co., (New York: McKinsey & Co., November 18, 1988), 1.

Page 20—Answered one critic: Edward J. Kane, *The Savings and Loan Insurance Mess: How Did It Happen?* (Washington, D.C.: The Urban Institute Press, 1989), 4.

CHAPTER TWO: *"Proper and Consistent Conduct"*

Page 34—The Capitol buzzed: Robin Toner, "Jim Wright Is Respected, but His Colleagues Are Concerned about His Tendency to Go it Alone," *New York Times*, April 3, 1989. A, 18.

Page 35—As Washington Post reporter: Tom Kenworthy, "Panel Drops Some Charges in Wright Ethics Inquiry," *Washington Post*, April 5, 1989, 1.

Page 36—In testimony given in: William K. Black, Deputy Director FSLIC, prepared for Subcommittee on Financial Institutions Supervision, Regulation and Insurance, United States House Committee on Banking, Finance and Urban Affairs, 100 Cong., 1st Sess., June 9, 1987; printed in *Fraud and Abuse by Insiders, Borrowers, and Appraisers in the California Thrift Industry: Hearing Before a Subcommittee of the [United States House] Committee on Government Operations*, 100th Cong., 1st Sess., June 13, 1987, 222–93 (hereafter, "Black Testimony").

Page 37—Black described a problem: "Federal Response to Criminal Misconduct and Insider Abuse in the Nation's Financial Institutions," *57th Report*, United States House Committee on Government Operations, 98th Cong., 2nd Sess., October 4, 1984; "Thrift Failures: Costly Failures Resulted from Regulatory Violations and Unsafe Practices," United States General Accounting Office, Report GAO/AFMD-89-62, June 16, 1989.

Page 37—Said Comptroller of the Currency Robert L. Clarke: "Remarks by Robert L. Clarke, Comptroller of the Currency, before the Exchequer Club, Washington, D.C.," January 20, 1988; printed in *Adequacy of Federal Efforts to Combat Fraud, Abuse and Misconduct in Federally Insured Financial Institutions: Hearing Before a Subcommittee of the [United States House] Committee on Government Operations*, 98th Cong., 2nd Sess., November 19, 1984, 1025–41.

Page 37—In October 1988: [Peter Barash], "Combating Fraud, Abuse and Misconduct in the Nation's Financial Institutions: Current Federal Efforts are Inadequate," *72nd Report*, United States House Committee on Government Operations, 100th Cong., 2nd Sess., October 13, 1988.

Page 38—Barash pointed: [Barash], *72nd Report*, 12, 10, 5–7.

Page 41—In October 1985, he told: Testimony of Edwin Gray before Subcommittee on Financial Institutions, United States House Banking Committee, Washington, D.C., 99th Cong., 1st Sess., October 17, 1985.

Page 42—At this point, however: [Richard J. Phelan], *Report of the Special Outside Counsel in the Matter of Speaker James C. Wright, Jr.*, United States House Committee on Standards of Official Conduct, 101st Cong., 1st Sess., February 21, 1989, 216–18 (hereafter, *Phelan Report*).

Page 43—Hall had gone to Wright: *Phelan Report*, 223–32.

Page 44—Wright called Gray: *Phelan Report*, 244, 248–49.

Page 45—The former president of the Dallas Home Loan Bank: *Phelan Report*, 262.

Page 45—As the Phelan Report concluded: *Phelan Report*, 265, 268.

Page 45—Wright now had a real grudge: *Phelan Report*, 271.

Page 46—To general astonishment, Barnard: *Phelan Report*, 251–52; *Federal Savings and Loan Insurance Corporation Recapitalization Act (H.R.27): Hearings before the [United States House] Committee on Banking, Finance and Urban Affairs*, 100th Cong., 1st Sess., January 21 and 22, 1987, 430–31.

Page 46—On January 29, Wright: *Phelan Report*, 210.

Page 46—The United States League of Savings Institutions said explicitly: *Congressional Record*, Senate, 100th Cong., 1st Sess., March 27, 1987, S4029–30.

Page 46—On March 2, Chairman Gray wrote: *Selected Speeches, Congressional Testimony, and Selected Correspondence of Edwin J. Gray*, Vol. 1 (Washington, D.C.: Federal Home Loan Bank System Publication Corporation, 1987), 131–35.

Page 47—On April 27, FSLIC sued Dixon: FSLIC in its Corporate Capacity v. Don R. Dixon, et. al. (United States District Court, Northern District of Texas), CA3-87-1102-G.

Page 48—Black ran into trouble: *Phelan Report*, 271–72.

Page 48—Black trudged up Capitol Hill: Black Testimony, 223, 224, 232.

Page 49—Danny Wall paid a courtesy visit: *Phelan Report*, 274–75, 276.

Page 50—Explained the Committee's report: *Statement of the Committee on Standards of Official Conduct in the Matter of Representative James C. Wright, Jr.*, United States House Committee on Standards of Official Conduct, 101st Cong., 1st Sess., April 13, 1989, 84.

Page 51—Pattern of institutionalized bribery: Brooks Jackson, *Honest Graft, Big Money, and the American Political Process* (New York: Alfred A. Knopf, 1988).

CHAPTER THREE: *The Edge of the Meltdown*

Page 53—"They gave us a Band-Aid . . .": Hal Lancaster, "United States Intervention in Southwest S&Ls Raises Industry Losses, Executives Say," *Wall Street Journal*, May 1, 1989, A16.

Page 54—Gov. Clements harrumphed: Jim McTague and Robert Trigaux, "Regulators Act to Avert Run on Texas S&Ls," *American Banker*, August 11, 1987, 1, 23.

Page 54—In Washington, Danny Wall: "Threat to Thrifts Dissipates in Texas," *American Banker*, August 14, 1987, 5, 8.

Page 55—Savings and loans, ironically, were the first to benefit: "Savings Deposits Soared in October," *New York Times*, December 5, 1987, 40.

Page 56—After several delays, Governor Clements released his report: "Report to the Honorable William P. Clements, Jr., Governor of the State of Texas," Governor's Task Force on the Savings and Loan Industry (Austin, Texas), January 25, 1988.

Page 58—The GAO kept close watch: "Failed Thrifts: Bank Board's 1988 Texas Resolutions," United States General Accounting Office, Report GAO/GGD-89-59, March 11, 1989.

Page 59—One reporter described: Lancaster, "U. S. Intervention," *Wall Street Journal*, May 1, 1989, A16.

Page 60—One of his planners told: "Thrift Crisis Poses Challenge to Bush's Attempt to Cut Deficit Without Resorting to New Taxes," *Wall Street Journal*, November 23, 1988, A16.

Page 61—Brady brought them: Peter T. Kilborn, "Officials Weighed Possibility of a Run on Savings Deposits," *New York Times*, February 9, 1989, A1, D15.

Page 61—Says Mullins: Interview by author with Robert R. Glauber and David W. Mullins, Jr., Washington, D.C., June 29, 1989.

Page 63—President Bush called: "President's News Conference on Savings Crisis and Nominees," *New York Times*, February 7, 1989, D8.

Page 63—In a scene like something from the depression: "Be Prepared . . . Develop a Crisis Plan," Video produced by United States League of Savings Institutions, recorded live, February 27, 1989, at meeting of Arizona League of Savings Institutions, Phoenix, Arizona.

Page 64—On the night of Sunday, February 5: Kilborn, "Officials," *New York Times*, February 9, 1989, A1, D15.

Page 65—Complained Congressman John La Falce: Letter from John J. La Falce to Alan Greenspan, February 22, 1989; letter from Alan Greenspan to John J. La Falce, February 27, 1989; Statement of the Honorable John J. La Falce, press release, Washington, D.C., March 7, 1989.

PART TWO—THE STRANGE CAREER
OF WILLIAM ISAAC

CHAPTER FOUR: *The Road to Washington*

Page 72—William Isaac was born: Interview by author with William Isaac, Washington, D.C., June 28 and 29, 1989 (hereafter "Isaac interview").

Page 73—About five years earlier, the Louisville bank: Interviews, FBI files.

Page 74—The troubles started: Metro-Dade police files.

Page 74—Kaki, they heard: Hank Messick, *Of Grass and Snow* (Englewood Cliffs, NJ: Prentice-Hall, 1979), 171–80.

Page 75—WFC would divert: FBI file.

Page 77—The National Bank of South Florida: Interview by author with Lou Frank, July 3, 1989; Letter of H. Joe Selby, Senior Deputy Comptroller for Bank Supervision, to the Honorable Doug Barnard, Jr., Chairman, Commerce, Consumer and Monetary Affairs Subcommittee, United States House Committee on Government Operations, March 29, 1985.

Page 78—Testified Robert Serino: Robert F. Serino, Director of Enforcement and Compliance, Office of the Comptroller of the Currency, Statement before Executive Session, United States House Select Committee on Narcotics Abuse and Control, 95th Cong., 2nd Sess., March 22, 1978.

Page 78—Examiners heard tales: Testimony of Jerome Sanford, *Banks and Narcotics Money Flow in South Florida: Hearings Before the [United States Senate] Committee on Banking, Housing and Urban Affairs*, 96th Cong., 2nd Sess., June 5 and 6, 1980, 33–35.

Page 78—During this period, Moscow Narodny: Martin Tolchin, "Russians Sought United States Banks to Gain High Tech Secrets," *New York Times*, February 16, 1986, A1.

Page 78—A Cuban government defector: Interviews by author with Jose Luis Llovio-Menendez, New York City.

Page 78—A Metro-Dade police wiretap: State of Florida v. Alberto San Pedro, (11th Circuit, District of Florida), Case No: 86-4118; Transcript labelled Case No: 258612-F, August 22, 1985.

Page 79—In 1978, a joint FBI and DEA Task Force: Hilda Indan and Helga Silva, "Dade Banks Turn over Records in Drug Probe," *Miami News*, March 24, 1978, 1.

Page 79—Later he developed a bad habit: United States v. Juan Evelio Pou-Mencia, (United States District Court, Southern District of Florida) 79-311-CR; United States v. Juan Evelio Pou-Mencia, (United States District Court, Southern District of Florida) 81-563-CR.

Page 80—Villoldo joined the bid: Corporation records, Florida Secretary of State's office, Tallahassee, Florida.

Page 80—A cryptic and unexplained passage: United States Senate Committee on Foreign Relations, Subcommittee on Terrorism, Narcotics and International Operations, *Drugs, Law Enforcement and Foreign Policy*, (Washington, D.C.: United States Government Printing Office, 1989), 146–47.

Page 80—"The Comptroller has clearly stated . . .": Letter of Guillermo Hernandez-Cartaya to Juan Evelio Pou, Coral Gables, Florida, August 16, 1977; Affidavit of Ray L. Corona submitted with "Supplemented and Renewed Motion for Recusal," in the matter of Sunshine State Bank, Federal Deposit Insurance Corporation Administrative Hearing, Case No. FDIC 83-252b&c, (hereafter "Corona affidavit"), 3–4.

Page 80—The active help of the Louisville Bank: Corona affidavit, Financing Agreement, August 26, 1977.

Page 81—During the week of December 19: Corona affidavit, 3, 4.

Page 82—Frank explained: Testimony of Lou Frank, United States v. Ray L. Corona and Rafael Corona (United States District Court, Southern District of Florida), 84-853-CIV transcripts, Vol. 8, 8 (hereafter "Frank testimony").

Page 83—Corona claims: Corona affidavit, 3.

Page 83—Had Isaac been pushy?: Frank testimony, 19.

Page 84—In a curious parallel: Corporate Records, Republic of Panama and State of Florida; Interview by author with Fernando Capablanca, Miami, FL.

Page 84—There were prosecutions: United States v. Guillermo Hernandez-Cartaya, et al. (United States District Court, Southern District of Florida), 81-23-CR.

Page 85—Assistant United States Attorney R. Jerome Sanford: Interview by author with R. Jerome Sanford.

Page 85—At the end of 1978, a Justice Department memo: Memo from John P. Lydick to WFC Files, September 6, 1978; George J. Mouldson, attorney, Fraud Section, Criminal Division, Justice Department, to Mark F. Richard, Chief, Fraud Section and John C. Keeney, Deputy Assistant Attorney General, Criminal Division, December 12, 1978.

Page 85—Something about Monomeros: Isaac interview.

Page 85—A small group of journalist buffs: John Cummings, "Miami Confidential" *Inquiry*, August 3 and 24, 1981, 19–24; Penny Lernoux, *In Banks We Trust* (Garden City, NY: Anchor Press of Doubleday, 1984), 143–68; and Jonathan Kwitney, *Endless Enemies: The Making of an Unfriendly World* (New York: Congdon & Week, 1984), 25, 247–48.

CHAPTER FIVE: *The Butcher Revels*

Page 88—Jake is now serving: Interview by author with Jacob F. Butcher, Atlanta Prison Camp, Atlanta, GA, August 30, 1987 (hereafter "Butcher interview").

Page 89—It ultimately cost: Letter from Alvin E. Kitchen, Assistant Director, FDIC, to author, Washington, D.C., August 2, 1989. The total as of that date for eight Butcher banks in liquidation was $1,066,636,716.

Page 89—When I first met Butcher: Butcher interview.

Page 89—The green light had been on: "Borrowed Money, Borrowed Time: The Fall of the House of Butcher," *The Tennesseean* and the *Knoxville Journal*, Nov. 18, 1983, 20–21.

Page 90—Jesse Barr, Jake's right-hand man: Interview by author with Jesse Barr, Renaissance Unit, Lexington Federal Correctional Institution, Lexington, Kentucky (hereafter "Barr interview").

Page 91—A card on file: Released in lawsuit, FDIC v. Aetna Casualty & Surety Company (United States District Court, Eastern District of Tennessee, Northern Division [Knoxville]), CIV 3-85-1242.

Page 92—In November, Blanton beat: Hank Hillin, *FBI Codename TENNPAR: Tennessee's Ray Blanton Years* (Nashville, TN: Pine Hall Press, 1985), 41, 414–15.

Page 92—Bert Lance explained: Testimony of Thomas B. Lance, in *Matters Relating to T. Bertram Lance: Hearing Before [United States Senate] Committee on Governmental Affairs*, Washington, D.C., 95th Cong., 1st Sess., July 15 and 25, 1977, 56.

Page 93—Carter campaigned for him: Hillin, *Codename TENNPAR*, 291.

Page 93—He pulled strings with President Carter: Joe Dodd, *Exposé: The Real Story Behind the Knoxville World's Fair* (Knoxville: Joe Dodd, 1982), 79–104; Kenneth Y. Tomlinson, *Reader's Digest*, November 1979.

Page 95—Other losses hit in 1980: Memorandum from Patrick J. McDonough, review examiner, to the Board of Review and the Board of Directors, FDIC; "Jacob F. Butcher and his Related Banking Interests" (undated), from Aetna files, plaintiff's exhibit #795.

Page 95—The "financial wizard" behind C.H., Jr.: "Borrowed Money," 14–15.

Page 96—Defrocked banker named Jesse Barr: Barr interview.

Page 96—Jesse was rising: "Borrowed Money," 10–11; my copy is annotated by Barr, but he made no changes in the section on his own biography.

Page 97—Jesse recalled amid the babble: Barr interview.

Page 99—Constant borrowing from the Fed Funds market: Letter from Jesse Barr to author, Lexington, KY, March 3, 1988.

Page 100—Mercantile National Bank had to sue: Mercantile National Bank at Dallas v. Jake F. and Sonya Butcher (United States District Court, Northern District of Texas), CA3-83-821.

Page 100—What did the Louisville bankers know: Interview by author with A. Stevens Miles, Louisville, KY, July 24, 1985, and with Leonard V. Hardin, Louisville, KY, July 25, 1985.

CHAPTER SIX: *"I Think We Had Them"*

Page 102—Stated George M. Little, Jr.: Deposition of George M. Little, Jr., First State Bank of Wayne County v. City and County Bank of Knox County, et al. (United States District Court, Eastern District of Kentucky at London), CIV-83-141, 128 (hereafter "Little deposition").

Page 103—He had stumbled on a trace: Little deposition, 120–23.

Page 103—Little kept worrying: Little deposition, 96–98.

Page 104—His report proved him incorrigible: Report of Examination, UAB Johnson City, State of Tennessee Department of Banking, December 14, 1979, Confidential Section, 22.

Page 104—"It really hit the fan": Little deposition, 95–98, 129.

Page 105—As Little said: Little deposition, 95–98, 129.

Page 105—His lawyers had unearthed them: Butcher interview.

Page 106—Two-day congressional hearing: *Federal Supervision and Failure of United American Bank (Knoxville, TN), Hearings before a Subcommittee of the [United States House] Committee on Government Operations,* Washington, D.C., 98th Cong., 1st Sess., March 15 and 16, 1983 (hereafter *UAB-Knoxville hearings*).

Page 106—Plus a scathing report: [Peter Barash], "Federal Supervision and Failure of United American Bank in Knoxville, TN, and Affiliated Banks, *Twenty-Third Report* [United States House] Committee on Government Operations" 98th Cong., 1st Sess., (Washington, D.C.: United States GPO, 1983) (hereafter *"Barash Report"*).

Page 107—A letter from the Federal Reserve Bank: Letter from Richard A. Dill, Federal Reserve Bank of Atlanta, to O.B. Rutherford, chairman of board, City & County Bank of Powell at Powell, TN, July 19, 1972.

Page 107—OCC dealt briefly: *Barash Report,* 17.

Page 108—Former Comptroller of the Currency: Interview by author with John G. Heimann, New York City, NY, (hereafter "Heimann interview").

Page 108—Two papers: Memo from Roy E. Jackson, Regional Director, FDIC, to John J. Early, Director, Division of Bank Supervision, October 20, 1977, from Aetna case files.

Page 110—Conversation with the Butchers: James L. Sexton, Assistant Memphis Regional Director, memo to files, November 18, 1977; cf, *Barash Report*, 19–20.

Page 110—FDIC Chairman Isaac defended: UAB-Knoxville hearings, 16.

Page 111—Butcher began: Roy Jackson, Regional Director, FDIC, memo to files, February 23, 1978.

Page 111—On January 15, 1979, Sexton: *Barash Report*, 23–29.

Page 112—The higher politics of the FDIC board of directors: Heimann interview. Isaac interview.

Page 112—Sprague does, however, recall: Interview by author with Irvine H. Sprague, Alexandria, VA (hereafter "Sprague interview").

Page 113—The Barnard subcommittee report: *Barash Report*, 32.

Page 114—After the application languished: A. David Meadows, Regional Director, Memphis, memo to files, July 30, 1982.

Page 114—Isaac claimed, to the contrary: Isaac interview; Interview by author with David Meadows. Washington, DC.

Page 115—Former FDIC examiner Robert Shober: Interview by author with Robert Shober, Louisville, KY.

Page 115—One of the stranger episodes: Jeffrey C. Gerrish, regional counsel, FDIC, memo to files, January 21, 1983.

Page 117—As one critic said: Mountjoy Trimble, Second Amended Complaint, First State Bank of Wayne County v. City and County Bank of Knox County, et al. (United States District Court, Eastern District of Kentucky at London), CIV-83-141 State case, op. cit.

Page 117—The Comptroller of the Currency stopped: Telephone interview by author with H. Joe Selby.

Page 117—On January 25, Regional Director Meadows: Jeffrey C. Gerrish, regional counsel, FDIC, memo to file, February 2, 1983.

Page 117—Adams called: Little deposition.

Page 118—Jake went to court: UAB-Knoxville hearings, 156–70.

Page 118—In a marathon: UAB-Knoxville hearings, 199–202; Butcher interview.

Page 119—The FDIC Board met in Washington: Irvine H. Sprague, *Bailout: An Insider's Account of Bank Failures and Rescues* (New York: Basic Books, 1986), 272–73n.

Page 120—Sprague, who has written: Sprague interview.

Page 120—A bleary William Isaac: "C&C, Butcher banks declared healthy by federal examiners," *Knoxville Journal*, February 17, 1983, 1.

Page 120—Sasser vouched for him: Sprague interview. Butcher interview.

Page 121—The FDIC's Jim Sexton wrote back: Letter from James Sexton to R. Gene Smith, March 17, 1983; Letter from Leonard V. Hardin to R. Gene Smith, February 22, 1983; Neil Welch, memo to files, April 21, 1983.

Page 122—Louisville law firm: Reporter's notes, *Louisville Times*.
Page 124—The last word: Butcher interview.

CHAPTER SEVEN: *Darkness at Sunshine State*

Page 126—Tony Fernandez fled: Transcript of proceedings, United States v. Gerardo Jorge Guevara, Ray L. Corona, Rafael L. Corona, Manuel Lopez-Castro and William Vaughn (United States District Court, Southern District of Florida at Miami), 84-853-CR, Vol. 2, 96-106 (hereafter, "Fernandez Transcript").

Page 127—Tony said he first met Ray Corona: Fernandez Transcript, Vol. 3, 330, 343–55.

Page 128—"You do not want to make the Colombians mad": Fernandez Transcript, Vol. 5.

Page 128—Alvero-Cruz's cheapness: Fernandez Transcript, Vol. 3, 354.

Page 128—Fernandez was relieved: Fernandez Transcript, Vol. 3, 358–59.

Page 128—Silver-haired Hungarian refugee: Martha Branigan, "A Tax-Haven Service Landed Its Proprietor in Some Shady Affairs," *Wall Street Journal*, April 17, 1986, 1.

Page 129—Samos nonetheless opposed: Fernandez Transcript, Vol. 3, 358.

Page 129—Lou Frank, tried to soften the blow: Rafael Corona, Fernandez Transcript, Vol. 21, 4483.

Page 129—They took a Lear jet: Fernandez Transcript, Vol. 3, 370–76.

Page 131—He assumed a new identity: Fernandez Transcript, Vol. 4, 632.

Page 131—An FDIC examiner commented: Alan W. Heifetz, Administrative Law Judge, "Initial Decision," In the Matter of Sunshine State Bank, FDIC Administrative proceedings, FDIC-83-252b&c, 6, 8–12 (hereafter "Heifetz decision").

Page 132—Weird things: Heifetz decision, 13, 37; Lyle V. Helgerson, Assistant Regional Director, FDIC, memo to files, October 7, 1983.

Page 132—The Dallas office called: Heifetz decision, 27–30.

Page 132—All-American tradition of shady dealing: Cavanagh Communities Corporation, Form 8 (Amendment to Form 10-K) filed with Securities and Exchange Commission, Washington, D.C., April 28, 1983, 2–4.

Page 133—State officials by now were firmly: Heifetz decision, 26; Administrative Hearing Transcript, 3517–19.

Page 133—"The judge went back . . .": Heifetz decision, 36; Sunshine State Bank v. FDIC (United States Court of Appeals, 11th Circuit), CIV-85-5741, March 18, 1986.

Page 134—"The curious aspect of distilling . . .": Heifetz decision, 4.

Page 134—Attorney Shevin had a few hours: "Order," In the Matter of X,Y,Z Bank (Circuit Court, 11th District, Florida, General Jurisdiction Division), Case No. 85-3134-CA17, August 2, 1985.

Page 134—For the FDIC's regional examiners: Sprague interview. and others.

Page 135—A pervasive political weakness: James Ring Adams, "Losing the Drug War: Drugs, Banks and Florida Politics," *American Spectator* September 1988, 20–24.

Page 136—On January 25, 1985, Roy Corona: "Supplemental and Renewed Motion for Recusal," In the Matter of Sunshine State, August 19, 1985, 2–3.

Page 137—The FDIC board brushed aside: "Decision and Order on Respondents' Supplemental and Renewed Motion for Recusal," In the Matter of Sunshine State, August 19, 1985, 2–3.

Page 138—The FDIC had no trouble: FDIC v. Sunshine State Bank (United States District Court, Southern District of Florida at Miami), 86-0875-CIV; Susan Sachs, "The Bank that Wouldn't Die: Bank Saga— Bad Loans, Odd Deals," *The Miami Herald*, July 6, 1986, 1A, 12A.

PART THREE—INTERLUDE: THE OHIO BANK CRISIS

CHAPTER EIGHT: *The Friends of Marvin Warner*

Page 146—Born in 1919 in Birmingham: Polk Laffoon IV, "How Marvin Warner Ramrods His Empire," *Cincinnati Post*, August 28, 1976, 1; Polk Laffoon IV, "Warner Pulled Up His Sleeves and Plunged into Real Estate," *Cincinnati Post*, August 30, 1976, 9.

Page 147—Arky was born: Richard Wallace and Jim McGee, "Lawyer with Ties to E. S. M. Kills Himself," *Miami Herald*, July 24, 1985, 1A, 14A.

Page 147—This fatal friendship: James Lyons, "How Many Hats Can Steve Arky Wear?," *The American Lawyer*, May 1985, 86–93; Lou Frank, memo to Donald L. Tarleton, Regional Administrator, Comptroller of the Currency, February 15, 1977 (hereafter "Frank memo"); *Ohio Savings and Loan Crisis and Collapse of E. S. M. Government Securities, Inc., Hearing before a Subcommittee of the [United States House] Committee on Government Operations*, 99th Cong., 1st Sess., April 3, 1985, 1049–65, 1075.

Page 148—His colleagues lived like gamblers: Thomas Tew, Receiver of E. S. M. Group, Inc., "Report on the Condition of the E. S. M. Companies," Securities and Exchange Commission v. E. S. M. Group, Inc. et al. (United States District Court, Southern District of Florida at Fort Lauderdale), 85-6190-CIV, 142–47 (hereafter "Tew Report"), March 1985.

Page 148—The high living was a front: Tew Report, 42–52.

Page 149—Some lenders did ask: Tew Report, Appendix G.

Page 150—The outfit had aroused suspicions: Frank memo.

Page 151—I asked about the connection: Interview by author with Dan Fromhoff, North Miami, FL, March 30, 1988.

Page 152—By May, Atlanta: William Nortman, Associate Regional Administrator, Miami, Branch Office, SEC, Action Memorandum, File Nos. A-914, A-915, A-918, May 13, 1977.

Page 152—The Arky, Freed firm went to court: Lyons, *Amer. Lawyer*, 88–90.

Page 153—Their nerve aroused Warner's interest: Deposition of Marvin L. Warner, In the Matter of American Bancshares, Inc., SEC file No. A-962, November 28, 1979, 82.

Page 154—He furiously pulled strings: William Nortman, memo to file, SEC file No. A-962, January 24, 1979.

Page 155—Warner always insisted: Marvin L. Warner to Editor, *Wall Street Journal*, May 5, 1985.

Page 155—The raid produced the indictment of the bank: United States v. The Great American Bank of Dade County, et al. (United States District Court, Southern District of Florida), 82-720-CR.

Page 156—A former member of Lewis's staff: Background interview.

Page 157—Its own suspicions about Argent: Memo from Stephen B. Woodrough, July 21, 1977.

Page 157—Home State copped a plea: United States v. Home State Savings Association (United States District Court, Southern District of Ohio at Cincinnati), CR-80-74; James C. Cissell, United States Attorney, Southern District of Ohio, "News Release," December 15, 1980.

Page 158—The losses increased: Tew Report, 35, 42–46.

Page 159—Warner and Ewton "were umbilically tied together": David Satterfield, "Millionaire Drained E. S. M., Ex-Officer Says," *Miami Herald*, August 8, 1986, 1A, 20A.

Page 160—Perez Sandoval became formidable: James Ring Adams, "A Lawyer's Death and a Trail of Broken Banks," *Wall Street Journal*, August 22, 1985.

Page 161— Warner counterpunched: Home State Financial, Inc. v. Juan Vicente Perez Sandoval, Division of Administrative Hearings, State of Florida, Case No. 84-1115.

Page 161—Government investigators later charged: "Banco de Commercio: Irresponsible Banking," *VenEconomy Monthly*, June 1985, 14–18; Banco de Commercio v. Juan Vicente Perez Sandoval (Circuit Court, 11th Judicial District, Dade County, Florida, General Jurisdiction Division), Case No. 85-37648 CA12.

Page 162—Warner had taken control of ASLA: Minutes, Board of Directors, American Savings and Loan Association.

Page 163—The deal hit the fan: ASLA Board minutes, July 31, 1984; ASLA Board minutes, September 10, 1984; Shepard Broad to Marvin Warner, Miami, FL, January 4, 1985.

Page 164—At a management committee meeting: Minutes, Asset-Liability Committee, ASLA, May 25, 1984; "Trustee's Objection to Proof of Claim . . . ," and amended complaint, In re. E. S. M. Government Securities, In C. Tew v. American Savings and Loan Association (United States District Court, Southern District of Florida in Fort Lauderdale) 85-6254-CIV, 6-23.

Page 164—Like a huckster with a live one: Letter from Ronnie R. Ewton to Marvin Warner, Fort Lauderdale, FL, June 4, 1984.

CHAPTER NINE: *The Time Bomb Explodes*

Page 166—"You may be losing . . .": Memo from Sylvester Hentschel to Clark Wideman, October 8, 1982. Exhibit in files of Joint Select Committee on Savings and Loans, 116th Ohio General Assembly, in State Library, Columbus, Ohio.

Page 167—Then he wrote Chief Examiner Kurt A. Kreinbring: Sylvester F. Hentschel, "Remarks" page, 1982 Home State Examination, returned to Chief Examiner Kurt A. Kreinbring, February 3, 1983. Ohio Joint Select Committee files.

Page 167—Hentschel put his concern right on the front: Report of Examination, Home State Savings Association, Division of Building and Loan Associations, Department of Commerce, State of Ohio, July 10, 1982, 2. Ohio Joint Select Committee files.

Page 168—Wideman argued: Interview by author with Clark Wideman, Columbus, Ohio, August 27, 1985; James Ring Adams, "How Home State Beat the Examiners," *Wall Street Journal*, September 3, 1985.

Page 168—Wideman's successor: Interview by author with Lawrence Huddleston, Columbus, Ohio.

Page 169—A special investigating committee: "Protecting the Depositor," Report and Recommendations of the Joint Select Committee on Savings and Loans, 116th Ohio General Assembly, February 1, 1986. 22-25.

Page 170—Some of these blows: Satterfield, *Miami Herald*, August 8, 1986.

Page 171—Huddleston put his staffing request: Memo from C. Lawrence Huddleston to Warren W. Tyler, July 5, 1984. Ohio Joint Select Committee files.

Page 171—Before leaving, he wrote a memo: (Lawrence Huddleston), "Accomplishments of the Division of Savings and Loan Associations, February 1983–November 1984." (undated). Ohio Joint Select Committee files.

Page 172—A "Celestial" to the last: Memo from C. Lawrence Huddleston to the Honorable Richard Celeste, Governor of Ohio, January 10, 1985. Ohio Joint Select Committee files.

Page 173—In May, Warner called: James Ring Adams, "The Friends of Marvin Warner," *Wall Street Journal*, September 3, 1985; Campaign Contribution Reports, Files of Ohio Secretary of State, Columbus, Ohio.

Page 173—Celeste said: Adrienne Bosworth, Herb Cook, Jr., and Max S. Brown, "Should Celeste Have Closed the S&Ls?," *Columbus Monthly*, May 1986, 44-51.

Page 174—According to one sharp critic: Edward J. Kane, "How Incentive-Incompatible Deposit-Insurance Systems Fail" (typescript), October 24, 1988. 11.

Page 177—Professor Kane drew a number of cynical conclusions: Kane, "Deposit-Insurance Systems," 14–15, 20–21.

CHAPTER TEN: *The Seamless Web (I)*

Page 181—Denton helped float the WFC: Interviews, FBI informant report.

Page 182—Aldereguia, a former veterinarian: Interviews.

Page 183—According to the *Miami Herald*: Joe Crankshaw and Patrick Riordan, "Cuban Secret Police Letter to Spy in Miami Is Found," *Miami Herald*, March 15, 1978, 1.; Gloria Marina, " 'I'm Not Samuel': Ex-WFC Aide Denies That He's Cuban Spy," *Miami Herald*, March 19, 1978, 1.

Page 184—Dr. Bernardo Benes: Interview by author with Bernardo Benes, North Miami, FL.

Page 187—The most dramatic rise: Brad Kuhn, "The Quiet Influence of Richard Swann," *Orlando Sentinel*, May 22, 1989, A1, A5; James Ring Adams, "Florida Politics and the Power of Pull," *Wall Street Journal*, August 1, 1989.

Page 189—Half a million of the proceeds: "Borrowed Money," *Tennesseean* and *Knoxville Journal*, 7, 8.

Page 189—"I think S&Ls in Florida were the key": Undated notes in Aetna files.

Page 190—A shadowy Geneva multi-millionaire named Bruce Rappaport: Seth Lipsky, ed., *The Billion Dollar Bubble and Other Stories from the* Asian Wall Street Journal (Hong Kong: *Asian Wall Street Journal*, 1979), 1–41; Seth Lipsky, "Lucrative Link: How Bruce Rappaport Built Shipping Fortune with Pertamina Deals," *Wall Street Journal*, February 11, 1977, 1; Deposition of Bruce Rappaport, Martropica Compania Naviera, S.A. v. Perushaan Pertambangan Minyak Dan Gas Bumi Negara (Pertamina), (Supreme Court of the State of New York, County of New York) Index No. 13258/76.

Page 192—An SEC court filing: "Memorandum of Points and Authorities . . . ," SEC v. Marvin L. Warner, et al. (United States District Court, Southern District of Florida in Fort Lauderdale), 86-6742-CIV, May 5, 1987.

Page 192—The SEC has accused Warner: "Opposition of the Securities and Exchange Commission to motions . . . ," Marvin L. Warner v. United States Securities and Exchange Commission (United States District Court, Southern District of Florida in Fort Lauderdale) 85-2740-CIV, 14.

PART FOUR—THE EDUCATION OF EDWIN GRAY

CHAPTER ELEVEN: *The Making of an Outcast*

Page 195—Ed Gray flew to Dallas: Interview by author with Ed Gray, correcting the docudrama version in the *Washington Post* (hereafter

"Gray interview"); cf. David Maraniss and Rick Atkinson, "In Texas, Thrifts Went on a Binge of Growth," *Washington Post*, June 11, 1989, 1.

Page 200—According to the FDIC, Merrill had become: William Isaac, "A Statement on Brokered Deposits," Subcommittee on General Oversight and Investigations, (United States House) Committee on Banking, Finance, and Urban Affairs, 99th Cong., 1st Sess., July 16, 1985.

Page 203—David Lamar Faulkner was born: Dennis Cauchon, "S&L Trial: 'Folk heroes' or crooks?" *USA Today*, February 27, 1989, 1B; "In Empire's Wake, a Dynasty Shakes," *American Banker*, February 7, 1984, reprinted in *Adequacy of Federal Home Loan Bank Board Supervision of Empire Savings and Loan Association, Hearing before a Subcommittee of the (United States House) Committee on Government Operations*, April 25, 1984, 565. (Hereafter, *Empire Hearings*.)

Page 204—His celebrations: Maryln Schwartz, "It Was a Texas-Size Wedding," *Dallas Morning News*, November 7, 1983.

Page 204—At the Southfork Ranch: Maryln Schwartz, "Big Buckskins . . . For Cattle Barons, It's Always Leather Weather," *Dallas Morning News*, June 23, 1985.

Page 205—The two had been close friends: Allen Pusey, "Mattox Receives $200,000 from Developer Faulkner," *Dallas Morning News*, January 26, 1986; Ronnie Dugger, "Jim Mattox: Two Inquiries," *Texas Observer*, June 16, 1989, 1, 4–8.

Page 205—One of Faulkner's associates: Dugger, *Texas Observer* 6.

Page 205—Conducting what Ed Gray later called: *Empire Hearings*, 77.

Page 205—The "land flip": Allen Pusey, "Fast Money and Fraud," *New York Times Magazine*, April 23, 1989, 30–34.

Page 207—Bowman, the Texas S&L commissioner: *Empire Hearings*, 46.

Page 208—Gray's first reaction: Gray interview.

CHAPTER TWELVE: *Two, Three, Many Empires*

Page 211—This was exactly the pattern: M. Ray Perryman, "The Estimated Economic Impact of Excessive Construction Financing in the Savings and Loan Industry on the Economies of Texas and the Dallas/ Fort Worth Area, A Study Submitted to the *Dallas Morning News*," (Waco, Texas: M. Ray Perryman Consultants, 1987).

Page 212—Not only were bankers symbols: Quoted in James Ring Adams, *Secrets of the Tax Revolt* (San Diego: Harcourt Brace Jovanovich, 1984), 208–9.

Page 214—He sponsored a congressional investigation: *The Failure of Citizens State Bank of Carrizo Springs, Texas, and Related Financial Problems, Hearings before the Subcommittee on Financial Institutions Supervision, Regulation, and Insurance of the (United States House) Committee on Banking, Currency, and Housing*, 94th Cong. 2nd Sess., (Washington, D.C.: Government Printing Office, 1976), November 30–December 1, 1976.

Page 214—In a foreshadowing of the Butchers' loan shuffle: Allen Pusey, "Problems, Players Surfaced in '70s Scandal," *Dallas Morning News*, December 23, 1988.

Page 215—Beebe was omni-present behind the scenes: Allen Pusey, "Beebe's Network Cast Long Shadow in Thrift Industry," *Dallas Morning News*, December 23, 1988.

Page 215—According to the fascinating study, *Inside Job*: Stephen Pizzo, Mary Fricker, and Paul Muolo, *Inside Job, the Looting of America's Savings and Loans*, (New York: McGraw-Hill, 1989), 231.

Page 216—Carlos Marcello, the legendary head: Cf. John H. Davis, *Mafia Kingfish: Carlos Marcello and the Assassination of John F. Kennedy* (New York: McGraw-Hill, 1989), 7–21.

Page 216—*Inside Job* reports: Pizzo, et al., *Inside Job*, 188, 236; Pusey, "Beebe's Network."

Page 217—Pusey of the *Dallas Morning News*: Pusey, "Beebe's Network;" see also, Allen Pusey, "Network Fueled $10 Billion S&L Loss," *Dallas Morning News*, December 4, 1988.

Page 217—Dixon, a short, driven figure: Byron Harris, "Break the Bank!" *Texas Monthly*, January 1988, 88. By 1975, he said in one deposition: Sworn Statement of Don R. Dixon, February 12, 1987, Exhibit M to "Exhibits to Plaintiff's Memorandum of Law in Support of its Motions for Temporary Restraining Order . . .," Federal Savings and Loan Insurance Corporation v. Donald R. Dixon (United States District Court, Northern District of Texas in Dallas), CA3-87-1102-G.

Page 218—a man of expensive tastes: Dana Dixon, "Gastronomique—Fantastique!" released in FSLIC v. Dixon; James Ring Adams, "The Big Fix," *American Spectator*, March 1989.

Page 220—testified Vernon officer Gregory McCormick: Sworn statement of Gregory Scott McCormick, Exhibit E to Plaintiff's Memorandum, FSLIC v. Dixon.

Page 220—the friendly institutions: Minutes, Board of Directors, Vernon Savings and Loans; Paul Duke, Jr., "Easy Money: How Texas S&L Grew into a Lending Giant and Lost $1.4 Billion," *Wall Street Journal*, April 27, 1989, A1, A8; Pizzo, et al., *Inside Job*, 199–201.

Page 220—Vernon's other borrowers: Vernon minutes; Pusey, "Network Fueled"; Pizzo, et al., *Inside Job*, 199–201.

Page 222—Both bought casinos from Morris Shenker: Pusey, "Network Fueled"; Pizzo, et al., *Inside Job*, 171–75.

Page 222—*Inside Job* speculated: Pizzo, et al., *Inside Job*, 173–75.

Page 223—After this flight: Vernon minutes.

Page 223—Harris brought to light: Byron Harris, "Other People's Money, The Savings and Loan Crisis," special report broadcast on WFAA-TV, Dallas, February 14, 1989.

Page 224—But the most colorful, and sleaziest: Byron Harris, "The Party's Over," *Texas Monthly*, June 1987, 110–13.

Page 224—Jack Brenner, one of Dixon's employees: Harris, February 14, 1989 broadcast.

Page 224—A Vernon officer confessed: John V. Hill, "Plea Agreement and Factual Résumé," United States vs. John V. Hill, (United States District Court for Northern District of Texas in Dallas), CR3-88-59, March 24, 1988.

Page 224—But it was McBirney's last party: Harris, "The Party's Over," 111; Pizzo, et al., *Inside Job*, 2.

Page 225—"We knew what was going on": Telephone interview by author with Art Leiser, August 3, 1989.

Page 225—Bowman's ties to the "Texas 40": Steve Klinkerman, "United States Expands Probe of S&Ls," *Dallas Times Herald*, August 27, 1987.

Page 226—The expansive developer Tom Gaubert: Aubrey B. Harwell, Jr., "Report of Independent Counsel Aubrey B. Harwell, Jr. to Chairman Edwin J. Gray, Federal Home Loan Bank Board," Regarding Certain Agreements between Thomas M. Gaubert and the FSLIC (Nashville, Tennessee: Neal & Harwell, April 21, 1987), 12–79.

Page 227—Almost all the funds in the PAC: "East Texas First" Reports, Federal Election Commission, 1985.

Page 228—North Dallas Task Force indicted: United States vs. Robert H. Hopkins, Jr., E. Morten Hopkins and John W. Harrell (United States District Court, Northern District of Texas in Dallas), CR3-89-008-G; Brooks Jackson and David Rogers, "Wright Took More Free Plane Trips, Source Says," *Wall Street Journal*, May 8, 1989, A18; Byron Harris, "A PAC of Lies: The Commodore Savings Case," *Wall Street Journal*, July 18, 1989.

Page 228—Gaubert's dispute: *Phelan Report*, 240–53.

Page 229—Don Dixon took a different approach: Adams, "The Big Fix," *American Spectator*, 22.

Page 232—As the *Phelan Report* put it: *Phelan Report*, 206, 213–16.

Page 233—The Ethics Committee turned its back: *Phelan Report*, 194–96, 278.

CHAPTER THIRTEEN: *Nemesis*

Page 234—Even now, Gray can't discuss it: Gray interview.

Page 236—After the 1984 election, Regan: Donald F. Regan, *For the Record* (San Diego: Harcourt Brace Jovanovich, 1988), 220–29.

Page 238—Keating, the owner of Lincoln Savings: Diane Solov, "Keating Learned from Lindner," *Dayton (Ohio) Daily News*, May 21, 1989.

Page 238—Political pull helped Lindner: (James Ring Adams), "I'm All the Parties," *Wall Street Journal*, September 3, 1985; Roy L. Harris, Jr., "Fighting Back: Keating, Under Attack in Lincoln S&L Mess, Blames the Regulators," *Wall Street Journal*, July 18, 1989. A1, A10. *Federal Regulation of Direct Investments by Savings and Loans and Banks; and Condition of the Federal Deposit Insurance Funds, Hearings before a Sub-*

committee of the (United States House) Committee on Government Operations, February 27 and 28, 1985. (Washington, D.C.: Government
Printing Office, 1985), 4–7. (Hereafter, Investment Hearings.)

Page 240—Keating took the stand: Investment Hearings, 210–14.

Page 240—Greenspan added: Investment Hearings, 78.

Page 240—One March 1985 piece: Monica Langley, "Too Cozy?
Chief United States Regulator of S&Ls Draws Fire for Ties to Big
Thrifts," Wall Street Journal. March 22, 1985, A1.

Page 240—At the end·of 1985, Keating: Gray interview; Interview
by author with Shannon Fairbanks,

Page 241—One of the regulators who did go over: Testimony of
Lawrence W. Taggart before United States House Banking Committee,
San Francisco, California, January 13, 1989, (typed transcript) 116–24,
148. (Hereafter, "San Francisco Hearings.")

Page 241—So Taggart sat down and wrote a letter: Letter from
Lawrence W. Taggart to Donald Regan, August 4, 1986; read into the
San Francisco Hearings record by Banking Committee Chairman Henry
Gonzalez.

Page 242—Keating later claimed credit: Roy Harris, Wall Street
Journal, July 18, 1989.

Page 243—According to a leak to the New York Times: Kenneth E.
Noble, "Thrift Units' Regulator, Under Inquiry, Resigns," New York
Times, May 2, 1987.

Page 243—Gray remembers being called, alone: Letters: From John
McCain to Edwin Gray, May 25, 1989; From Edwin Gray to John
McCain, May 30, 1989; From Alan Cranston to Edwin Gray, June 7,
1989; From Edwin Gray to Alan Cranston, June 15, 1989.

Page 245—This time, Black took notes: Handwritten notes by William Black, April 9, 1987, typed as memo to Edwin J. Gray, April 10,
1987.

Page 248—Following routine: Gray interview; "For Charlie Keating,
The Best Defense Is a Lawsuit," Business Week, May 1, 1989, 32.

Page 248—He had good reason to let the issue ride: Letter from
Edwin J. Gray to Jim McTague, American Banker, April 25, 1989.

Page 249—Wall started meeting: Jim Calle and John Dougherty,
"Keating Discussed Firing Wright Foe," Arizona Tribune, June 6, 1989.

Page 251—This regulator-swapping: Testimony of Frederick D.
Wolf, San Francisco Hearing, January 13, 1989.

Page 251—In early 1988, the Detroit News: Michael Clements and
Roger Martin, "Execs of Firm Probed by Feds Are Riegle Contributors,"
Detroit News, February 28, 1988. 1A, 14A.

Page 251—The syndicated columnist: Warren Brookes, "Bailing
Cranston Out?" Washington Times, July 26, 1989.

Page 252—The accountants Kenneth Leventhal & Company: Kenneth Leventhal & Company, Report to Squire, Sanders & Dempsey, July
14, 1989.

Page 254—A month later, he released a statement: Alan Cranston,
"Contribs4," (press release) July 17, 1989.

Page 254—Charles Keating gave it a suitable epitaph: David J. Jefferson, "Keating of American Continental Corp. Comes Out Fighting," *Wall Street Journal*, April 18, 1989.

PART FIVE—THE BIG FIX

CHAPTER FOURTEEN: *The Seamless Web (II)*

Page 257—One real surprise: *Phelan Report*, 130–34.

Page 258—During his resignation speech: Affidavit of Louis A. Farris, Jr., *Congressional Record*, House, May 31, 1989, H2241.

Page 259—The alert Dallas reporter Byron Harris: Byron Harris, broadcast, WFAA-TV, Dallas, April 19, 1989; Allen Pusey, "Beebe's Network."

Page 259—In 1985, he had free use: Brooks Jackson, "Wright Took '85 Trip on Jet Paid for by Ex-Official of Texas S&L," *Wall Street Journal*, April 28, 1989, A16.

Page 260—Harris noted in his broadcast: Byron Harris, broadcast, April 19, 1989.

Page 261—The Freeman affidavit: Affidavit of John A. Freeman, *Congressional Record*, House, May 31, 1980, H2240-41.

Page 261—Ling now became more interesting: Home State Financial, Inc., Form 10-K, Amended, 1983, Securities and Exchange Commission file number 0-3897, 11–14.

Page 262—James Ling introduced: Interview by author with James Ling, Dallas.

Page 263—They happened on a national bank: "Stipulation by and between the Division of Gaming Enforcement and Southmark Corporation, Syntek Investment Properties, Inc. and Syntek West, Inc." In the Matter of Southmark Corporation, a Proposed Holding Company of Greate Bay Hotel and Casino, Inc. doing business as The Sands, New Jersey Casino Control Commission, Trenton, New Jersey, April 10, 1986, 114–26 (hereafter "Stipulation").

Page 264—Phillips bought stock in Novus: "Stipulation," 127–40.

Page 264—Anthony Spilotro, a murderous mafioso: Cf. Steven Brill, *The Teamsters* (New York: Pocket Books, 1978), 219–28.

Page 264—Bossier, a Louisiana state bank: Pizzo, et al., *Inside Job*, 248–50.

Page 266—The junk bond–thrift network: Charles R. Babcock, "Coelho Changes Account of Investment," *Washington Post*, May 14, 1989, A1, A14.

CHAPTER FIFTEEN: *The Greatest Crime*

Page 274—The man in charge of the study: Testimony of Frederick D. Wolf, Assistant Comptroller General, before San Francisco Hearings, 20–23.

Page 276—Warning Signs Of a Failing Thrift: Cf. James Ring Adams, "The S&L 'Rescue': Masking a Broader Crisis" (Boston: H. C. Wainwright & Co.) Economics, newsletter, June 1989.

EPILOGUE: *Paying the Price*

Page 281—"These things are always worse . . . ": Adrienne Bosworth, Herb Cook, Jr., and Max S. Brown, "Should Celeste Have Closed the S&Ls?," *Columbus Monthly*, May 1986, 44–51.

Page 281—The highest estimate to date: G. Christian Hill, "A Never-ending Story; An Introduction to the S&L Symposium," *Stanford Law & Policy Review*, Spring 1990, 24.

Page 283—This low-balling persisted: Charles A. Bowsher, Comptroller General of the United States, "Resolving Failed Savings and Loan Institutions: Estimated Costs and Additional Funding Needs," presented before the United States House Committee on Ways and Means, 101st Cong., 2nd Sess., September 19, 1990.

Page 285—In a bankruptcy claim: In re *The Drexel Burnham Lambert Group, Inc.,* (United States Bankruptcy Court, Southern District of New York) Chapter 11, Case No. 90 B 10421, "Consolidated Proofs of Claim of the Federal Deposit Insurance Corporation and of the Resolution Trust Corporation." (Hereafter, "Drexel claim.")

Page 286—To the federal regulators, Centrust owner David L. Paul: *Resolution Trust Corporation v. David L. Paul, et al.,* (United States District Court, Southern District of Florida) CIV—90-1477.

Page 286—Like other S&L owners with yachts: *Centrust Bank, State Savings Bank, Hearing before the United States House of Representatives Committee on Banking, Finance, and Urban Affairs,* 101st Cong., 2nd Sess., March 26, 1990, 324.

Page 288—The FDIC and the Resolution Trust Corporation filed: Drexel claim, 7–9.

Page 290—According to one document from the hearings: *Silverado Banking, Savings and Loan Association, Hearings before the United States House of Representatives Committee on Banking, Finance and Urban Affairs,* 101st Cong., 2nd Sess., May 22 and 23, 1990, 532.

Page 292—Henkel maintained: *Investigation of Lincoln Savings and Loan, Hearings before the United States House of Representatives Committee on Banking, Finance, and Urban Affairs,* 101st Cong., 1st Sess., Part 3, October 31 and November 7, 1989, 181. (Hereafter, "Lincoln Hearings.")

Page 292 (footnote)—John Connally's bribery: James Reston, Jr., *Lone Star: The Life of John Connally* (New York: Harper & Row, 1989), 480–81.

Page 293—The attorneys for the thousands: *Sarah B. Shields, et al. v. Charles H. Keating, Jr., et al.* (United States District Court, Central District of California) CIV-89-2052, Fifth Consolidated Amended Class Action Complaint, 128–34.

Page 294—Keating kept detailed: "Excerpts from Keating's 'Political Diaries' " *National Mortgage News*, October 15, 1990, 22.

Page 295—Before Benston emerged: Telephone interview with Durward Curlee, October 18, 1989; Telephone interview with George Benston, October 24, 1989; See also, James Ring Adams, "Don Regan's Big Fix; Now It's Broke," *New Republic*, November 13, 1989, 16–18.

Page 297—House Banking Committee chairman Gonzalez expressed amazement: *Lincoln Hearings*, 5.

Page 297—Dochow eventually took charge: James Ring Adams, "Beyond the Keating Five; Friendly Regulators," *National Review*, March 19, 1990, 36–38.

Page 299—Lisa Walleri charged: *Lisa Walleri and Dan Walleri* v. *The Federal Home Loan Bank of Seattle, et al.* (United States District Court for the District of Oregon) CIV—90-855.

Page 300—John F. Downey, deputy director: Testimony of John F. Downey before the United States House of Representatives Budget Committee Task Force on Urgent Fiscal Matters, October 25, 1990. 101st Cong., 2nd Sess. Cf. Stephen Labaton, "S.L. Inquiry Harassment Is Detailed," *New York Times*, October 26, 1990, D1, D6.

Page 302—Senator Howard Metzenbaum: Jeff Gerth, "Misuse of Savings Bailout Reported in Texas Purchase," *New York Times*, July 8, 1990 A1, A12.

Page 304—In an article in the *Stanford*: Joseph Grundfest, "Lobbying into Limbo: The Political Ecology of the Savings and Loan Crisis," *Stanford Law and Political Review*, March 1990, 28.

Page 305—These anemic results revived: Cf. James Ring Adams, *The Secret History of the Tax Revolt* (San Diego, CA: Harcourt Brace Jovanovich, 1984), 81–83.

Page 307—Recounting Keating's strategy: Richard L. Berke, "Witness Recalls Keating Plan of 'Buying Access' in Senate," *New York Times*, December 15, 1990, A1, A11.

Page 308—This is some of what he read: William Proxmire, "Take the Pledge, No More Special Interest Money," *Roll Call*, September 17, 1990.

Page 309—These structural changes: Cf. James Ring Adams, "The S&L Debacle: What Taxpayers Should Know," *The Heritage Lectures No. 287* (Washington, D.C.: The Heritage Foundation, 1990), 5–6.

Index